Social Implications and Challenges of E-Business

Feng Li
University of Newcastle upon Tyne, UK

INFORMATION SCIENCE REFERENCE

Hershey · London · Melbourne · Singapore

Acquisitions Editor:	Kristin Klinger
Development Editor:	Kristin Roth
Senior Managing Editor:	Jennifer Neidig
Managing Editor:	Sara Reed
Assistant Managing Editor:	Sharon Berger
Copy Editor:	Heidi Hormel
Typesetter:	Jamie Snavely
Cover Design:	Lisa Tosheff
Printed at:	Yurchak Printing Inc.

Published in the United States of America by
Information Science Reference (an imprint of IGI Global)
701 E. Chocolate Avenue, Suite 200
Hershey PA 17033
Tel: 717-533-8845
Fax: 717-533-8661
E-mail: cust@idea-group.com
Web site: http://www.info-sci-ref.com

and in the United Kingdom by
Information Science Reference (an imprint of IGI Global)
3 Henrietta Street
Covent Garden
London WC2E 8LU
Tel: 44 20 7240 0856
Fax: 44 20 7379 0609
Web site: http://www.eurospanonline.com

Library of Congress Cataloging-in-Publication Data

Social implications and challenges of e-business / Feng Li, editor.

        p. cm.

Includes bibliographical references and index.

Summary: "This book explores the social implications and challenges of E-Business and E-Commerce regarding social inclusion and exclusion, the social shaping of e-business technologies, the changing nature and patterns of work and social activities, and online identity, security, risks, trust and privacy. It also explores the applications of E-Business technologies and principles in non-business activities and the challenges involved"--Provided by publisher.

  ISBN 978-1-59904-105-6 (hardcover) -- ISBN 978-1-59904-107-0 (ebook)

  1. Electronic commerce--Social aspects. 2. Electronic data interchange--Social aspects.. 3. Information society--Economic aspects. I. Li, Feng, 1965-

  HF5548.32.S633 2007

  381'.142--dc22

                           2006033767

British Cataloguing in Publication Data
A Cataloguing in Publication record for this book is available from the British Library.

Table of Contents

Section I
Opportunities and Challenges in E-Government and E-Learning

Detailed Table of Contents

Section I
Opportunities and Challenges in E-Government and E-Learning

This chapter highlights some of the differences that occur when higher education is provided by e-learning provisions and argues that the challenges that students face and the differences in student:tutor and student:student interactions are sufficiently different to warrant such degrees being awarded under a separate qualification classification. Drawing on research carried out by Ashridge into the realities of getting started in e-learning, and a literature review of e-student and e-tutor issues, the argument is made that actually succeeding at this form of learning requires additional skills, motivation and discipline that should be more widely recognised, and that this would be best achieved through a separate qualifications classification.

Mentoring has been widely known for its ability to enhance the career development, and to provide psychosocial support, for more junior organizational members. Through the use of computer mediated communication technology, e-mentoring may allow individuals to bridge geographic and time differences. This chapter focuses on whether computer mediated communication technology will allow for true mentoring relationships to develop, as well as what personal characteristics may be necessary to grow these virtual relationships. A model and proposition for future research are offered.

Alaska is the largest and most sparsely populated state of the United States of America. Extreme weather patterns and extreme cultural diversity compound the challenge of delivering quality education to state residents in remote areas. This chapter introduces the challenges associate with delivering e-learning in Alaska, reviews the historical evolution of distance learning networks and summarizes present achievements and future opportunities. The analysis includes K-12 education, college and professional continuing education.

This chapter introduces games-based e-learning as a means of providing enriching and stimulating learning experiences within higher education and training. It highlights how e-learning has evolved and the developments that have opened the way for games-based e-learning, giving examples of specific applications. This chapter will explore the implications, challenges and barriers to games-based e-learning, and identify a number of future trends.

This chapter integrates the relationship management among three groups of key stakeholders in e-government, which include government itself, its citizens and employees. It examines the literature regarding the underlying rationale of a successful e-government, and develops and empirically tests an evaluation system for the usability of government Web site which supports the relationship management among citizens, government employees, and public services.

This chapter introduces a framework of mobile policing, and examines how it was implemented in Thailand to improve the effectiveness and efficiency of crime control and also provide services to citizens. The system not only simplifies the collection, storage and retrieval of crime data but also uses Bayesian analysis to give constantly refined predictions of the risks of crime in different localities, along with the factors influencing the risk levels. The chapter also discusses the evaluation of the system by users.

This chapter presents a framework for measuring the usability and content usefulness of Web sites by using the benchmarking approach. It describes the purpose of evaluation, metrics used, and processes through which Web benchmarking can be performed. A total of 46 criteria were identified as the benchmarking metrics. The framework was tested for its applicability by evaluating four political Web sites in Malaysia. The results demonstrated that the framework is easy to follow, and would be particularly useful for organisations intending to benchmark the overall usability and content usefulness of their Web sites against those of their competitors.

Section II
Social Shaping, Construction, and Consquences of E-Business

This chapter explores how relationships are defined in scholarly literature, and then examines how consumers define what they perceive to be the crucial attributes of a relationship in general and with an (online) organization in particular. The results indicate that the notion of relationship has to be redefined for online communication and interaction. The practical implications for designing the interaction process with online users are highlighted.

This chapter investigates the social implications of managing project stakeholders with a special account of e-project management. The authors argue that project management portals are indispensable in project collaboration and coordination. A detailed analysis of project stakeholders and project management portals presented in this chapter allows for a thorough review of the strengths and weaknesses of the e-project approach. It provides the basis for understanding the social challenges of modern ICT solutions in e-project management.

Using the product and services innovation failures literature, this chapter develops a framework to help understand why so many Internet-based business-to-consumer (B2C) "dotcom" companies failed to fulfil their initial promise. It places B2C dotcom ventures on a continuum of need-solution context of innovations, in conjunction with the notion that seller/buyer perceptions about the scope of innovations are not necessarily concordant. Using case evidence, the chapter illustrates the explanatory power of the framework and contributes to e-commerce issues by clarifying why, despite resource availability, many early B2C firms failed due to misjudged perceptions of sellers and/or buyers.

This chapter discusses the role that trust and power play in shaping the use of electronic markets (EM) to support exchange relationships with suppliers that exhibit predominantly transactional characteristics. The study finds that EM is used to take advantage of a superior power position in order to achieve cost reductions, breeding mistrust and eroding the suppliers' bargaining power. The findings support the argument that social relational characteristics such as trust and power are significant factors in shaping the use of EM in transaction oriented relationships.

This chapter investigates open source software/free software (OSS/FS) from three perspectives: motivations that lead to OSS/FS, the organization of OSS/FS communities and the economic theory as a means of explaining the manifold phenomenon. It analyzes the social implications that lie underneath the OSS/FS diffusion, together with the social processes that take place in OSS/FS communities, in an effort to enhance our understanding of the diverse mechanisms that disseminate OSS/FS rapidly.

There are substantial inequalities in access to, and use of the Internet. These inequalities build on enduring social and economic inequalities that have themselves been rooted in previous rounds of the development of electronic technologies and which have largely resisted public policies designed to remedy them. Recent public policies have attempted to remedy digital disadvantage but there is little evidence that they are fundamentally transforming them. This chapter highlights the enormous challenges involved and explores the pros and cons of several new approaches.

Chapter XIV

The chapter argues that the innovation, adoption and diffusion of ICTs bear the hallmark of technological determinism in which social, economic and political factors are underplayed. By way of contrast, the chapter considers the merits of a social shaping approach to the analysis of innovation in ICTs, to assess the prospects for ameliorating the digital divide between developed and developing countries and for stimulating economic development in the latter through the promotion of e-business. The chapter suggests how future research on the social shaping of ICTs, e-business, and the digital divide between developed and developing nations can meet the challenges discussed herein.

Foreword

The relationship between technological change and business organisations has long fascinated scholars in management and related sciences. However, advancing our understanding of this relationship has remained as elusive as any problem in the field of management. Do new technologies have specific requirements to which business and other organisations have to adapt in order to survive? If so, what are the implications of this for business strategy, organisational design and human resources? Or is it more the case that new technologies are shaped by the context of their use, where it is prevailing norms, values, cultures and so forth, that have a decisive role in determining how particular technologies are deployed and implemented? If so, why is it that some organisational/institutional contexts are able to use the enabling features of new technologies to transform them, whilst others seem more adept at appropriating new technologies to shore up existing systems, processes and practices, or provide significant barriers and resistance to change? Another approach is to 'question the questions' and ask if the explanations we are seeking are best framed in terms of a competing proposition that either the requirements of a technology or the social context of its use shapes the outcomes of technological change? Is it more meaningful, for example, to consider dynamics of the interaction between the technical and the social as more symbiotic, rather than see them as separate and distinct entities acting on each other in some way? The papers in this collection provide an attempt to come to terms with some of these issues in the context of the 'new technology' of our time, the Internet. Of course, what is 'new' about the Internet needs to be carefully dissected as do claims about its capacity for the transformation of the way we do business or deliver public services. At the same time, we need to be careful about our assumptions with regard to the capacity of different types of organisations and sectors to appropriate these new technologies and what we really mean when we talk of 'barriers' or 'resistance' to change. Moreover, we also need to do more than just stand back and analyse these issues but also use these insights to provide practical guidance to the managers, professionals, public officials and many others who are wrestling with these challenges in their daily work lives. However, as the various contributors to this informative volume show, things are not always as they at first seem. Indeed, we may have to re-examine some of our fundamental assumptions in areas such as system development, business models and strategy, and the management of organisational change, if we really are to be able to 'transform' business and government.

Ian Mcloughlin
University of Newcastle upon Tyne

Ian Mcloughlin (I.P.Mloughlin@ncl.ac.uk), is the director of the Business School and codirector of the Centre for Social and Business Informatics at the University of Newcastle upon Tyne (UK). A leading expert on social informatics, his research has focused on technology and organization; new forms of work, organization and employment relationship; managing change and project management; social informatics and sociotechnical systems; and the development and deployment of the technologies of e-government. In the last few years, he led a series of large research programs, including Advanced Multi-Agency Service Environment (AMASE), funded by the EPSRC; Advanced Environments for Smart Organisational Portals (AESOP), funded by the European Commission; and Framework for Multi-Agency Environments (FAME), funded by the Office of the Deputy Prime Minister (UK). He is a member of the Executive Committee of the Association of Business Schools and council member of the British Academy of Management.

Preface

Are we in the midst of a second Internet boom? If so, how it was different from the first boom of the late 1990s, which went bust spectacularly in 2001? As the stock market recovered rapidly from the dot.com crash, there have been some marked changes in the way that the Internet and e-business has evolved. In particular, behind the headlines, such as the multibillion dollar purchase of Skype by eBay and Google's sky-rocketing share prices, many smaller but innovative and profitable dot.coms have been launched, and numerous private and public sector organisations are being radically transformed. Most importantly, many radical changes predicted during the late 1990s, but dismissed during the aftermath of the dot.com crash, are materalising.

In many ways, the Internet boom itself has never stopped. Even during the stock market downturn, people from all over the world continued to join the Internet to search, chat, e-mail, play and spend money. In the business world, and in governmental and other organisations throughout the world, new strategies, new business models and new organisational designs have been introduced. The way we work, play, communicate, learn and shop has been significantly transformed; and the boundaries between sectors, products, services, channels and organisations are increasingly eroded. Most importantly, the distinctions between work, home, education, leisure and so on are increasingly blurred (Li, 2006).

E-business is not limited to the private sectors; the public sectors also are experimenting with new ways of information and services delivery via electronic channels and are actively facilitating and shaping the development of infrastructure and services. However, the challenges have been extremely complex and many e-government and e-public services initiatives have failed to deliver the anticipated benefits, and there have been numerous project failures. More significantly, the development of e-business is facilitating profound social changes and is itself shaped by a plethora of social forces. Due to the rapid pace of developments, many such issues have not been systematically examined. In 2005, I edited a special issue of the *Journal of Electronic Commerce in Organizations* (*JECO*) on the "Social Aspects of E-Business," in my capacity as the chair of the E-Business and E-Government Special Interest Group (SIG) of the British Academy of Management (BAM) (Li, 2005). However, due to the limited space in the journal's special issue, many significant issues were left out. This edited book will provide the capacity to present a greater number of papers in order to address these emerging issues in a more comprehensive fashion.

Social Implications and Challenges of E-Business

For several decades, we have been exploring the changing business environment as a result of the rapid development of information and communications technologies (ICTs) and the knowledge-based, networked, information economy. The Internet is particularly significant because it is facilitating profound social—as well as economic—changes. As Kelly (1997) forcefully argued:

We have been awash in a steadily increasing tide of information for the past century. Many successful knowledge businesses have been built on information capital, but only recently has a total reconfiguration of information itself shifted the whole economy ... the grand irony of our times is that the era of computers is over. All the major consequences of stand-alone computers have already taken place. Computers have speeded up our lives a bit, and that's it. ... In contrast, all the most promising technologies making their debut now are chiefly due to communication between computers—that is, to connections rather than to computations. And since communication is the basis of culture, fiddling at this level is indeed momentous. (p. X)

Social-science thinking on ICTs and social, economic and organisational developments have been dominated by two distinct traditions. One tradition is concerned with the "impacts" or "effects" of ICTs on social and economic variables, although the crude technological determinism, which was the hallmark of this approach, and the notion of technology as an exogenous variable in social and economic changes have become increasingly untenable. The alternative major tradition has focused on the socio-economic shaping, including social construction, of technology (Mackenzie & Wacjman, 1999). The ESRC Virtual Society programme in the UK has emphasised that technologies rarely have the "effects" or "impacts" that might be anticipated from their stated technological functionality, capabilities and characteristics. Rather we need to reframe our analytical frameworks to anticipate "counterintuitive" outcomes and seek to explain and understand these as part of a process whereby technologies are shaped in use (or nonuse) in specific contexts (Woolgar, 2002).

As the Internet and related technologies and services continue to penetrate into every corner of our society and personal lives, new ways of working and living become possible, but the way technologies is used will be shaped by a plethora of social forces. All these issues need to be systematically investigated in order to understand the profound social implications and challenges of e-business. To highlight this point, some examples are explored briefly below.

Privacy in a Networked World

For years, most of us routinely gave away information about ourselves to different organisations (e.g., postal code, home phone number and date of birth). In fact, many of our personal records, held by different organisations, are listed publicly. Until recently this was largely not problematic and represented a minimal threat to our privacy because these records were widely scattered in different places, such as libraries, city halls and courthouses around the country. However, with the rapid development of the Internet and our exponentially improved ability to search, mine and manipulate data, the situation has changed radically. When public records are aggregated into an individual profile, they can become a powerful—and potentially dangerous—tool. An entire data-brokerage industry has emerged in recent years to provide such services to anyone who can afford to pay, and with minimal skills and equipment, many simple requirements can be fulfilled through a do it yourself (DIY) approach.

This is not just limited to highly sensitive personal information. If you are a UK resident, your postal code can quite accurately identify the property you live in, which can be matched with a free, property-price database on the Internet. This will provide a fairly accurate indication of the value of your property. Your car registration information (model of car and year of registration) and a free database of used-car prices on the Internet can yield information about the value of your car. Such simple information could then be combined to indicate the income level of your household, which then could be used for the effective promotion of different products and services. The potential for further combinations with other information is enormous and if not adequately regulated and actively monitored, can be misused and abused by different organizations and individuals for different purposes.

The *E-Commerce Times* reported that *The Chicago Tribune* managed to find the identities, work places, post office box addresses and telephone numbers for hundreds of CIA employees in the United States and abroad by using only public records. The data were derived from telephone listings, real estate transactions, voting records, legal judgments, property tax records, bankruptcies, business incorporation papers and so on. What is particularly alarming is that "with only a credit card number, the *Tribune* was able to obtain nearly all the information it had acquired from data providers. That included the names of clandestine CIA operatives assigned to U.S. embassies" (Crewdson, 2006).

If even the CIA cannot keep such information safe, then everyone should be concerned. Our information is not limited to what is stored in different public records—just imagine what our banks, supermarkets and credit card companies know about us. Through records such as the loyalty-card schemes, supermarkets know exactly what we buy each week, which can be used to maximize revenue and profit, and improve the effectiveness of promotions. More worryingly, our credit card companies know exactly where we shop, eat, entertain, travel, and stay. When such information is harnessed and built into an individual profile, our privacy could be under serious threat, if the use of such information is not tightly regulated. Are existing measures sufficient? Or are new legislations necessary to adequately protect us against misuse of such information? The difficulties involved in enforcing existing and new rules are also enormous. Many other serious issues, such as identity theft, are just beginning to emerge and the full implications are not yet understood. Such issues will certainly need to be systematically investigated.

Living in 'Two Spaces': MMORPG Meets the Real World

In 2001, colleagues and I published a paper titled, "Between Physical and Electronic Spaces: Implications for Organizations in the Information Economy" (Li, Whalley, & Howard, 2001). In that paper, we argued that with the rapid development of ICTs, a new electronic space has emerged that coexists and sometimes intertwines with the physical space of our "real" physical world. This significantly increases the complexity and flexibility of our space economy for organisations and individuals, and increasingly we have to live in "two spaces." Although the misconception about the "death of distance" and "end of geography" in the information economy has largely been dismissed, the full implications—and the enormous complexity—in our space economy are yet to be fully appreciated. As the "two spaces" continue to evolve and intertwine at unprecedented complexity and speed, numerous new issues have emerged.

For example, millions of people play online role-playing games that also are known as massively multiplayer online role-playing games (MMORPGs). In these games, a large number of players interact with one another in a virtual world either using their existing identity in the physical world or, more often than not, through a new virtual identity that might not even be remotely linked to the identity of the player in the physical world. Examples of such games include Second life, EverQuest, World of Warcraft and Entropia Universe, to name a few. MMORPGs are immensely popular, with several commercial games reporting millions of subscribers. In most of these games, players assume a different identity (from their physical world identity), which evolves through interactions with the virtual identities of other players in the electronic space.

It should be noted that significant economic activities take place in these virtual worlds. Large amounts of real-world money is spent on the virtual characters, and the wealth generated in the virtual world can be easily converted into real money through the services like eBay. For example, in Second Life alone, residents spend an equivalent of $5 million each month for virtual products and services for their virtual characters, and this figure is rapidly growing. Many virtual entrepreneurs, such as fashion designers for online characters, have quit their real-world jobs to focus on their virtual-world businesses—and the virtual dollars they earn in these games can then be converted into real-world money (Hemp, 2006).

In December 2004, a 22-year-old gamer made history by spending $26,500 (£13,700) on an island that exists only within the game Project Entropia, an MMORPG that allows thousands of players to interact with each other. The Australian gamer, known by his gaming moniker, Deathifier, bought the island in an online auction (BBC, 2004). The virtual island includes a gigantic abandoned castle and beautiful beaches ripe for the development of beachfront virtual property for different virtual characters. Deathifier made money from his investment by taxing other gamers, who came to his virtual land to hunt or mine for gold. He also sold plots to people who wished to build virtual homes on his virtual island.

Living through those virtual characters—also know as Avatars—can be an intense social experience, and many players spend as much as 40 hours a week in those worlds. Many commercial organisations already advertise in these virtual worlds, and some even developed their own MMORPGs for their targeted audience (e.g., The Coca-Cola Company's Coke Studios and Wells Fargo bank's Stagecoach Island) (Hemp, 2006). In many ways, the virtual world is as real as the physical world. Real commercial transactions and social interactions take place between the virtual identities of different players, whether they are from the same city or the other side of the world. Within the virtual world, players can set up virtual businesses that sell products and services to other virtual players; and the wealth generated can be spent on other virtual products or services, or converted into real money for spending in the physical world.

In fact, from an e-business perspective, the evolution of the virtual world will significantly extend the range and scale of activities because, in addition to the existing categories of e-business activities between individuals and organisations in the physical world via electronic channels (such as, B2B and B2C), these activities are also developing in parallel within the virtual world and have enormous business and social implications. For example, you can set up a Web development company to develop e-commerce systems for virtual companies inside a MMORPG, which will create new categories of e-businesses, such as virtual business to virtual consumer (VB2VC) and virtual business to virtual business (VB2VB). Furthermore, such virtual relations can be extended to interact directly with the physical world, so a virtual service can be sold to real businesses in the physical world—virtual business to physical business (VB2PB) or vice versa. One example is a company serving the physical world marketing their products via virtual companies inside MMORPGs. Such developments will significantly complicate the interplay between the physical and the virtual spaces and entities.

For a marketer, for example, these developments raise serious challenges. How effective would it be for a physical-world brand to be marketed within the virtual world, perhaps inside a particular MMORPG? Should the marketer be targeting the Avatars inside the game, or the real players behind the Avatars? The social implications will be profound. The meaning of the real/physical and the virtual will need to be redefined; and our social interactions with one another and with businesses and other organisations will need to be significantly extended. MMORPGs are an example where the virtual world significantly extends our physical world, and the interplay between the physical and the virtual creates numerous opportunities and challenges with economic and profound social implications. Many of these issues are still poorly understood and systematic research is urgently needed.

E-Government, E-Public Services and E-Learning

In 2000 *The Economist* magazine famously announced that after e-commerce and e-business, the next Internet revolution would be e-government (*The Economist*, June 28, 2000). The UK government set itself an ambitious target for the provision of public services electronically, that by the end of 2005 every public sector that can be provided online must be online. It also wanted to make the UK the best place in the world for e-commerce. Billions of pounds have since been invested in central and local governments, the health services and other public-sector organisations in order to achieve the target, with £14 billion per year being spent on computer systems and service (Cross, 2005). Similar initiatives have been launched by governments all over the world, not only in developed countries, but also in an increasing number of developing countries.

This book defines e-business broadly and regards e-government and e-public service as a subset of e-business—the use of Internet and related technologies to transform public services and the organisations providing them. However, due to the profoundly different issues and challenges in public services compared with the commercial sectors, e-government and e-public services have increasingly becoming an area of study in its own right (Li, 2006).

E-business in the private sector is profoundly different from e-government and e-public services in several ways. For private sector businesses, the dominant logic is relatively clear and simple: any business needs to make more money than it spends in the long term; it needs to generate adequate returns for its investors; and it needs sufficient cash to keep it going. There are many other stakeholders, such as employees, managers and the government, but the dominate logic for private-sector business is simple—to generate profit for its shareholders, even though it has responsibilities for employees and for the wider community. Recently, considerable attention has been paid to issues such as corporate social responsibility but the dominate logic of business in the private sector remains unchanged (Bakan, 2004). In contrast the logics in the public sector are much more complicated. There are multiple, sometimes equally powerful, stakeholders, and many public-sector organisations exist to protect the weak and disadvantaged. Many public services have no alternatives so they have captive audience.

The differences, and sometimes conflicts, between the different logics—and between different strategic objectives—are often difficult to reconcile. What works in the private sector rarely works in the public sector in the same fashion, even after serious adaptation and adjustment (Li, 2006). There have been numerous high-profile failures of major e-government projects throughout the world, highlighting the enormous challenges involved.

In education, significant investments have been made by both the private and public sectors in the name of e-learning. The result has been somewhat less than spectacular, and there have been many high-profile failures. From an e-business perspective, the Internet and related technologies can be used in two different ways in facilitating teaching and learning. On the one hand, the technologies can support and supplement existing modes of teaching and learning by continuing to do what we used to do better or differently. Most existing e-learning initiatives perhaps fall into this category. However, on the other hand, it is possible to use the Internet and related technologies to enable radically different and far more effective modes of teaching and learning in ways not possible or not even imaginable in the past. For example, my teenaged son learned to play the electric guitar almost exclusively using free resources on the Internet, including free literature as well as tips from other guitar enthusiasts in various online forums and chat rooms with Web cams and online chats. When I talked about this at a recent ORACLE Executive Learning Workshop, a number of colleagues said that their children did exactly the same thing. This example indicates not only the enormous untapped potential of e-learning, but also, perhaps, that we are missing a trick in our pursuit of e-learning?

The Purpose and Structure of this Book

This book is part of our effort to address the profound social implications and challenges of e-business and improve our understanding of how the development of the Internet and e-business shapes, and are shaped, by various social forces; and the difficulties and challenges involved in applying e-business technologies and principles to public services and other nonbusiness activities. The vast range of topics involved means this book will only begin to address issues in this complex, rapidly evolving area, rather than providing a systematic exploration of the field. Papers selected for this volume will explore the social implications and challenges of e-business and e-commerce in terms of social inclusion and exclusion and the digital divide; the social shaping of e-business technologies; the changing nature and patterns of work and social activities; and online identity, security, risks, trust and privacy. The authors also will explore the applications of e-business technologies and principles in public services and nonbusiness activities and the challenges involved.

As such, this book will be structured into two main sections. The first section will look at the challenges and opportunities involved in applying the Internet and related technologies in government, public service and other noncommercial sectors. The second section will examine issues in the broad area of social shaping and construction of the Internet and related technologies, and the enormous social implications and challenges of e-business.

Section I: Opportunities and Challenges in E-Government and E-Learning

In Section I, seven papers have been selected. In Chapter I, Blass, Ettinger, and Holton of Ashridge Business School (UK) highlight some of the differences that occur when higher education is provided through e-learning and argues that the challenges that students face and the differences in student-tutor and student-student interactions are sufficiently different to warrant that such degrees be awarded under a separate qualification classification. Drawing on research carried out at Ashridge into the realities of getting started in e-learning and a literature review of e-student and e-tutor issues, the argument is made that actually succeeding at this form of learning requires additional skills, motivation and discipline that should be more widely recognised and that this would be best achieved through a separate qualifications classification. Such a classification also would enable issues surrounding quality and standards to surface, ensuring that e-learning degrees are equivalent to their more traditionally taught counterparts.

Godshalk of the Pennsylvania State University (USA) offer a model and various propositions that investigate whether computer-mediated communication (CMC) technology allows the development of e-mentoring relationships. Specific environmental conditions, such as the social influences of peers, supervisors and the organisation's culture, as well as personal characteristics, are posited as antecedents of an individual's choice to use CMC and subsequent engagement in an e-mentoring relationship. E-mentoring is clearly a new tool individuals may use to enhance their careers, yet the social implications of this phenomenon are still under investigation. The real challenges surrounding e-mentoring involve what effect, if any, the lack of face-to-face interaction has on dyad members, their organisation and their career progression. Given our technology-driven environment, understanding who might adopt, pursue and gain from e-mentoring relationships is a new research direction that will make a significant contribution to our literature.

Hoanca and Mock of the University of Alaska Anchorage (USA) examines how e-learning technologies have emerged as a cost-effective, interactive means of delivering quality teaching to even the most isolated locations in Alaska. Additionally, the ability to archive content and to access it at will, in an asynchronous manner, is highly suited to the different learning styles and different learning rates of the various populations in the state. This chapter introduces the challenges associated with delivering e-learning in Alaska, reviews the historical evolution of distance-learning networks, and summarizes present achievements and future opportunities. The analysis includes K-12 education, college and professional continuing education. For the state of Alaska, geography, climate and cultural diversity make distance education highly desirable for providing quality education options to all state residents. E-learning technologies provide multimedia-rich learning content, can adapt to a variety of bandwidth channels and allow for interactive but asynchronous interaction.

Connolly and Stansfield of the University of Paisley (UK) introduce games-based e-learning as a means of providing enriching and stimulating learning experiences within higher education and training. It highlights how e-learning has evolved and the developments that have opened the way for games-based e-learning by giving examples of specific applications. Through gaining a better understanding of the implications, challenges and barriers to games-based e-learning, educators, practitioners and developers will be able to make better use of and gain substantial benefit from these exciting learning technologies. The chapter also will identify some future trends in relation to e-learning and games-based e-learning.

Chang and Chen of YuanPei Institute of Science and Technology, Taiwan, introduce a CRM-based e-government usability services framework by exploring the relationship among the different e-government stakeholders and by integrating internal and external customers in public services. An evaluation system for the usability of government Web sites is developed and empirically tested, which supports the relationship management between citizens and government employees. They also suggest a number of issues for future research.

Boondao of the Ubon Rajathanee University (Thailand) and Tripathi of the Asian Institute of Technology (Thailand), explore the field of e-policing and introduce a framework of mobile policing for crime control and citizen services, derived from the system requirements of both police and citizens. They examine how an e-policing system is using this framework to improve the effectiveness and efficiency of crime control and also providing services to citizens. In particular, the system not only simplifies the collection, storage and retrieval of crime data but also uses Bayesian analysis to give constantly refined predictions of the risks of crime in different localities, along with the factors influencing the risk levels.

Hassan of the Northern University of Malaysia and Li of the University of Newcastle upon Tyne (UK) use a benchmarking approach to develop a structured framework for evaluating Web sites' usability and the usefulness of their content. The chapter describe the purpose of the evaluation, metrics to be used and processes through which Web benchmarking can be carried out. Several methods were used including content analysis of literature and expert review. A total of 46 criteria were identified that can be used as the benchmarking metrics. The framework was tested for its applicability by evaluating four political Web sites in Malaysia. The results proved that the framework is easy to implement and would be particularly valuable for those who intend to benchmark the overall usability and usefulness of their Web sites against those of their competitors.

Section II: The Social Shaping, Construction, and Consequences of E-Business

In Section II, seven papers have been selected that explore the social implications and challenges of e-business. Treiblmaier of Vienna University of Economics and Business Administration (Austria) investigates the influence of the Internet on relationships between consumers and vendors. In the precomputer era, relationships always implied a social dimension, which modern technology tries to mimic by learning about customers' needs and addressing them individually. Treiblmaier investigated how relationships are defined in scholarly literature and how consumers define what they perceive to be the crucial attributes of a relationship, in general, and with an online organization, in particular. The chapter concludes that the notion of relationship has to be redefined for online communication and interaction, and offers practical implications for designing the interaction process with online users

Jovanovic, Mihic, and Petrovic of the University of Belgrade (Serbia), explore the social implications of managing project stakeholders with particular reference to e-project management, including the architecture and importance of project management (PM) portals and the way they are related to e-projects. The authors argue that PM portals are indispensable in project collaboration and coordination and are closely related to e-projects, since the portals play a key role in both the PM implementation and an adequate incorporation of and discussion with all project stakeholders. The authors believe that a detailed analysis of project stakeholders and PM portals presented in this chapter allows for a thorough review of strengths and weaknesses of the e-project approach, and it will provide the basis for understanding the social aspects of modern ICT solutions in e-project management.

Pandya of Northeastern Illinois University (USA) and Dholakia of the University of Rhode Island (USA) explore B2C failures by introducing an innovative theoretical framework. Using the product and services innovation failures literature, this chapter develops a framework to help understand why so many Internet-based B2C "dot.com" companies failed to fulfil their initial promise. Viewed collectively, B2C dot.com crashes constitute an initial wave of failure of an entirely new class of technology-driven services. Such services sought to inform, promote, sell and deliver B2C items in radically unfamiliar ways. Besides ignoring basic precepts of sound business practice, unsuccessful B2C firms failed to realize they were marketing *innovative services*. The authors place B2C dot.com ventures in a need-solution context of innovations, in conjunction with the notion that seller/buyer perceptions about the scope of innovations are not necessarily concordant. Matched perceptions between sellers and buyers lead to success. Sellers as well as buyers, however, can misjudge the nature and scope of innovations. Using case evidence, the chapter illustrates the explanatory power of the framework and contributes to e-commerce issues by clarifying why, despite resource availability, many early B2C firms failed due to misjudged perceptions of the sellers and/or buyers

Bunduchi of the University of Aberdeen Business School (UK) discusses the role that social relational characteristics, such as trust and power, play in shaping the use of a particular type of e-business application—electronic markets (EM). The analysis is based on a case study of an EM in the electricity sector. The study finds that the use of EMs to take advantage of a superior power position to achieve cost reductions breeds mistrust and erodes suppliers' bargaining power. The findings support the argument that social relational characteristics, such as trust and power, are significant factors in shaping the use of EM in transactionally oriented relationships

Lakka, Lionis, and Varoutas of the University of Athens (Greece) investigate the social aspects of open-source software (OSS), also known as free software (FS). They discuss OSS/FS from three perspectives: motivations that lead to OSS/FS, the organization of OSS/FS communities and the economic theory as a means of explaining the phenomenon. The chapter analyses the social implications behind OSS/FS diffusion, together with the social processes that take place in OSS/FS communities in an effort to enhance our understanding of the diverse mechanisms that disseminate OSS/FS rapidly.

Bonney, Komolafe, and Tait of the Robert Gordon University (UK) explore digital inequality. They argue that there are substantial inequalities in access to and use of the Internet. These inequalities are built on enduring social and economic inequalities that are rooted in previous rounds of the development of electronic technologies and have largely resisted public policies designed to remedy them. Rapid developments in the use of the Internet have great potential for commercialisation and democratization, but digital inequality means that this potential is not always exploited to the advantage of the poorer sectors of the community. Recent public policies have attempted to remedy digital disadvantage, but there is little evidence that they are fundamentally transforming them. Constant innovation enables the more advantaged sectors to advance their position, while many are still excluded from compensatory attempts at catch-up. An increasing body of experience suggests new approaches, but the magnitude of the challenge of ending digital inequality should not be underestimated.

Finally, Genus and Nor of the University of Newcastle upon Tyne examine the digital divide from a social shaping of technology perspective. The digital divide is a phenomenon associated with disparities between groups and societies in the adoption and diffusion of electronic ICTs and e-business practice. The chapter argues that, in rhetoric at least, the innovation, adoption and diffusion of ICTs bear the hallmark of technological determinism (i.e., that of a technical imperative) in which social, economic and political factors are underplayed. By way of contrast, the chapter considers the merits of a social-shaping approach to the analysis of innovation in ICTs to assess the prospects for ameliorating the digital divide between developed and developing countries and for stimulating economic development in the latter through the promotion of e-business. The chapter suggests how future research on the social shaping of ICTs, e-business and the digital divide between developed and developing nations can meet the challenges discussed therein.

What is Next?

Despite the radical changes we have witnessed in the last 10 years or so, we have probably only seen the tip of an iceberg and barely scratched the surface of the e-business phenomenon. The papers presented in this book, as well as those included in the special issue of *Journal of Electronic Commerce in Organizations* (Li, 2005), represent our attempts in making sense of the complex social implications and challenges of e-business. We hope this book will be relevant to academics and practitioners interested in the social aspects of e-business in private- and public-sector organisations. It should be particularly useful to researchers, postgraduate and undergraduate students, businesses and information systems professionals, and management consultants interested in the broad context of e-business, the social forces that shape the development of the Internet and e-business, and the social changes and challenges brought about by such developments. This is still a rapidly evolving and expanding area, and more research is clearly needed.

REFERENCES

BBC. (2004). Gamer buys $26,500 virtual land. In *BBC News.* Retrieved from http://news.bbc.co.uk/1/hi/technology/4104731.stm

Bakan, J. (2004). *The corporation: The pathological pursuit of profit and power.* London: Constable.

Crewdson, J. (2006). Data mining easy as using credit card. *The eCommerce Times.* Retrieved from http://www.ecommercetimes.com/story/8OHZcAKhyleruS/Data-Mining-Easy-as-Using-Credit-Card.xhtml

Cross, M. (2005, October). Public sector IT failures. *Prospect*, 48-53.

Hemp, P. (2006, June). Avatar-based marketing. *Harvard Business Review*, 48-57.

Kelly, K. (1997). New rules for the new economy. *Wired Magazine* (5.09). Retrieved from http://www.wired.com/wired/archive/5.09/newrules.html?topic=&topic_set=

Li, F. (2005). Social aspects of e-business. *Journal of E-Commerce in Organisations, 3*(2, Special Issue).

Li, F. (2006). *What is e-business? How the Internet transforms organisations*. Oxford: Blackwell.

Li, F., Whalley, J., & Williams, H. (2001). Between physical and electronic spaces: Implications for organizations in the information economy. *Environment and Planning A, 33,* 699-716.

Mackenzie, D., & Wacjman, J. (1999). *The social shaping of technology.* Buckingham, UK: Open University Press.

Woolgar, S. (2002). *Virtual society? Technology, cyberbole, reality*. London: Oxford University Press.

Acknowledgments

This book would not have been possible without the contributions, support, encouragement and criticisms of numerous people. The call for paper was initially distributed through the E-Business and E-Government Special Interest Group (SIG) of the British Academy of Management (BAM) and subsequently widely distributed to academics and practitioners all over the world. Potential authors initially submitted an extended abstract, indicating the approaches and main focuses of their papers and how they intended to contribute to the central theme of the book. After a careful screening process, the authors of 25 abstracts were invited to submit full chapters, which went to reviewers. Most papers were reviewed by two independent referees, and, in a few cases, when there are major disagreements between the referees; the opinion of a third referee was consulted. In the end, only 14 papers were accepted for the book. As you can imagine, a large number of authors and referees contributed to the process.

First of all, I would like to thank all authors who submitted papers for this book. Due to the large number of submissions received, reviewing all the papers was no trivial task. I would like to thank everyone who helped with the review process. Without their timely efforts and constructive criticisms, this book would not have been possible. Unfortunately, I am unable to thank each of them individually here due to the large number of people involved, but their support is greatly appreciated.

The publisher has been very supportive throughout the process, and the enthusiasm, professionalism, efficiency and timely reminders have kept the project going without major glitches. I am particularly grateful to Dr Mehdi Khosrow-Pour, editor-in-chief of the *Journal of Electronic Commerce in Organizations* and Jan Travers, managing director, Kristin Roth, development editor, and Michelle Potter, development editor, all of IGI Global. Without their support and encouragement, this project would not have been completed so smoothly.

Any errors remain the responsibility of the authors.

Feng Li
University of Newcastle upon Tyne, UK

Section I
Opportunities and Challenges in E-Government and E-Learning

Chapter I
Differing Challenges and Different Achievements:
The Case for a Separate Classification for Qualifications Undertaken by E-Learning

Eddie Blass
Ashridge Business School, UK

Andrew Ettinger
Ashridge Business School, UK

Viki Holton
Ashridge Business School, UK

ABSTRACT

Higher education has traditionally been provided in universities through lectures, seminars and tutorials, and other social mechanisms of learning where students interact in less formal settings. This chapter highlights some of the differences that occur when higher education is provided by e-learning provisions and argues that the challenges that students face and the differences in student-tutor and student-student interactions are sufficiently different to warrant that such degrees be awarded under a separate qualification classification. Drawing on research carried out at Ashridge Business School, UK, into the realities of getting started in e-learning, and a literature review of e-student and e-tutor issues, the argument is made that actually succeeding at this form of learning requires additional skills, motivation and discipline that should be more widely recognized, and that this would be best achieved through a separate qualifications classification. Such a classification would also ensure that e-learning degrees are equivalent to their more traditionally earned counterparts.

INTRODUCTION

Until the Internet boom, higher education was mainly offered in three formats: full-time, part-time and a traditional form of distance learning of self-directed study around paper-based guides (with tutor support via telephone), supplemented with residential blocks and summer schools that provided an interactive element. There were also some corporate programs being provided, but these were delivered in the form of a combination of the previous formats. E-learning differs from the other forms of delivery because it changes the element of tutor-student and student-student interaction so that it occurs through computer-mediated technology, rather than face to face or even over the telephone. Hence the communication process becomes asynchronous and does not take place in real time. Drawing on research into e-learner experiences reported in the literature, and primary research carried out at the Ashridge Business School, UK, this chapter argues that this difference needs much stronger recognition than it currently has, and, as such, a separate qualifications classification should be drawn up to take into account these differences to ensure that quality standards are maintained by e-learning providers of higher education.

In May 2004, Ashridge Business School published a research report based on a multimethod investigation into organizations' experiences introducing e-learning. Sixteen organizations were case studied through a series of interviews, observations and document data collection, and 29 of their "virtual learning resource centre" (VLRC) client companies participated in a survey to ensure that the learning from the case studies was applicable to a wider population. Many of the case study organziations were early pioneers into e-learning (such as, Mercer and Xerox Europe), while others had only engaged in e-learning initiatives more recently (such as, Logicom, Volvo and Electrocomponents). While not all the organziations involved in the Ashridge research

were pursuing higher-education awards specifically, the experiences of the learners, developers, implementers and tutors involved are still directly comparable. They had to learn to interact for the purposes of learning through computer-mediated technology, and their employees had to both work and study which is typical of the e-learner, rather than them being full-time students. However, it should be noted that the learners that are discussed in this chapter, in the context of the corporate e-learning experiences, did not have the additional benefit of an award at the end of their efforts to add to their motivation. The case study data is discussed throughout the chapter to illustrate the key points being made.

Although e-learning has not been the panacea that some expected at the start of the 21st century, it may yet be. The expansion of e-learning has not materialized as quickly as initially predicted, but this does not mean that it will not happen in an elongated time frame. As Diebold (1996) observes, things usually take much longer to happen that you expect them to, and you cannot anticipate what people will do with a new technology. The dot.com boom and bust cycle highlighted that technology can be ahead of the market, as illustrated by the fact that consumers were not quite ready for the anytime, anywhere shopping experience. The same could be said of e-learning. Some universities, for example, invested heavily in developing e-learning courses that have not recruited enough students to be viabile (e.g., the Global University Alliance and Universitas 21), although the market in some areas is buoyant (e.g., the University of Phoenix). Media companies also have moved into this territory (such as, Worldwide Learning, part of the News International Group), but have failed as yet to establish a worthwhile market.

Arguably the development of e-learning is being carried out by the wrong people. Academics are being "encouraged" within some institutions to put their wares "online," and this is exactly what they are doing—putting lecture materials online. This is not good e-learning, and not surprisingly, it is not selling well or showing signs of being successful. In essence, it is a substandard degree offering. Birchall and Smith (2002) confirm that the quality of e-learning offerings is seen as variable, so the potential for loss of e-learning credibility is great. They also found UK business schools using e-learning for knowledge transference only, rather than any behavioral learning, and hence only using it for lower levels of qualifications. This strategy is particularly doomed to failure as learner maturity affects the success of adult learning (Delahaye, Limerick, & Hearn, 1994), and lower-level learners are less likely to have developed the requisite maturity in their learning processes to succeed at such e-endeavors. Students who are newer to learning require more social interaction to aid the learning process.

In addition to the developers of e-learning being the "wrong" people, the current users also might be. Schofield and Rylance-Watson (2002) found that e-learning was best suited to reflectors and theorists, the introvert, the self-starter and for those comfortable with information technology (IT)—not the average personality profile. E-learning needs sophisticated learners, but sophisticated learners do not necessarily want to undertake e-learning. They may prefer other more familiar, social learning strategies. Dupuis (1998) looks at how school students use technology, both in terms of receiving from and contributing to its development, and predicts that when that generation become students in higher education, then there will be real change. School students are growing up learning to interact socially through technology, rather than having to learn this as a new form of social interaction.

So too might the universities be "wrong" for e-learning. Barnett (2000) claims universities need to adapt to a world of supercomplexity, suggesting the concept of supercomplexity as being beyond post-modernity. He defines it as "that form of complexity in which our frameworks for understanding the world are themselves problematic" (2000, p. 76) such that universities need new ways

of understanding themselves and need to be revolutionary, rather than norm-enforcing. However, in reality the opposite is true. Universities themselves are not adapting to providing e-learning but are trying to cope with it within their existing norms, cultures and structures. Abeles (2005) finds that within universities, most academics who are working in the arena of e-learning are worrying about changes at the microlevel, rather than seeing the change in the landscape.

Manicas (2000) identifies higher education as being at the brink. He identifies the forces from the past that have shaped the current system, including a symbiosis of science, industry and the state; industrialization and urbanization; democracy; and accelerating demands for specialized knowledge. The forces that he predicts are globalization, computer-mediated technologies and the affordability of higher education as participation increases. In such a world, Rooney and Hearn (2000) can see three scenarios for the university of the future: the do-nothing scenario, which lets the momentum of history and the uncertainty of the future determine strategy; the commodified university, which uses technology that is available to move towards a commodified model of knowledge distribution; or the online learning community, which uses technology to connect students and increase the diversity of knowledge through networks. The role of e-learning in each will vary greatly in terms of its purpose and underlying philosophy. Currently we can see universities engaging in the first two scenarios, either doing nothing or developing e-learning materials/courses as commodities. However, there are indications that some organizations are moving into the third scenario, learning communities, such as Ashridge's VLRC. This is a new area for education that is evolving as it emerges.

Margules (2002) is more fatalistic about the impact of technology on learning. "Like it or not, the storage and distribution of information, and the associated teaching and learning pedagogy aided by technology, is now undermining the more traditional methods of teaching, learning and research" (2002). His vision sees e-learning ultimately replacing traditional classroom-based teaching. When you consider the number of students undertaking e-MBAs, compared to class-taught MBAs, he could be right. The challenges for businesses and the social implications of such a wholesale shift would be massive. Given the focus on knowledge transfer at the expense of behavioral skills being witnessed in e-learning qualifications (Birchall & Smith, 2002), there is a danger that a proliferation of such qualifications will result in a form of social de-skilling in the workplace.

Despite all this recognition of change in the higher-education sector, be it changes to the current way of working, resistance to changes in the current model, or simply recognition of forces for change that are shaping the future direction of higher education, little is being done to accommodate the change in the current system. Rather than embracing the changes and recognizing the differences stemming from new ways of learning, which are technologically enabled or enhanced, universities are "fitting" the technology into their current forms, structures and modus operandi, largely ignoring the social implication that the e-challenge is posing.

London (2003) interviewed Greg Papdopoulos, a technical guru, about e-learning and the speed of its development. Papdopoulos' view is that:

E-learning is all about content. And there is no technology that accelerates the creation of great content—in fact, delivering online makes it harder. ... The mistake the schools, colleges and universities (and companies) have made is to think that effective e-learning content could be developed in-house by a few dedicated amateurs. They need to develop a computer application with a pedagogical user interface. ... Real life obstacles, such as human obstinacy and penny-pinching, tend to slow the advance of technology revolutions. (London 2003, p. 6)

We are being too closed minded in our consideration of e-learning, focusing on the knowledge content rather than the social interface.

The differences between traditional and e-learning methods are too great for such a close-minded view, and the challenges that e-learning poses are being left to students to resolve. Computer-mediated learning, e-learning, online learning, asynchronous-learning networks or whatever you wish to call such advances bring significantly different challenges to students. They require the development of different skills sets and are dependent on different success factors than those of traditional students. The tutor's role is different; the learning experience is different; the learning process is different, and as such, so should be the qualification. Pond (2001) acknowledges that many traditional academic and professional accrediting bodies are struggling with the sometimes blatant mismatches between traditional accrediting paradigms and new educational realities.

New paradigms require new solutions, and rather than trying to squash e-learning into traditional qualification models, why not give it a qualification classification of its own? Rather than receiving a Bachelor of Arts or Science degree in their chosen subject, students could receive a Bachelor of E-Learning degree. This moves us away from the BA in business studies or BS in environmental science to a BE in business studies or in environmental science, if the courses were undertaken predominantly through e-learning. Rather than offering traditional degrees, virtual universities should be offering virtual degrees, and their difference should be recognized. This is not to say that virtual degrees are better or worse, they are simply different. By recognizing these differences in terms of the challenges of the e-learning process and to the quality criteria, new standards and frameworks can then be established to ensure that such provisions are indeed of an equivalent standard to the more traditional provisions. Traditional quality assurance is based on the "was the instructor a content expert?" and "have the learners demonstrated mastery of the information?" model (Pond, 2001, p. 186), which allows students to make a judgment on the quality of the institution. This is proving to be an inappropriate model for e-learning as many institutions are struggling with the validation and quality monitoring of their e-learning qualifications. A number of alternatives are suggested. Julien (2005) suggests a framework for accreditation of e-trainers across Europe, while Pond (2001) suggests accrediting the learner rather than the institution.

THE E-STUDENT

Miller and Dunn (1996) define a virtual university as "a learner-oriented organisation that provides educational services to adults at the place, time, pace and in the style desired by the learner" (p. 71). While e-learning is theoretically available to anyone, anywhere, not everyone makes a good e-student. Schrum and Hong (2002) identified seven dimensions that they found to be critical success factors for adults enrolling in e-learning. Firstly, and obviously, there is access to the tools. If a student has difficulty accessing the technology there will be obvious difficulties in succeeding with the learning as they will be restricted in their abilities to "attend" the learning. The UK Ministry of Defence found this to be a key barrier to the implementation of e-learning in their workplace. Once difficulties arose with access to the technology or using the materials, the project lost credibility quickly. Volvo also had difficulties because broadband is not universally available, and Mercer Human Resource Consulting found that the superior technological infrastructure in the United States meant the United Kingdom staff was offered a lesser provision.

Secondly, and building on the access issues, is technological competence. Not only do students need to have access to the technology, but they need to be experienced and comfortable using the technology. Alexander (2001) found that students' information and communications technology (ICT) skills have an impact on participation in e-learning activities. It is a significant challenge for students to have to learn the technology, as well as the content of a course, when undertaking e-learning. B&Q appointed a coach in each of its stores to help overcome problems such as these. This also brought a social element into the e-learning process in its early stages as there was someone for employees to physically talk to if they experienced difficulties, rather than having to use e-mail to communicate.

The next three factors all relate to the learning process. The third critical success factor is learning preference. The students need to be able to recognize their own abilities and styles of learning in order to ask questions of the materials or modify their learning techniques as necessary for the online environment. This suggests a certain maturity in learning and an understanding of the learning process. Breaking the learning down into bite-sized chunks can help engage some otherwise disaffected e-learners, but it is not always appropriate to the content.

The fourth factor is study habits and skills, which builds directly on the third factor. Here the researchers found that learners appreciated the greater control over their learning, yet with this appreciation came responsibility. The learners needed to be self-disciplined enough to prepare for "class" and to do the assignments without the monitoring and guidance of a physical teacher watching over them. All the companies that took part in the Ashridge study indicated that one of the biggest barriers to e-learning was "lack of time" on the part of the participants. The ability and discipline of building e-learning into the day's activities should not be underestimated. People find it easier to build a meeting or other social interaction into their diaries, than they do half an hour of personal space for e-learning. This factor also may be partly dependent on the fifth factor—the students' goals and purposes. What is it that is motivating the student to undertake the studies in the first place? This has a huge impact on completion rates. Stating these motivations explicitly at the start of the course can help the student focus and stay on course. Some organizations have made some of their e-learning compulsory, and this has improved success rates compared to when the learners felt they had a choice.

The final two factors relate to the nature of the student themselves. Lifestyle factors can have a significant impact on students' completion rates. The student must be able to find the time to do the studies, so dependents, children, exceedingly demanding jobs (in terms of hours in the office) and other demands can reduce the time available for the student to study. Lifestyle factors, in a sense, can reduce the accessibility a student has to the learning technology. Highly social individuals will find they have less time available for e-learning, than those that prefer time to themselves, as e-learning is an activity that requires time to oneself.

The final factor is personal traits and characteristics. Students who succeed at e-learning tend to have a strong sense of commitment, willingness and self-discipline. That is not to say that traditional classroom students do not need these traits also, but they have a greater bearing on the success rates of online students than they do for traditional students. While a traditional student may succeed as a result of peer and tutor pressure, an e-learning student will not feel the same social pressure and hence will not succeed without self-discipline and commitment, and this should be recognized in their success. Bob Hesketh at Mercer Human Resource Consulting recognizes that:

E-learning is not always going to be people's first choice. ... Going on a residential training programme, meeting and socializing with colleagues is something that is highly valued by people ...

Working with a group is more rewarding for most people than working alone and the discussion with others often helps the learning process.

In the higher-education sector not all of the e-learners will be full-time students, but all of them will be influenced by the activities they engage in during the rest of their day. Volvo Trucks, for example, found that those members of their staff who spent all day, every day working at a personal computer (PC) did not want to learn at their PC, also. They were overdosed on technology before e-learning came into the equation and so were unlikely to want to swap off-site training days for PC-based learning. SkillSoft, on the other hand, interviewed more than 200 employees in 14 countries about their e-learning experiences (20% of which were compulsory e-learners), and they found that 93.5% enjoyed their e-learning experiences and 98% would recommend it to others (Baldwin-Evans, 2004).

Self-discipline and motivation in this context cannot be understated. Kerker (2001) reflected on his many e-learning experiences, having started many but not finished any at all, and concluded that, *"when not confronted with a learning deadline, I postpone the learning experience"* (p. 3). He missed the facility of being able to ask questions in real time and lacked the patience to wait for an answer. He liked being spoon-fed by a live person, who led him from one piece of information to the next, made difficult concepts simple and exciting to understand, and motivated, directed and encouraged him. While these issues could be addressed in an online environment, they would not be as "instant" as Kerker wanted, nor as "live" or as "social." Kerker illustrates nicely the fact that e-learning qualifications require "more" from a student than a traditional qualification does. He had succeeded in traditionally taught qualifications, but somehow lacked the discipline, stamina, interest and/or motivation to persevere with e-learning.

A Darwinist analogy is offered by Schrage (1999) who sees the "Harvard/Stanford model being replaced by the Wal-Mart/Amazon.com get-it-when-you-think-you-need-it model" (p. 224) and argues that "offering training resources to employees—to be used on their own time, of course—smacks of a Darwinism that presumes people who want to get ahead will actually subsidize their company's training 'investment'" (p. 224). According to Schrage's ideas, Kerker would not survive as one of the fittest.

Yet this may all change soon. Dupuis (1998) studied school children and how their use of technology is changing their learning and development in their formative years. She found that:

Not only are kids consumers of pre-packaged products, but some also become creators in this digital world. Many students work on collaborative projects, such as creating web pages or building rooms in Doom. In environments like chat rooms they learn to share ideas, question people's integrity, voice personal opinions, and accept others with backgrounds and ideas unlike their own. (p. 13)

As such she predicted that the future generation coming to college will distrust traditional institutions and authority and may prefer online learning options. Having grown up with technology, they will not have any of the "lack of technological experience" barriers that Schrum and Hong (2002) identified as being critical to success, and they already will be using technology as a social media.

This adds a challenge for e-learning material developers to keep their materials sufficiently dynamic and engaging to hold the attention of the next generation, who have been brought up with Play Stations and computer games that give "virtual reality" a dimension of its own. Simply providing text online will not suffice as e-learning materials. Unless the materials become more creative, dynamic and engaging in their format and content, with a mechanism for social interaction, then e-learning is not likely to succeed with the coming generations as it will be viewed as an old-fashioned, out-of-date, isolated mode of learning. There is a danger that e-learning could shift from being too new for the market to being too out of date for the market, without actually reaching a point of market appreciation.

There is always the possibility that future generations will find traditional classrooms even worse. Bourne, McMaster, Reiger and Campbell (1997) experimented with a course that they offered in both face-to-face (FtF) and asynchronous learning networks (ALN) formats and found that after the first few class periods few students attended the lecture sessions preferring the ALN mode. Eighty percent of the students liked the ALN and only 20% were uncomfortable without the traditional lecture. They also found no observable differences between men's and women's usage of the course materials and that non-native English speakers performed at least as well as English speakers, which is not always the case with classroom based learning. Non-native English speakers may find the ability to go back over materials as many times as they like a helpful feature of e-learning, as well as being able to work at their own pace, rather than the pace set by the instructor.

The "anytime" facility of ALN was used by students to shift their learning patterns, often to the middle of the night, however the "anywhere" element was only applicable to those who were not collocated (ibid). Where students shared a dormitory, they did not want to use their computer conferencing, preferring instead to engage in FtF discussions, but where students were located at a distance from each other, the conferencing facilities were used as other forms of social interaction were not available. This suggests that it is "easier" to undertake face-to-face discussion than engage in computer conferencing, which may be due to a number of reasons. Firstly, FtF discussion is the norm with which we have grown up and been socialized to. Secondly, as naturally social animals, we like to engage with others in social activities, even if the focus of the socializing is on some form of formal learning experience. Alternatively, it may be speed driven; talking is faster than writing, and so forth. Whatever the reason, this highlights a key difference in the e-learning process, and it needs to be recognized and negotiated in gaining an e-qualification.

Williams (2002) found a reluctance among some students to post items in a discussion group as they were, "*intimidated by the permanence of contributions as opposed to easily forgotten and fleeting face to face comments*" (p. 267). They felt uneasy about having their thoughts publicly exposed for all to see and criticize. This suggests there is an element of bravery, self-confidence and/or openness in the e-learner that may not be apparent in the traditional classroom.

The need for engagement and active participation is highlighted by many (e.g., Mazone, 1998; Bourne et al., 2002) as being key to the success of online instruction, to the extent that a minimum amount of participation is suggested as a course requirement by some. This "forces" students out of their comfort zone into the "*exposed position*," which can be avoided by sitting quietly at the back of the traditional classroom. This again highlights the additional demands that e-learning places on students.

Other issues or problems that students may encounter with e-learning are highlighted by Fontaine (2002) in his discussion of "teleland." He identifies physical and psychological reactions to the strangeness of the e-ecology, which he calls "ecoshock." Symptoms of ecoshock include frustration, fatigue, clumsiness, anxiety, paranoia, depression, irritability and rigid thinking as the appropriateness of our normal or habitual ways of doing tasks becomes problematic, and we need to develop new strategies while remaining motivated. These issues do not arise for learners in traditional classrooms but need to be overcome by the e-learner in their new e-social environment.

Mercer was one of the first UK employers to develop e-learning and, therefore, has had longer than most to reflect on what helps or hinders e-learning. Bob Hesketh, the company's learning manager, has led the e-learning project from the mid-1990s. The conclusion of his experience is that whilst technology is important, "technology by itself will not make e-learning successful." He explains that although "it is possible to introduce an e-learning programme that's technically brilliant, the programme can still fail." Experience at Mercer has shown that e-learning is not always going to be people's first choice. Going on a residential program, meeting and socializing with colleagues is something that is highly valued by some people. They prefer to work with a group, finding it more rewarding than working alone, and the discussion with others often helps the learning process. The challenge for e-learning designers is to meet these learning needs and cater to these learning styles within a virtual environment.

THE ROLE OF THE E-TUTOR

Given that online learning has the ability to take place anywhere and at anytime, the role of the academic changes considerably. In the traditional classroom the tutor is there for the set time period of the class and interacts with the students during that time, which usually involves them giving some sort of "performance," often in the form of a lecture. As such the tutor's role is akin to the "sage on the stage." The tutor is the "font of all knowledge" and they impart this knowledge to the student. While it is possible for this performance to be recorded and replayed anywhere at anytime through video or other digital means, this simply replicates the performance as the "sage in a box," rather than transforming the experience into an online learning event. ALN that truly take advantage of the anywhere, anytime modality see the role of the tutor changing to the "guide on the side" (Bourne et al., 1997). No longer are they the font of all knowledge imparting the answers, but they become the resource to help guide, direct and facilitate student learning. This does not necessarily mean that the tutor is less engaged in the learning experience than in the traditional classroom; their engagement is simply different.

If it is done well, e-tutoring is a very time-consuming teaching strategy as planning involves understanding the context of the learning, the ICT itself, and the teaching and learning design (Alexander, 2001). In addition, much of the communication is one to one, and this cannot be avoided. "Students consistently rate communication and support from faculty and other students as having the major influence on their online learning experience" (Alexander, 2001, p. 242), so planning the social element in the online learning experience is also key. Hines (1996) sees the future role of the teacher as one of being an intermediary. They will act as intermediaries between students and the world of information, helping students draw on resources from around the globe. It will all be personal instruction, not class based, and the learning will be at the students pace.

Moshinskie (2001) highlights the role of the tutor in giving students the human touch, and combining push and pull strategies to get students through the course, that is the tutor should both require and inspire. Salmon (2002) calls for teachers to have passion and commitment, identifying the key issues for teachers and learners as being participation, emotions and time. Lawther and Walker (2001) found a lack of responsibility in their students for their own learning. Their tutors had to increase the number of personal consultations regarding assessments when delivering online, and students wanted regular milestones and feedback to help them pace themselves. This is supported by Canning's (2002, p. 40) findings that 35% of noncompleters of e-learning claimed, "more extensive support from their tutor," would have helped them complete their studies. The role of the e-tutor could be in danger of becoming a combination of providing a form of social pressure and administrative support.

A body of research is emerging on the importance of interaction in online learning. Murray (2003) suggests that people are realizing that online learning is not about ever more sophisticated technology but how that technology is used. As e-learning developers realize that the human side of teaching remains as important as it was in the pre-Internet era, interactive technologies could still hold the most potential for distance-learning designers. In addition, the training of the online instructor or e-tutor is paramount to the success of the online learning process (Gibbons & Wentworth, 2001). They suggest that prospective online facilitators need to learn to transfer the responsibility for learning to the learner through a combination of experiential learning and the use of the same collaborative learning models that they will be facilitating with students, that is they should learn to tutor online by studying online. This allows new e-tutors to gain an understanding of the differences in the online learner's experience, the online course delivery, and empathy for the needs and challenges that the learners face. This takes both time and commitment on the part of trainers but was the approach adopted by Coca-Cola Enterprises GB. They piloted e-learning on their human resources team which now understands from first-hand experience what helps and what hinders e-learning.

A key message stemming from the Ashridge Business School case studies is that e-learning must drive the technology and not the other way round. Information technology (IT) departments and academics need to be partners in the development of e-learning, not adversaries, and IT needs to be involved very early in the process.

THE E-LEARNING EXPERIENCE

If "pedagogy describes the traditional instructional approach based on teacher directed learning theory" and "andragogy describes the approach based on self-directed learning theory" (Gibbons & Wentworth, 2001, p. 1), then e-learning largely falls into the andragogical approach. De Boer and Collis (2002) take the educational model further than andragogy and propose that the use of Web sites as environments where learners can contribute to the learning resources of others means that the students become contributors as well as consumers in what De Boer and Collis term a "contributive pedagogy." They propose that courses should be redesigned online so that there are very few "lectures" but many activities that require Web site contributions.

Bourne et al. (1997) examined learning paradigms, comparing their traditional use with their implementation in ALNs. They found that the "learning by listening" paradigm traditionally represented as lectures could be represented as on-screen video but the lack of actual "presence" resulted in this being a relatively poor way of learning in ALNs. The "discovery learning" traditionally undertaken in a library benefited from ALNs, as Web searches could be much more effective. "Learning by doing" traditionally represented as laboratory work or writing/creating things could work well online but required investment in good learning modules and simulations, which are perhaps still lacking in most online learning environments. Finally, they saw the "learning through discussion and debate" paradigm as the one that potentially benefited most from ALNs. While it was difficult to engage a large class in discussion, needing smaller groups in traditional learning environments, the potential to scale up to many learners in ALNs could lead to a much richer discussion.

However, it is important to note that the online discussion is "different" when compared to face to face communication, as there is more time for reflection in the communication process—both from the students' and tutors' perspectives. Indeed, Bourne et al. (1997) identified "how to impart the 'closeness' of an intense face-to-face

interaction to ALN," as one of the issues remaining to be resolved with online learning. While they see the ALN as allowing the potential for social interaction to be scaled up in terms of the number of people joining a conversation, they recognize that the nature of the conversation process itself will be different.

This is one of the key factors that differentiates e-learning from face-to-face learning which underpins the argument for such qualifications being accredited separately. Face-to-face communication, debate and discussion are different forms of social interaction to asynchronous discussion through some form of written media (i.e., e-mail or a chat room). Even very fast typists cannot type at the speed at which they can talk, so the whole communication process is slowed down. Not only is it slowed down in terms of speed of expression, but it is slowed down with regard to speed of response as well. The message has to be written, posted, accessed and read before it can be responded to, rather than simply listened to. This process involves a different skills set. If you've ever read a transcript of an interview, you will see how the spoken word differs from the written word, as grammar, syntax, emphasis, use of pauses, punctuation and use of sub-sentences in the middle of a sentence (to name but a few) all make the reading of the transcript difficult to follow, while listening to the interview is easy. As such the ability to "converse" through some form of written ALN requires the ability to express yourself in written forms, not only to be understood, but also interpreted in the "tone of voice" that you intended.

The social psychological aspects of computer-mediated communication were examined by Keisler, Siegel, and McGuire (1987) and were found to be profoundly different from face-to-face communication. Issues of difference they identified in the communication process included time and information processing pressures, absence of regulating feedback, dramaturgical weakness, few status and position cues, social anonymity, computing norms and immature etiquette. While etiquette may have matured somewhat since 1987, the lack of regulating feedback and dramaturgical weaknesses in terms of lack of facial expression, body language and intonation still persist. Hudson's (2002) work supports these differences. He found that criticisms written online could come across as particularly harsh when not moderated by voice inflections or gestures. He offered suggestions that could help moderate the reception, suggesting that critical feedback should be given either about the concept or idea that the student has stated or the context in which the issues have arisen, rather than the student themselves.

The concept of community in the classroom was explored by Rovai (2002) who compared traditional and e-learning courses and identified four components of classroom community: interactivity; a sense of well-being of the student; the quality of the learning experience; and the effectiveness of the learning. His results suggested that there was no significant difference between ALNs and traditional classrooms in the overall sense of classroom community, but found that course design and pedagogy have a greater impact on community in the ALN course, than the traditional course. This may explain the disconnectedness and isolation that many other studies of e-learning report in their findings. Rovai did find some slight differences within the feelings of community, with traditional classrooms scoring higher with regards to similarity of learner needs, connectedness, friendship and group identity and ALNs scoring higher with regard to learners' feelings of recognition, the importance of learning in the course, thinking critically in the course, safety, and acceptance. This supports Schrum and Hong's (2002) critical factors for online success, as the motivation of the learners, their personal characteristics and learning preferences relate to those areas where the ALNs scored more highly. These relate to the task-driven interaction areas, rather than the socio-emotional areas that the traditional courses seem to score higher on.

Another difference in e-learning when compared to traditional learning is the application of multitasking to a form of multilearning. Crook and Barrowcliff (2001) observed undergraduate students usage of their computers on campus and found that users multitasked with several applications opened simultaneously. Of their sample, 47% had sessions exceeding five hours without a break, and on average they shifted between applications 79 times (with only 10% of time being accounted for by games). While it was common for sound and video players to be active in the background (akin to having the stereo on for background music), browsers were used most, followed by text, then e-mail. These findings suggest that students spend time looking for information and assimilating the data for use across subject areas. They also may "discuss" their findings with other students through e-mail as part of the social process.

CONCLUSION

E-learning clearly moves higher education into a new modus operandi. There are differences to be found with regard to the students, the tutors' role, the learning materials and the learning experience. It makes distance learning more "distant" than it was previously as there no longer needs to be any synchronous, real-time communication in the learning process. These differences define a whole new structure for qualifications that need to be monitored for quality assurance purposes now. Roger Betts, director of Imperial's distance learning MBA program said, "distance learning will always be the second best option. It is hard to see where technology will go, but it seems unlikely to compensate for the benefits of direct contact with students" (Anderson, 2003). While the only quality-assurance frameworks in position are those designed around some form of synchronous learning experiences, but they will never be appropriate for e-learning. Hence such qualifications will remain the second-best option in terms of quality assurance. A new framework is necessary now before there is a proliferation of e-learning offerings claiming to be of university-degree standard, when they are not.

There are a number of factors that could be contributing to the failure of anyone developing quality standards for e-learning. Firstly, there are difficulties surrounding the definition of e-learning itself. The term is used to refer to many different approaches, from an electronically delivered training material to more advanced media-rich content, such as video-streaming, and sophisticated "classroom tools." Secondly, there are the difficulties stemming from media hype that raises expectations unrealistically. Early e-learning, in particular, often took the form of text on screen, rather than text in a textbook. The education and training sector have been slow to integrate the creative opportunities that e-learning affords them. Learning could be made as exciting as a PlayStation game, but so far, it hasn't been.

Thirdly, in many universities and organziations, it was taken for granted that if the e-learning system was provided, people would use it. This has not turned out to be the case. It is like taking a horse to water but not being able to make it drink. E-learning needs to be marketed and introduced to students, rather than being thrust in front of them with them being left to get on with it.

There have also been problems with the technology itself. Despite efforts at standardization, compatibility between all courseware and learning-management systems is far from achieved, making collaborations such as Univesitas21 and the Global University Alliance partnerships in principle, rather than in practice. This has meant that purchasers have had to narrow down course selection to single platforms (Gold, 2003). Once standardization has been achieved, Singh and Reed (2002) see content becoming portable between university courses and learning-management systems, allowing different learning applications to share content and track data, giving greater variety in e-learning offerings and combinations.

The future for e-learning is uncertain. If universities continue to try and introduce it within their current structures and frameworks, they will fail, as they are trying to fit a square peg into a round hole. If, on the other hand, they embrace and exploit the differences that e-learning can offer, then they will expand the sphere of higher education beyond current expectations. However, they must address the issue of social interaction within e-learning, be it between tutor and student, or amongst students, as this appears to be a critical factor in e-learning success. This is a challenge both for the e-learning providers and the e-learners themselves. The demand for e-learning is increasing. Evans and Haase (2000) surveyed more than 2,500 people and found that 42% would be very likely to participate in online higher education if a particular course or program was offered that is not currently available. This could signal that the market is ready for a massive expansion and change in the provision. Recognizing the differences that e-learning offers by categorizing e-qualifications separately, with their own process for assuring quality could be a first step down this road. It would bring to the forefront the challenges that e-learning poses, ensuring that students have a much more realistic idea of the additional challenges they will face when undertaking their studies to those taught in a more traditional, social environment.

REFERENCES

Abeles, T. P. (2005). Institutional change in The Academy. *On the Horizon—The Strategic Planning Resource for Education Professionals, 13*(2), 63-68.

Alexander, S. (2001). E-learning developments and experiences. *Education and Training, 43*(4/5), 240-248.

Anderson, L. (2003, March 24). Fresh ways of learning at the touch of a finger. *Financial Times Special Report: Business Education*, p. I.

Baldwin-Evans, K. (2004). Employees and e-learning: What do the end-users think? *Industrial and Commercial Training, 36*(7), 269-274.

Barnett, R. (2000). *Realizing the university in an age of supercomplexity.* Buckingham, UK: SRHE and Open University Press.

Birchall, D., & Smith, M. (2002). *Scope and scale of e-learning delivery amongst UK Business Schools.* London: CEML.

Bourne, J. R., McMaster, E., Reiger, J., & Campbell, J. O. (1997). Paradigms for on-line learning. *Journal of Asynchronous Learning Networks, 1*(2), 38-56.

Canning, R. (2002). Distance or dis-stancing education? A case study in technology based learning. *Journal of Further and Higher Education, 26*(1), 29-42.

Crook, C., & Barrowcliff, D. (2001) Ubiquitous computing on campus: Patterns of engagement by university students. *International Journal of Human-Computer Interaction, 13*(2), 245-256.

De Boer, W., & Collis, B. (2002). A changing pedagogy in e-learning: From acquisition to contribution. *Journal of Computing in Higher Education, 13*(2), 87-101.

Delahaye, B. L., Limerick, D. C., & Hearn, G. (1994). The relationship between andragogical and pedagogical orientations and the implications for adult learning. *Adult Education Quarterly. 44*(4), 187-200.

Diebold, J. (1996). The next revolution in computers. In E. Cornish (Ed.), *Exploring your future: Living, learning and working in the information age.* (pp. 42-45). MD: World Future Society.

Dupuis, E. A. (1998, Fall/Winter) The times they are a changin: Students, technology and instructional services. *Reference Services Review,* 11-16, 32.

Evans, J. R., & Haase, I. M. (2000). What's ahead for online higher education: A consumer perspective. *Futures Research Quarterly, 16*(3), 35-48.

Fontaine, G. (2002). Presence in "teleland." In K. E. Rudestam & J. Schoenholtz-Read (Eds.), *Handbook on online learning: Innovations in higher education and corporate training* (pp. 23-52). London: Sage Publications.

Gibbons, H. S., & Wentworth, G. P. (2001). Andrological and pedagogical training differences for online instructors. *Online Journal of Distance Learning Administration, 4,*(3). Retrieved from http://www.westga.edu/~distance/ojdla/fall43/gibbons_wentworth43.html

Gold, M. (2003). Eight lessons about e-learning from five organisations. *American Society for Training and Development, 57*(8), 54.

Hines, A. (1996). Jobs and infotech. In E. Cornish (Ed.), *Exploring your future: Living, learning and working in the information age* (pp. 7-11). MD: World Future Society.

Hudson, B. (2002). Critical dialogue online: Personas, covenants and candlepower. In K. E. Rudestam & J. Schoenholtz-Read (Eds.), *Handbook on online learning: Innovations in higher education and corporate training* (pp. 53-90). London: Sage Publications.

Julien, A. (2005). Classifying e-trainer standards. *The Journal of Workplace Learning, 17*(5/6), 291-303.

Keisler, S., Siegel, J., & McGuire, T. W. (1987). Social psychological aspects of computer-mediated communication. In R. Finnegan, G. Salaman,

& K. Thompson (Eds.), *Information technology: Social issues—a reader* (pp. 247-2626). UK: Open University and Hodder & Stoughton.

Kerker, S. (2001). Confessions of a learning program dropout. *The New Corporate University Review, 9*(2)2-3, 10-11.

Lawther, P. M., & Walker, D. H. T. (2001). An evaluation of a distributed learning system. *Education and Training, 43*(2), 105-116.

London, S. (2003, March 24). The networked world changes everything. *Financial Times Special Report: Business Education*, p. VI.

Manicas, P. (2000). Higher education at the brink. In S. Inayatullah & J. Gidley (Eds.), *The university in transformation: Global perspectives on the futures of the university* (pp. 31-40). Westport, CT: Bergin & Garvey.

Margules, D. (2002). *University teaching and learning: Why a more flexible approach?* Retrieved from http://www.ioe.ac.uk/schools/leid/oet%20html%20docs/Margules_D.htm

Mazone, J. G. (1998). The essentials of effective online instruction. *Campus-Wide Information Systems, 16*(3), 104-110.

Miller, M. M., & Dunn, S. L. (1996). From the industrial to the virtual university. *Futures Research Quarterly, 12*(4), 71-84.

Moshinskie, J. (2001, August). Tips for ensuring effective e-learning. *HR Focus, 78*(8), 6-8.

Murray, S. (2003, March 24). Web based systems change the MBA landscape. *Financial Times Special Report: Business Education*, p. III.

Pond, W. K. (2001). Twenty-first century education and training: Implications for quality assurance. *The Internet and Higher Education, 4*(3/4), 185-192.

Rooney, D., & Hearn, G. (2000). Of minds, markets and machines: How universities might transcend the ideology of commodification. In S. Inayatullah & J. Gidley (Eds.), *The university in transformation: Global perspectives on the futures of the university* (pp. 91-104). Westport, CT: Bergin & Garvey.

Rovai, A. A. P. (2002). A preliminary look at the structural differences of higher education classroom communities in traditional and ALN courses. *Journal of Asynchronous Learning Networks, 6*(1), 41-56.

Salmon, G. (2002, April). *Hearts, minds & screens: Taming the future.* Keynote speech presented at the EduCAT Summit: Innovation in E-Education, Hamilton, New Zealand.

Schofield, N., & Rylance-Watson, E. (2002). *Management and leadership training and development delivered through e-learning outside the business schools.* London: CEML.

Schrum, L., & Hong, S. (2002). Dimensions and strategies for online success: Voices from experienced educators. *Journal of Asynchronous Learning Networks, 6*(1), 57-67.

Schrage, M. (1999). Sorry, no keg parties here. This university is on the desktop. *Fortune*, (11), 224.

Singh, H., & Reed, C. (2002). Demystifying e-learning standards. *Industrial and Commercial Training, 34*(2), 62-65.

Williams, C. (2002). Learning on-line: A review of recent literature in a rapidly expanding field. *Journal of Further and Higher Education, 26*(3), 263-272.

Chapter II
Social Implications
of E-Mentoring:
Development of an
E-Mentoring Model

Veronica M. Godshalk
Pennsylvania State University, USA

ABSTRACT

E-mentoring, also known as online mentoring or virtual mentoring, is changing the way that traditional mentor and protégé dyad members interact with each other. Mentoring has been widely known for its ability to enhance the career development, and to provide psychosocial support, for more junior organizational members. Through the use of computer-mediated communication technology, e-mentoring may allow individuals to bridge geographic and time differences. However, there is still much we do not know about e-mentoring and its social effects. This chapter focuses on whether or not computer-mediated communication (CMC) technology will allow for true mentoring relationships to develop, as well as what personal characteristics may be necessary to grow these virtual relationships. A model and proposition for future research are offered.

INTRODUCTION

It is indisputable that computer-mediated communication technology (CMC), that is the Internet, e-mail, instant messaging and related technologies, is changing the social landscape and the process of how we communicate with one another. Harris Interactive reported that more than 156 million adults, or 73% of the U.S. population age 18 and older, were communicating online in 2004. The Harris Interactive study characterized online users as representative of "mainstream" America in that 30% of users reported having a college degree or greater, and 48% noted annual household incomes of $50,000 or greater (Harris Interactive, 2004). Eurostat reports that close to 54% of European

Internet users link up every day or almost every day, and 82% link up weekly. In Europe, student use is particularly high (ranging from 42 to 96%) on a daily basis as is use by people educated at a graduate level (Eurostat, 2005).

As these individuals continue to use CMC, Kock (2004) suggests that this new digital media is creating new social situations and communication behaviors. Social scientists cannot entirely agree on what these social changes may be (DiMaggio, Hargittai, Neuman, & Robinson, 2001; Nie & Ebring, 2000; Lin, 2001) or if computer-mediated technology can substitute sufficiently for face-to-face (FtF) communication (Daft & Lengel, 1986; Daft, Lengel, & Trevino, 1987; Short, Williams, & Christie, 1976). Given the social implications of CMC use and the challenges facing the e-business environment, it is agreed that investigating these phenomena during the early stages of the new medium's diffusion and institutionalization is incredibly important research (DiMaggio et al., 2001).

E-mentoring is a recent social construction using CMC. Whether it is called e-mentoring, or online mentoring, telementoring, cybermentoring or virtual mentoring (Single & Muller, 2001), e-mentoring can be characterized as an ongoing, computer-mediated relationship that involves the receipt of mentoring functions between junior (inexperienced) and senior (more experienced) partners. E-mentoring relationships are evolving from traditional mentoring relationships due to CMC. Traditional, FtF mentoring involves the mentor providing psychosocial and vocational support functions. The setting and pursuit of goals for personal and professional development is an important element in the transfer of learning in mentor-protégé relationships, and mentors often offer feedback and information to help the protégé attain his or her goals (Godshalk & Sosik, 2003; Kram, 1985). Through the use of CMC, e-mentoring relationships are changing social patterns and communication styles, and allowing

e-mentors to provide similar support functions for e-protégés.

Mentors provide protégés with three broad functions: career development (i.e., exposure and visibility, coaching, protection, sponsorship, challenging assignments), psychosocial support (i.e., acceptance and confirmation, counseling, friendship) and role modeling (demonstrating, articulating and counseling regarding appropriate behaviors implicitly or explicitly) (Kram, 1985; Scandura, 1992). The career development functions provide vocational support and are associated with protégé outcomes, including enhanced knowledge, skills and abilities, opportunities for promotion, and increased compensation. Vocational support also is provided through role modeling, which allows protégés to understand appropriate interpersonal behavior and culture within the organizational context, and aids protégés in performing tasks and communicating well with superiors, peers and subordinates. The psychosocial functions provide socio-emotional (social) support and are associated with protégé outcomes, such as job and career satisfaction, career balance, and increased expectations of career success (Allen, Eby, Poteet, Lentz, & Lima, 2004; Dreher & Cox, Jr., 1996; Scandura, 1992; Wanberg, Welsh, & Hezlett, 2003).

E-mentoring appears to be a necessary form of relationship, given the technology-dependent environment within which we work and the need to interact using CMC. Increased use of communication technology expands opportunities for individuals to obtain information that will contribute to successful career advancement. Relying solely on FtF mentors may become impossible given the globalized workforce and geographically dispersed subject matter experts. In fact, Hamilton and Scandura (2003) stated that the key distinction between e-mentoring and traditional mentoring is in the amount of face-time between mentor and protégé. Many researchers have suggested that savvy professionals would be well advised to establish a network of developmental relationships (Baugh & Scandura, 1999; Higgins & Kram, 2001). This network can include individuals within and outside a person's organization or industry. The network allows the individual to consult experienced professionals, who might aid in navigating complex organizational, subject matter and career path issues. E-mentoring has the potential to provide individuals with such a developmental network, since many e-mentors may not be located within one's organization or even physically located close by. Students, too, may be aided by e-mentoring in that support can be given in understanding career and discipline-specific areas of study (Single & Muller, 2001; Single & Single, 2005). E-mentoring allows for an increase in the protégé's network structural diversity, that is, the range and density of a professional's network (Higgins, 2004).

Ensher and Murphy (2005) suggest that e-mentoring is a mutually beneficial relationship in which learning, career and emotional support occur primarily through computer-mediated means. Sproull and Kiesler (1999) note that given the rapid rise of the Internet and e-mail, it is likely that CMC will aid in developing relationships like e-mentoring relationships. Single and Single (2005) concluded that e-mentoring is an alternative mode of relationship that facilitates the expansion of mentoring opportunities. However, no research to date has investigated the possibility of whether or not CMC users are able to develop highly interpersonal relationships, like mentoring relationships. Also, we need to understand what personal characteristics and environmental conditions are necessary to support such relationships. This is because even traditional mentoring relationships can become dysfunctional (Eby & McManus, 2004; Scandura, 1998), and e-mentoring must deal with the environmental CMC distance and personal issues, such as a lack of nonverbal cues, informal and misunderstood communications and delayed feedback, that might cause e-mentoring relationships to fail.

Therefore, the purpose of this chapter is to investigate whether or not CMC technology will allow for the development of e-mentoring relationships, and what personal characteristics are necessary on the part of the e-mentor and e-protégé. A model will be developed and propositions will be offered for future research. Theory will be garnered from the mentoring literature, communication media and business communication literatures, and sociology. Since e-mentoring is a new avenue by which individuals are transforming their careers via the Internet, an investigation of the social implications of this phenomenon is warranted. Given our technology-driven home, school and work environments, understanding who might adopt, pursue and gain from e-mentoring relationships seems an appropriate research direction that will make a significant contribution to our literature.

Can CMC Users Develop an Environment to Support Highly Interpersonal, E-Mentoring Relationships?

Since the advent of CMC, the development and emergence of the Internet in the early 1980s and widespread use over the last decade, researchers have been reflecting on: "A general question raised by the diffusion of CMC systems is the extent to which human communication is altered by such media" (Rice & Love, 1987, p. 86). Communication technologies are transforming the nature, form and temporal aspects of work. Compared to traditional means, electronic-communication technology carries more information faster, at a lower cost and to more people. However, the process of how we communicate with each other has been altered, that is, no longer FtF, creating a variety of social issues in many settings.

Specifically, social implications regarding the use of technology can be found impacting human relations in organizational settings (Gephart, 2002). CMC shortens the time between events and their consequences, reduces internal and external organizational buffers, increases the number and variety of people involved in decision making, increases vertical and horizontal communication, and allows or increases interorganizational interdependence (Hinds & Kiesler, 1995; Huber 1990; Sproull & Kiesler, 1999; Rice & Gattiker, 2001). The emergence of virtual relationships and communities, which are distinct from social communities, highlights the diffuse, globalized and digitized nature of today's CMC-based organizations (Gephart, 2002). Communication technologies affect the potential for and dynamics of information exchange as well as interpersonal relationships (Flanagin & Waldeck, 2004). Communication-technology use, therefore, has the potential to reduce uncertainty about the organization, develop positive connections with others, and give novice employees the ability to learn "the ropes" from experienced individuals, who may or may not be organizational members (Flanagin & Waldeck, 2004).

While the many benefits of CMC have been noted extensively, CMC technology is not without drawbacks. CMC has been identified as a less personal, less socio-emotional or more task-oriented medium by some researchers (Connolly, Jessup, & Valacich, 1990; Hiltz, Johnson, & Turoff, 1986; Rice & Love, 1987). CMC (specifically, e-mail) is considered a very "lean" communication channel, because nonverbal cues are not present. Media, such as videoconferencing or the telephone, are considered richer because of the inclusion of sound or expression, which encourages paralanguage cues. Two theories, social presence theory (Short et al., 1976) and media richness theory (Daft et al., 1987), are aligned with these descriptions of CMC. Social presence theory classifies communications media along a continuum according to various degrees of "awareness" of the other person. This theory posits communication is effective when the medium has the appropriate social presence required for the level of interpersonal involvement necessary for the task. Media richness theory categorizes communications media

along a continuum of "richness," where the media is able to transmit nonverbal cues, provide feedback, convey personality traits and support the use of natural language. Daft and Lengel (1986) note that FtF communication is considered the "richest" media and is most effective for reducing discussion ambiguity. E-mail, on the other hand, is not considered very rich because of inherent limitations in offering nonverbal cues and providing immediate feedback. Thus, the general conclusion of early CMC research is that, "CMC, because of its lack of audio or video cues, will be perceived as impersonal and lacking in normative reinforcement, so there will be less socio-emotional content exchanged" (Rice & Love, 1987, p. 88).

Contrasting these perspectives, other researchers suggest that more enhanced use of CMC has given rise to new theories and models to explain media-use behavior. Walther (1996) has posited that CMC users are able to develop highly interpersonal, online relationships. His model, using social information processing theory, assumes that communicators using CMC, like other communicators, are driven to develop social relationships.

To do so, previously unfamiliar users become acquainted with others by forming simple impressions through textually conveyed information ... The key difference between ... CMC and FtF communication has to do not with the amount of social information exchanged but with the rate of social information exchanged [his italics]. (Walther, 1996, p. 10)

CMC communications take longer to decipher because of the lack of nonverbal cues, hence these relationships make take longer to develop. Walther suggests that when users have time to exchange information, build impressions, compare values and provide timely feedback, CMC allows for highly interpersonal relationships to develop. Walther states that when users expect to have a long term association, CMC is no less personal than FtF.

While Walther (1996) suggests that CMC may be inefficient when compared with FtF communications, there is less reason to think that as was once thought. Empirical studies are supporting his claims. Studies have found that due to insurmountable factors, like social influences or geographic distances, users may choose "lean" communications media (like e-mail) and then modify their behavior to make up for the lack of "social presence" or "richness" associated with the media's use (Fulk, Schmitz, & Steinfeld, 1990; Lee, 1994; Markus, 1994; Ngwenyama & Lee, 1997). Researchers purporting theories of social influence (Fulk et al., 1990; Fulk, 1993) and social construction of reality (Lee, 1994) stress that the dyad's social influences (peer, cultural or communication schema similarity) have a stronger affect on the individual's use of communication media, than does the media's traits (social presence or richness). That is, when individuals experience influences from peers or superiors to use CMC or when the organization's culture embraces CMC as a primary mode of communication, individuals with these social influences will similarly embrace and use the dominant communication schema. Also, when individuals understand that geographic and time differences are commonplace in their globalized work environments, they are motivated to use the communication technology available to them to develop relationships that may assist in their completion of assignments (Hammer & Mangurian, 1987; Dimmick, Kline, & Stafford, 2000). Therefore, it appears that group norms and social influences may have greater impact on the individual and his choice of communication technology than the richness of the media's traits. The following propositions are hence offered regarding these environmental conditions:

Proposition 1: *E-mentoring dyad members, who experience high levels of social influence regard-ing the use of communication technology, such as peer or supervisor influence, or the organization's cultural influence, will be more likely to use CMC and more actively engaged in an e-mentoring relationship than those who do not experience social influence.*

Proposition 2: *E-mentoring dyad members who experience greater geographic distance and time differences will be more likely to use CMC and more actively engaged in an e-mentoring relationship than those who do not experience geographic distance and time differences.*

What Personal Characteristics are Necessary to Support E-Mentoring Relationships?

Other theories are available to inform our notions of how CMC may allow for highly interpersonal, e-mentoring relationships and specific characteristics potential e-mentors and e-protégés should demonstrate. Walther's (1992) relationship development theory and Carlson and Zmud's (1999) channel expansion theory emphasize that it is the user's knowledge and experience base that allows the individual to participate in increasingly rich communication over time. Dyad members reach out (even using CMC), and may go out of their way, to develop relationships. CMC users may invoke knowledge-building experiences, that is, previous experience with the communication technology, the discussion topic, the organizational context or the dyad coparticipant, to enhance their relationship. Carlson and Zmud found strongest support for CMC-channel experience and experience with the communications partner, as well as some support for organizational context experience, as indicators of perceived media richness. Based on these findings, e-mentoring partners should build their relationships on previous experiences with CMC use, the organizational context and previous FtF communication (if possible) with the partner.

Kock (2004) suggests that the higher the similarity in communication schema alignment, the lower the degree of cognitive effort required, hence the more effective the e-mentoring communications. While individuals may differ on how they choose to communicate with others due to cultural or other learned behaviors, fundamental differences affect communication negatively (Tan, Watson, & Wei, 1995). Specifically, when schema misalignment exists, Kock suggests an increase in "the amount and intensity of communication necessary to accomplish collaborative tasks and reach a shared understanding of concepts and ideas needed to complete tasks" (2004, p. 337). A communication schema misalignment (i.e., communication verbiage or contextual misunderstandings, differences in rate of feedback response or even humor misinterpretations) will detract from the e-mentoring relationship, since dyad members will experience a more task-oriented focus and less personal communications and therefore identify less with the e-mentor (Postmes, Spears, & Lea, 2001).

The more the e-mentor and e-protégé have cognitively adapted to the CMC medium, the lower the degree of cognitive effort required and, therefore, the more effective the relationship. The individual's use of knowledge-building experiences permit the user to perceive the media channel as increasingly rich (while the media's traits remain constant) and allow for effective interpersonal communication. These theories argue that the participants' knowledge, experience, communication schema similarity and informed use of the communication technology enhances the relationship, more so than the richness or complexity of the technology itself. Therefore,

Proposition 3: *E-mentoring dyad members who have greater knowledge-building experience, such as experience with e-mail use (CMC), the communication partner or organizational context, will be more likely to use CMC and more*

actively engaged in an e-mentoring relationship than those who have low levels of knowledge and communication experience.

Proposition 4: *E-mentoring dyad members with similar communication schema will be more likely to use CMC and more actively engaged in an e-mentoring relationship than dyads with more diverse communication schema.*

Further, evidence is available to suggest other individual personality characteristics may enhance the e-mentoring relationship. Recent studies on online communities have found that these communities provide their participants with social support (Rheingold, 1993). Social support is gained from participants interacting with each other and finding common interests, since most interaction between online actors is cognitively and affectively based. Compared to real-life social networks, online communities are more often based on participants' shared interests, rather than shared demographic characteristics (Wellman & Gulia, 1999). Perceived similarity, that is shared attitudes and values, has been found to be more positively related to effective e-mentoring relationships than actual demographic similarity (Ensher, de Janasz, & Heun, 2004). Chicoat and DeWine (1985) found that audioconferencing partners produced higher ratings of their partner's attitude similarity, social attractiveness and physical attractiveness than did those partners using video or FtF communications. So it may be that perceptions of similarity, regardless of the type of media used, are more important in establishing and maintaining CMC-based e-mentoring relationships. Hence,

Proposition 5: *E-mentoring dyad members with high levels of perceived similarity will be more likely to use CMC and more actively engaged in an e-mentoring relationship than dyads with low levels of perceived similarity.*

Two other individual-level variables, self-monitoring and communication apprehension, have been suggested as important factors in the socialization process because of their focus on self-presentation and interpersonal communication competence (Flanagin & Waldeck, 2004). These variables are core concepts related to the uncertainty reduction theory that postulates that individuals engage in interactive strategies, such as direct communication, to obtain relevant information from others (Berger, 1979). Self-monitoring is related to one's interest in obtaining information from others in the environment. Self-monitoring is defined as a pragmatic self-presentation that assists individuals in identifying oneself with regard to the specific social situation and roles that are present (Snyder, 1987). High self-monitors pay close attention to the social situation and adapt their behavior accordingly. High self-monitors strive to understand the dynamics of their environment and behave in a way that is acceptable to those around them, all while causing minimal disruption to others (Snyder & Coupland, 1989). In order to reduce uncertainty in their environment, high self-monitors would find the most inconspicuous mechanism by which to gather information. Flanagin and Waldeck suggest that high self-monitors would readily use CMC to gather the necessary information that would allow them to fit into and feel comfortable about their environment. These researchers state that high self-monitors "may regard e-mail as a way of obtaining information from trusted others in an unobtrusive manner" (Flanagin & Waldeck, 2004, p. 150). Low self-monitors, on the other hand, may be more apt to rely on traditional FtF channels of communication, since they are less selective and socially adept in understanding when, how and why to ask for information (Sypher & Sypher, 1983) and are less afraid to reveal their uncertainties (Flanagin & Waldeck, 2004). Therefore:

Proposition 6: *E-mentoring dyad members who are high self-monitors will be more likely to use CMC as a primary mode of communication and will become more actively engaged in an e-mentoring relationship than low self-monitors.*

Communication apprehension (CA) can be defined as "an individual's level of fear or anxiety associated with either real or anticipated communication with another person" (McCroskey, 1997, p. 82). Individuals with high CA tend to respond to situations in which they feel anxious by avoiding or withdrawing from communication. In work settings, high CAs are perceived as less competent, less attractive, potentially less successful, productive and satisfied on the job, and as having more difficulty in establishing relationships with co-workers than their more verbal counterparts. High CAs are less likely to receive supervisory positions and are more likely to be dismissed from their jobs than low CAs (Richmond, 1997). However, given CMC advantages in providing a forum for information sharing without the discomfort of FtF interaction and other characteristics, such as anonymity and absence of status differences, (Postmes et al., 2001; Weisband, Schneider, & Connolly, 1995), high CAs will more readily use CMC to establish relationships and gather necessary information than would their low CA counterparts. In fact, low CA individuals may relish and miss the FtF interactions that allow them to differentiate themselves from high CAs. While it is acknowledged that low CAs will probably engage in e-mentoring relationships at the same rate (or possibly at a greater rate) as high CAs, it is believed that high CAs will use CMC as a primary mechanism for communication due to their inherent apprehension towards FtF communication. Hence,

Proposition 7: *E-mentoring dyad members who have high CA will be more likely to use CMC as a primary mode of communication than individuals low in CA.*

Future Research Opportunities

Taken together, these propositions support Walther's (1996) and Carlson and Zmud's (1999) assertions that CMC allows for highly interpersonal relationships to develop, especially when e-mentoring dyad members use knowledge-building experiences, perceive similarities in attitudes, values, and communication schema, and appreciate their self-monitoring and CA behaviors. Also, the propositions suggest that given certain environmental conditions, such as the social influences received from peers, supervisors and the organization's culture, as well as geographic and time differences, e-mentoring may act as a suitable proxy for traditional mentoring relationships. By taking the time necessary to learn about each partner, e-mentoring relationships can be long-term, healthy relationships, regardless of their CMC format. Reported findings from Mentornet (2004), a formal e-mentoring program for college women designed to assist them with remaining in the science field, found that:

- Fifty percent of respondents reported that the e-mentoring program filled a gap in their support system.
- More than 50% reported greater confidence in their chosen area of study and felt they would succeed in their careers.

- Close to 40% of respondents said they would be applying at the e-mentor's company for a job after graduation.
- No differences were found in relationship satisfaction for same-race versus cross-race pairings.
- Some women of color reported increased self-confidence due to their e-mentoring relationship.

Clearly, this anecdotal data suggests that e-mentoring is working. Most of the data we have today about the effectiveness of e-mentoring is anecdotal in nature. Figure 1 articulates the relationship between all the variables of interest discussed in this chapter. The model and propositions noted herein need empirical testing, as do future propositions and hypotheses about potential variables. In order to understand how e-mentoring affects employees and what social implications it creates, researchers need to investigate the processes inherent in e-mentoring relationships. Differences between formal and informal e-mentoring relationships, the time and distance effect of CMC on e-mentoring, and the personal characteristics of who will be successful in e-mentoring relationships are burgeoning research opportunities. Further investigation is necessary so that we might understand the nuances

Figure 1. Antecedents and outcomes of e-mentoring relationships

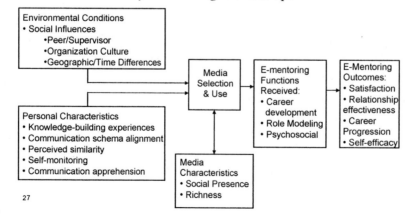

associated with the antecedents and outcomes of e-mentoring functions provided.

Ensher, Heun, and Blanchard (2003) state that while the majority of research on e-mentoring relationships focuses on formal programs, such as MentorNet, there is evidence that spontaneous relationships are blossoming through use of CMC technology. Ensher et al. suggest that researchers examine the similarities and differences of e-mentoring when comparing formal and informal relationships. The traditional mentoring literature has investigated formal and informal programs and found informal programs to be more advantageous for dyad members (Wanberg et al., 2003). However, while looking at similarities and differences in formal and informal relationships will inform the literature, it will be a challenge for researchers to investigate (and gather data on) informal e-mentoring relationships due to their casual nature and virtual format. In the meantime, there are many opportunities to examine formal programs and to understand how long these relationships last, what type of influences participants feel in formal programs, how mentoring functions are received, and what outcomes occur for dyad members and their organizations. The literature will be greatly informed should researchers gather data from all parties—the e-mentor, e-protégé and their employers. Agreement on variables of interest has been found to provide greater insight and reduces reporting biases by respondents (Godshalk & Sosik, 2000; Sosik & Godshalk, 2004).

The social implications of CMC on e-mentoring relationships needs to be investigated as we move further away from having a majority of traditional, FtF relationships and towards having a majority of relationships based on use of CMC technology. Early researchers were emphatic that FtF relationships could not be adequately replicated through the use of technology (Connolly et al., 1990; Daft et al., 1987; Rice & Love, 1987; Short et al., 1976). Because of today's social influences on employees, the geographic

and time differences that must be overcome to complete assigned tasks, and the commonplace use of communication technology, employees are forging relationship through use of CMC with some success (Carlson & Zmud, 1999; Walther, 1992, 1996). E-mentoring researchers need to empirically examine how mentoring functions are received in an online format and what outcomes occur for both protégés and mentors. Also, the effects of time and distance should be analyzed. Do e-mentoring relationships flourish because of, or in spite of, time and distance constraints? How long can such relationships last without FtF interactions? Can audio and video technologies be adequate surrogates for FtF e-mentoring interactions?

Finally, our model posits certain personal characteristics that would make individuals more likely to use CMC and, therefore, to become more actively engaged in e-mentoring relationships. There may be other individual difference variables that should be considered to understand who might participate in e-mentoring programs. Quantitative surveys of e-mentoring program participants will provide such data. Such investigations will inform organizations who plan to offer formal e-mentoring programs. It may be that certain individuals are predisposed for success in an e-mentoring environment, while others may be less interested and engaged.

CONCLUSION

This chapter has offered a model and various propositions to investigate whether or not CMC technology will allow for the development of e-mentoring relationships. Specific environmental conditions, such as the social influences of peers, supervisors and the organization's culture, as well as personal characteristics, are posited as antecedents of an individual's choice of CMC use and subsequent engagement in an e-mentoring relationship.

E-mentoring is clearly a new tool individuals may use to enhance their careers, yet the social implications of this phenomenon are still under investigation. The real challenges surrounding e-mentoring involve what effect, if any, the lack of FtF interaction has on dyad members, their organization and their career progression. Given our technology-driven environment, understanding who might adopt, pursue and gain from e-mentoring relationships is a new research direction that will make a significant contribution to our literature. It is hoped that future empirical exploration will shed some light, for both researchers and practitioners, on how e-mentoring will positively affect careers in the 21st century.

REFERENCES

Allen, T.D., Eby, L.T., Poteet, M.L., Lentz, E., & Lima, L. (2004). Career benefits associated with mentoring for protégés: A meta-analysis. *Journal of Applied Psychology, 89*(1), 127-136.

Baugh, S. G., & Scandura, T. A. (1999). The effects of multiple mentors on protégé attitudes toward the work setting. *Journal of Social Behavior & Personality, 14*(4), 503-521.

Berger, C. R. (1979). Beyond initial interaction: Uncertainty, understanding and the development of interpersonal relationships. In H. Giles & R. St. Clair (Eds.), *Language and social psychology* (pp. 89-102). Oxford, UK: Basil Blackwell.

Carlson, J. R., & Zmud, R. W. (1999). Channel expansion theory and the experiential nature of media richness perceptions. *Academy of Management Journal, 42*(2), 153-170.

Chicoat, Y., & DeWine, S. (1985). Teleconferencing and interpersonal communication perception. *Journal of Applied Communication Research, 18*, 14-32.

Connolly, T., Jessup, L. M., & Valacich, J. S. (1990). Effects of anonymity and evaluative tone on idea generation in computer-mediated groups. *Management Science, 36*, 97-120.

Daft, R. L., & Lengel, R. H. (1986). Organizational information requirements, media richness and structural design. *Management Science, 32*(5), 554-571.

Daft, R. L., Lengel, R. H., & Trevino, L. K. (1987). Message equivocality, media selection, and manager performance: Implications for information systems. *MIS Quarterly, 11*(3), 355-366.

DiMaggio, P., Hargittai, E., Neuman, W. R., & Robinson, J. P. (2001). Social implications of the Internet. *Annual Review of Sociology, 27*, 307-336.

Dimmick, J., Kline, S., & Stafford, L. (2000). The gratification niches of personal e-mail and the telephone. *Communication Research, 27*(2), 227-248.

Dreher, G. F., & Cox, T. H., Jr. (1996). Race, gender and opportunity: A study of compensation attainment and the establishment of mentoring relationships. *Journal of Applied Psychology, 81*, 297-308.

Eby, L. T., & McManus, S. E. (2004). The protégé's role in negative mentoring experiences. *Journal of Vocational Behavior, 65*(2), 255-275.

Ensher, E. A., de Janasz, S. C., & Heun, C. (2004). *E-mentoring: Virtual relationships and real benefits.* Paper presented at the Academy of Management Annual Meeting, New Orleans, LA.

Ensher, E. A., Heun, C., & Blanchard, A. (2003). Online mentoring and computer-mediated communication: New directions for research. *Journal of Vocational Behavior, 63*, 264-288.

Ensher, E. A., & Murphy, S. E. (2005). *How successful mentors and protégés get the most out of their relationships.* San Francisco: Jossey-Bass.

Eurostat.(2005). *Statistics in focus: Industry, trade and services—population and social conditions—science and technology, 25*. Retrieved April 29, 2006, from http://epp.eurostat.cec. eu.int/cache/ITY_OFFPUB/KS-NP-05-025/EN/ KS-NP-05-025-EN.PDF

Flanagin, A. J., & Waldeck, J. H. (2004). Technology use and organizational newcomer socialization. *Journal of Business Communication, 41*(2), 137-165.

Fulk, J. (1993). Social construction of communication technology. *Academy of Management Journal, 36*(5), 921-950.

Fulk, J., Schmitz, J., & Steinfeld, C. W. (1990). A social influence model of technology use. In J. Fulk & C. W. Steinfeld (Eds.), *Organizations and communication technology* (pp. 117-140). Newbury Park, CA: Sage.

Gephart, R. P. (2002). Introduction to the brave new workplace: Organizational behavior in the electronic age. *Journal of Organizational Behavior, 23*, 327-344.

Godshalk, V. M., & Sosik, J. J. (2000). Does mentor-protégé agreement on mentor leadership behavior influence the quality of mentoring relationships? *Group & Organization Management, 25*, 291-317.

Godshalk, V. M., & Sosik, J. J. (2003). Aiming for success: The role of learning goal orientation in mentoring relationships. *Journal of Vocational Behavior, 63*, 417-437.

Hamilton, B. A., & Scandura, T. A. (2003). E-mentoring: Implications for organizational learning and development in a wired world. *Organizational Dynamics, 31*(4), 388-402.

Hammer, M., & Mangurian, G. E. (1987). The changing value of communications technology. *Sloan Management Review, 28*(2), 65-72.

Harris Interactive. (2004, September 8). *156 million (73%) adults in U.S. are now online; 44% of them have broadband* (press release). Retrieved February 13, 2006 from http://www.harrisinteractive.com

Higgins, M. (2004). *Developmental network questionnaire.* Cambridge, MA: Harvard Business School Publishing.

Higgins, M. C., & Kram, K. E. (2001). Reconceptualizing mentoring at work: A developmental network perspective. *Academy of Management Review, 26*, 264-288.

Hiltz, S. R., Johnson, K., & Turoff, M. (1986). Experiments in group decision making: Communication process and outcome in face-to-face versus computerized conferences. *Human Communication Research, 13*, 225-252.

Hinds, P., & Kiesler, S. (1995). Communication across boundaries: Work, structure, and use of communication technologies in a large organization. *Organization Science, 6*, 373-393.

Huber, G. P. (1990). A theory of the effects of advanced information technologies on organizational design, intelligence, and decision making. In J. Fulk & C. W. Steinfeld (Eds.), *Organizations and communication technology* (pp. 237-274). Newbury Park, CA: Sage.

Kock, N. (2004). The psychobiological model: Towards a new theory of computer-mediated communication based on Darwinian evolution. *Organization Science, 15*(3), 327-348.

Kram, K. E. (1985). *Mentoring at work.* Glenview, IL: Scott, Foresman and Company.

Lee, A. S. (1994). Electronic mail as a medium for rich communications: An empirical investigation using hermeneutic interpretation. *MIS Quarterly, 18*(2), 143-157.

Lin, N. (2001). *Social capital: A theory of social structure and action.* New York: Cambridge University Press.

Markus, M. L. (1994). Electronic mail as the medium of managerial choice. *Organizational Science, 5,* 502-527.

McCroskey, J. C. (1997). Willingness to communicate, communication apprehension, and self-perceived communication competence: Conceptualizations and perspectives. In J. A. Daly, J. C. McCroskey, J. Ayres, T. Hopf & D. M. Ayres (Eds.), *Avoiding communication: Shyness, reticence, and communication apprehension* (pp. 75-108). Cresskill, NJ: Hampton.

Mentornet, (2003). *2002-2003 program evaluation highlights.* Retrieved on January, 26, 2006, from http://www.mentornet.net

Ngwenyama, O. K., & Lee, A. S. (1997). Communication richness in electronic mail: Critical social theory and the contextuality of meaning. *MIS Quarterly, 21*(2), 145-167.

Nie, N. H., & Ebring, L. (2000). *Internet and society: A preliminary report.* Stanford, CA: Institute for the Quantitative Study of Society.

Postmes, T. T., Spears, R., & Lea, M. (2001). Communication and commitment in organizations: A social identity approach. *Group Processes & Intergroup Relations, 4*(3), 227-246.

Rheingold, H. (1993). *The virtual community: Homesteading on the electronic frontier.* Reading, MA: Addison-Wesley.

Rice, R. E., & Gattiker, U. E. (2001). New media and organizational structuring. In F. M. Jablin & L. L Putnam (Eds.), *The new handbook of organizational communication* (pp. 544-581). Thousand Oaks, CA: Sage.

Rice, R. E. & Love, G. (1987). Electronic emotion: Socioemotional content in a computer-mediated network. *Communication Research, 14,* 85-108.

Richmond, V. P. (1997). Quietness in contemporary society: Conclusions and generalizations of the research. In J. A. Daly, J. C. McCroskey, J. Ayres, T. Hopf & D. M. Ayres (Eds.), *Avoiding communication: Shyness, reticence, and communication apprehension* (pp. 257-268). Cresskill, NJ: Hampton.

Scandura, T. A. (1992). Mentorship and career mobility: An empirical investigation. *Journal of Organizational Behavior, 13,* 169-174.

Scandura, T. A. (1998). Dysfunctional mentoring relationships and outcomes. *Journal of Management, 24*(3), 449-468.

Short, J., Williams, E., & Christie, B. (1976). *The social psychology of telecommunications.* London: Wiley.

Single, P. B., & Muller, C. B. (2001). When e-mail and mentoring unite: The implementation of nationwide electronic mentoring program. In L. Stromei (Ed.), *Implementing successful coaching and mentoring programs* (pp. 107-122). Cambridge, MA: American Society for Training and Development.

Single, P. B., & Single, R. (2005). E-mentoring for social equity: Review of research to inform program development. *Mentoring & Tutoring, 13*(2), 301-320.

Snyder, M. (1987). *Public appearances/private realities: The psychology of self-monitoring.* New York: W. H. Freeman.

Snyder, M., & Coupland, J. (1989). Self-monitoring processes in organizational settings. In R. A. Giacalone & P. Rosenfeld (Eds.), *Impression management in the organization* (pp. 7-20). Hillsdale, NJ: Erlbaum.

Sosik, J. J., & Godshalk, V. M. (2004). Self-other rating agreement in mentoring: Meeting protégé expectations for development and career advancement. *Group & Organization Management, 29*(4), 442-469.

Sproull, L., & Kiesler, S. (1999). Computers, networks and work. *Scientific American, 265*(3), 116-123.

Sypher, B. D., & Sypher, H. E. (1983). Self monitoring and perceptions of communication ability in an organizational setting. *Personality and Social Psychology Bulletin, 9,* 297-304.

Tan, B. C., Watson, R. T., & Wei, K. (1995). National culture and group support systems: Filtering communication to dampen power differentials. *European Journal of Information Systems, 4*(2), 82-92.

Walther, J. B. (1992). Interpersonal effects in computer-mediated interaction: A relational perspective. *Communication Research, 19,* 52-90.

Walther, J. B. (1996). Computer-mediated communication: Impersonal, interpersonal, and hyperpersonal interaction. *Communication Research, 23,* 3-43.

Wanberg, C. R., Welsh, E. T., & Hezlett, S. A. (2003). Mentoring research: A review and dynamic process model. *Research in Personnel and Human Resource Management, 22,* 39-124.

Weisband, S. P., Schneider, S. K., & Connolly, T. (1995). Computer mediated communication and social information: Status salience and status differences. *Academy of Management Journal, 38*(4), 1124-1151.

Wellman, B., & Gulia, M. (1999). Net surfers don't ride alone: Virtual community as community. In B. Wellman (Ed.), *Networks in the global village* (pp. 331-367). Boulder, CO: Westview.

Chapter III
Social Implications of Distance Education in Alaska

Bogdan Hoanca
University of Alaska Anchorage, USA

Kenrick Mock
University of Alaska Anchorage, USA

ABSTRACT

Alaska is the largest and most sparsely populated state in the United States of America. Extreme weather patterns and extreme cultural diversity compound the challenge of delivering quality education to state residents in remote areas. E-learning technologies have emerged as a cost-effective, interactive means of delivering quality teaching to even the most isolated locations in the state. Additionally, the ability to archive content and to access it at will, in an asynchronous manner, is highly suited to the different learning styles and different learning rates of the various populations in the state. This chapter introduces the challenges associated with delivering e-learning in Alaska, reviews the historical evolution of distance-learning networks, and summarizes present achievements and future opportunities. The analysis includes K-12 education, higher education and professional continuing education.

INTRODUCTION

Alaska is a state faced with special circumstances, in particular limited availability of basic infrastructure, extreme weather and wide cultural diversity. By offering low-cost access from almost anywhere, the ability to archive content and being able to randomly access any section of this content, and ability to deliver multimedia over a variety of bandwidth channels, e-learning technologies have become critically important in Alaska, from elementary school to post-graduate levels. Most of the social implications are positive, but we point out some of the negative consequences of e-learning as well.

GEOGRAPHY AND DEMOGRAPHY OF THE STATE

In January 1959, Alaska was the 49th state to join the United States of America. Among U.S. states, it has the largest area (572,000 square miles equaling one-seventh of country's total area), but a comparatively tiny population: 627,000 inhabitants in the year 2000 or 0.2% of the U.S. population (Alaska, 2000). The population density in Alaska in the year 2000 was 1.1 people per square mile, as opposed to the U.S. average of 79.6 people per square mile. Roughly half of the state's population lives within driving distance of the three largest urban centers: Anchorage (271,000 inhabitants), Fairbanks (31,000 inhabitants) and Juneau (31,000 inhabitants). The rest of the population lives in rural areas, many in small villages of just a few hundred inhabitants. Many of these small and remote communities are accessible only by airplane and some are accessible seasonally by boat. There are fewer than a dozen roads Alaska and they primarily connect the major population centers. The state capital, Juneau, is not on the road system.

Although Alaska is part of a "first world" nation, many Alaskan citizens live in conditions more typical of "third world" countries. Many of the small villages do not have indoor plumbing, have limited and unreliable electric utilities, and have a telephone system that may not operate in extreme weather. Extreme weather is often the norm rather than the exception.

As in many other areas of the United States, part of the population diversity is due to immigration. More intriguing, the ancient inhabitants of the area, the ancestors of the Alaskan Natives themselves exhibit extreme diversity. Alaskan Natives are a diverse group of people, speaking 20 languages across seven language families. Beyond the language differences, hunting, fishing, and social habits also make the Alaska Native cultures of Yupik & Cupik, Inupiak, Athabascan, Aleut & Alutiiq, Eyak, Tlingit, and Haida & Tsimshian stand out from each other.

The Alaska Native Lands Settlement Act (ANCSA) of 1971 granted approximately one-ninth of Alaska's land and $962.5 million in cash compensation to Alaskan Natives in exchange for land claims to most of Alaska. There are 12 Regional Native Corporations, endowed with land and financial resources, with shareholders living in the respective regions, as well as a 13th corporation "at-large," which includes Natives not living within any of the Regional Corporations areas. This 13th entity was endowed only with financial resources but no land. Beyond just representing the local interests of Alaskan Natives, these corporations have become significant economic players in the state (some even nationwide) and have adopted significant roles in better serving the educational needs of the regions where they operate.

All three urban centers have local colleges and universities, as well as satellite locations of these campuses in neighboring communities, but many villages can only access these urban centers by air. A 1998 study by McDiarmid, Goldsmith, Hill, and Hull found that 60% of Alaskan students live within 20 road miles of one of the three main university campuses, while another 25% are within 20 road miles of one of the satellite campuses. This leaves 15% of the state's students unable to attend university courses within a daily commute. Given the almost equal split between urban and rural populations in the state, these statistics indicate an unde-representation of the rural population in education. Still, interestingly enough, Alaska's percentage of the population aged 25 and older who are high school graduates is 88.3%, higher than the 80.4% U.S. figure. The percentage of people with bachelors' degrees or higher is 24.7%, also higher than the

U.S. average of 24.4%. Part of the reason for this relatively high percentage of educated citizens is an extensive network of distance-education facilities throughout the state.

HISTORY AND CHALLENGES OF EDUCATION IN ALASKA

According to Darnell (1970), the first mention of a school for Alaskan Natives is in 1786, when a Russian fur trader opened an establishment on Kodiak Island to teach young Natives arithmetic, Russian and Christian values. As in many other cases of colonized indigenous populations, Christian education in Alaska was intended to "reclaim" the Natives and teach them a "useful trade." Integration in the school system occurred not by design but simply because of lack of funding for separate schools. As a consequence, the curriculum was almost exclusively Western and often involved sending young Natives to boarding schools, some of which were outside the state.

The combination of Western curriculum, alien to the Alaskan Natives, and the forced removal of young Native students to boarding schools away from their community had significant negative effects on the performance of the students. Across the cultural diversity of Native populations, one common theme is the importance of family and community connections. With these connections removed at a critical formative time, many of the Native students sent to boarding schools committed suicide, others were unable to perform at satisfactory levels and only few of them succeeded in their education.

After statehood, school administration switched to a state-level system, then to a regional- or district-based system. Initially, high schools were opened as regional institutions until a landmark suit, *Molly Hootch vs. the State of Alaska*. Citing the high dropout rates and severe cultural shock that plagued Alaska Native students in boarding schools, the suit argued

that the state was discriminating against Native students by forcing them to spend nine months a year away from home. The consent decree in 1976 forced the state to provide a minimum level of high school facilities in each village with an elementary school. The legal battles pitting the rural Alaskan population against the state of Alaska continue, most recently with the *Moore vs. State of Alaska*, which challenges the overall availability of funding for rural schools.

The No Child Left Behind Act poses additional challenges, because it requires teachers to be qualified in the subject matter they teach. A small school with a small number of students cannot afford to recruit and retain a large number of teachers; moreover, it is difficult to imagine two or three teachers qualified in teaching all of the subject matters required for students in grades K-12. One of the major implications of distance education is the ability to provide quality instruction in the local language and culture, by sharing qualified teachers among several village schools in a district.

Statistics about the school performance of Alaskan Natives are striking. Although Alaskan Natives represent about 23% of the public school population, they comprise 30% of school dropouts and only 18% of graduates. This low success rate is certainly not due to lack of motivation to succeed. Sponder (1990) reported that Alaskan Natives were highly motivated by a desire to earn a college degree. Distance delivery was important, because it enabled students to remain in their villages while studying. An earlier study of Alaska Native students (Chu & Culbertson, 1982) also concluded that Alaskan Natives are just as eager to get an education as the general population but that they have much lower expectations. The study points out that even those students who drop out of school because of "not liking school" plan to resume their studies in the future. Students tend to drop out because of factors in their surrounding socio-economic environment, not because of a lack of motivation. Distance education, especially self-paced asynchronous environments, allow more flexibility in dealing with these socio-economic factors and increase the likelihood of academic success.

Another reason for the low success rates of Alaska Native students is the difference in language and culture between students and teachers, compounded by a lack of understanding of Native culture by teachers and school staff. In 1992, less than 5% of public school teachers were Alaskan Natives, while more than 89% were white. In particular, teachers recruited from outside the state tend to have little understanding of the culture and learning style of the local students. These teachers also tend to move on before they can gain much cultural understanding. A study on recruitment and retention of special education teachers notes that teachers from urban areas or from out of state tend to stay only for a short time in the rural districts that recruited them. Many of the teachers cannot get used to the isolation and lack of comforts that is part of village life (Schnorr, 1992).

Kleinfeld and Williamson McDiarmid (1986) found that a majority of village teachers in rural Alaska had been teaching for less than two years. Teachers were satisfied with the compensation and the school facilities, including small class size and the availability of technology and teaching materials. Paradoxically, teachers also were not troubled by cultural differences and had a good relationship with the students and the entire community. The sources of discontent were the remoteness and living conditions in the village, including the availability of food and medical care; the academic progress of the students; and the management of the local school district. Many of the teachers could not get used to the isolation and lack of comfort in village life. They worked for a few years, saved their income, then moved on to another job elsewhere.

Culture shock is strong enough to make some new teachers leave immediately. Rider (1982) cites a story of a couple of teachers, who upon arrival in the village, decided to stay on the plane and return immediately, without even disembarking. Other cases she includes in the paper indicate that the rural Alaskan environment can be challenging even for more seasoned outsiders. Travel is dangerous, with older planes often having to land in very limited visibility, which may be scary for the travelers on board. By training local teachers via distance education, both the cultural gap and the retention problems can be addressed at the same time.

SOCIAL IMPLICATIONS OF DISTANCE EDUCATION IN ALASKA

Alaskan citizens tend to be independent, unafraid of living in small, remote villages or isolated cabins in the middle of nowhere. This lifestyle required children to be home schooled, even before the Internet could help in the process. Students also may attend distance education courses because of religious reasons or because of capacity limits (especially for gifted or special education students). Additionally, and more pertinent to the Alaskan realities, distance education is an option for students with substance abuse, health conditions (including pregnancy) and those in prison (Cadigan, 1993).

Distance education is defined as the instructional setting where students and instructors are not in the same room (Moore & Kearsley, 1996). Several authors prefer the term mediated learning to highlight the fact that physical remoteness is not necessary. In fact, in many settings, distance-education courses are ideal for students who are within driving distance of the instructional facilities but who prefer the technology-mediated delivery for reasons mentioned above.

In 1936, distance education began in earnest when the state purchased elementary-education courses from the Calvert School in Baltimore, and secondary-level courses from the University of Nebraska. ACD (Alyeska Central School)

Alaska's Centralized Correspondence School (based in Juneau) offered courses to any Alaskan resident. Students enrolled individually but had opportunities to interact as a group, if several were enrolled in the same class. Course materials were mailed and student-teacher interaction was later facilitated through the University of Alaska (UA) computer network's e-mail system. Group interactions occurred via telephone conference calls. Classes were offered free to students, with school districts paying for the course materials and e-mail usage when the district purchased the course. Instruction was available for secondary and elementary curriculum (Willis, 1992). By 1987 e-mail delivery was utilized by nearly 1,000 students of the Centralized Correspondence Study program (Holznagel, 1992).

Starting in the 1970s, wider deployment of satellite technology made it possible to use audio- and videoconferencing, as well as closed-circuit television, to deliver courses. The delivery network underwent periods of abundance of resources alternating with years of scarcity, because state funding fluctuated with the level of oil revenues. Even early on, utilization of the satellite TV network was high, with K-12 courses offered during the day and university and continuing-education courses in the evening. Participants also took advantage of the network for social interaction. Community productions were broadcast, including such programs as "Ask an Alaskan," a quiz show from Bethel, and audioconferences among sixth grade "pen pals" in Alaska and Washington (LearnAlaska, 1985).

Implications for K-12 Education

Given that the vast majority of the state's high schools (241 of 298) have fewer than 100 students (Metzger, 2004), sharing teachers and instructional resources via distance delivery makes sense for the school districts. Even before the widespread use of the Internet, Alaska adopted electronic communications to support the delivery of distance courses. In the early 1990s, teachers across the state were already using e-mail in a combination of on-site and distance-delivered courses to train them on developing interdisciplinary learning modules for high school students (Bartman, 1992). Interestingly, even though technology is making inroads and more and more of the distance-education courses are delivered via the Internet, the oldest correspondence school in the state, the Alyeska Central School, still relies on postal mail for 90% of the work it does with students (Cavanagh, 2003).

Currently, the list of options for distance-delivered courses in Alaska includes a number of correspondence schools. One example, the Interior Distance Education of Alaska, a program of the Galena City School District, is available statewide (http://www.ideafamilies.org/). Started in 1997 with the intent of providing education options to 150 students in the Fairbanks area, the school has grown to several thousand students (3,000 by its second year). The school provides computing equipment, network connectivity and technical assistance, as well as a choice of curricular materials. Financial allotments are made available to enroll students in courses or course equivalents that cannot be delivered over distance (e.g., physical education or music). While some reports criticize the program for allegedly providing funds for family memberships for the local gym and for ski trips out of state, program officials contend that the expenses are lower than what it would take to pay for individual students at a local school (Cavanagh, 2004).

A list of success stories of rural students empowered by distance delivered courses is given as follows:

* Cadigan (1993) reports on a project involving eighth and ninth graders from eight high schools across the state who collaboratively built a remote-controlled underwater vehicle to collect samples from the waters in Prince William Sound. The communications

methods included primarily "telecommu-nications" (sic), but also telephone, fax and mail. Students interacted with three men-tors, all of them Alaskan Natives and two of them women: a civil engineer, a professor of electrical engineering in Fairbanks and a geologist in Barrow. Each site worked on a different component of the vehicle, although they all shared copies of all design ideas and of plans for the entire vehicle. An additional benefit of this remote interaction was to make available three Alaska Native role models to students beyond the immedi-ate community where the mentors lived and worked. Cadigan notes that "the enthusiasm at all sites was palpable and infectious."

- The Kuskokwim-Yukon School District broadcasts weekday math lessons via the Internet to 17 villages with 3,800 K-12 stu-dents. These villages can be as close as an 18-mile boat ride or 155 miles away, on an island in the Bering Sea (Gaither, 2004).

- In fishing villages on St. Paul and St. George islands in the Bering Sea, students take live music lessons with teachers from Anchor-age (Gaither, 2004). St. Paul students also can access online courses leading to a Cer-tificate in Web Technology, delivered from the University of Washington, and paid for by the local Native Corporation. Online lessons are combined with phone- and vid-eoconferencing time, as well as help from a local teaching assistant and lab coordinator (Distance Education Report, 2004). The St. Paul community had only 600 residents ac-cording to the 2000 census.

- Students in Savoonga, dubbed the "Walrus Capital of the World," took part online in preparatory math classes for the high-school graduation qualifying exam in algebra I. As a result of this distance-delivery mechanism, attendance rates increased significantly (students perceiving the new way to learn as fun), and algebra test scores increased by almost 90% (Distance Learning, n.d.).

- Alaskan village students traveled virtually to the Smithsonian Institute, the Buffalo Zoo, NASA headquarters and even outer space. For example, through NASA's "Teaching from Space Program," students in Manoko-tak spent 20 minutes in live audio and video contact with astronauts aboard the Interna-tional Space Station (ADLP, 2005a).

- The FIRST LEGO League tournament brought together 39 teams statewide in 2003, competing on designing robots and solving scientific challenges. A team from Saint Michael's Island in the Bering Sea participated via videoconferencing. By 2005 the tournament expanded to include teams from Kodiak Island (ADLP, 2005b).

- One of the major events occurring during the Alaskan winter is the Iditarod sled dog race. More than 200 students in grades 4-12 from locations as far as Indiana and Texas participated in an online version of the race. They had to plan the race, assemble a dog team, train and care for the dogs, and develop race strategies (ADLP, 2005b).

- In the first worldwide kids conference, stu-dents from the Southwest Region School District, along with colleagues from 120 schools worldwide, presented to each other interactive, television-like educational pro-grams as well as musical performances (ADLP, 2005c).

- Using e-learning technologies, village stu-dents enroll for biweekly videoconferencing combined with online discussions about job opportunities, counseling and remote access to job fairs (GCI/CEO, n.d.).

The examples in this section have highlighted the multiple ways in which distance education is able to involve K-12 students in collaborative activities with peers across the state and across the world. E-learning technologies enable synchronous, media-rich interactions that make it possible for students to take classes with teachers from outside the local community and most likely outside the budgetary limits of the local school district. The availability of these course offerings also creates a path for these students to enter college, and distance education allows college students to continue to take courses in the local community.

Implications for College-Level Education

Through the university system, an effort has been made to bring higher-education courses to the rural villages via distance-delivery mechanisms. A study of distance-education needs (McDiarmid et al., 1998) revealed that more than 4,100 students took part in distance-education classes in 1997. At the time, the delivery methods relied heavily on one-way video, audioconferences and, to a lesser extent, the Internet.

More recently, a year 2000 study (Reyes & Bradley, 2000) includes quotes from a report by the University of Alaska Fairbanks that state that although Alaskan Natives comprised only 15% of the Alaskan population, they represented 25% of the distance-education students statewide. More strikingly, four courses had Alaska Native enrollments exceeding 40% and two had enrollments exceeding 50%. The most recent attendance figures for the academic year 2004-05 indicate 8,700 students on the Anchorage campus enrolled in distance-education courses (OPRA, 2005), 11% of the total undergraduate student body. Of these students, only 1,500 were taking only distance-delivered courses. The remainder (the majority, in fact) were taking both distance and traditional classes. This indicates that most students took distance education courses, even though they had the option to attend traditional courses. Moreover, 6% of the distance students were employees of the university, which eliminates any overhead due to commuting from work to school.

A snapshot of distance-delivered course offerings from the University of Alaska Distance Education Gateway (http://www.alaska.edu/distance) in fall 2005 is shown in Figure 1. Web-based instruction is now the most common form of distance instruction, comprising 43% of all distance offerings. Most Web-based courses involve static modules with little synchronous student-teacher interaction. Internet-based syn-

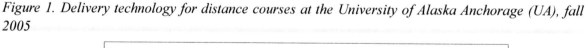

Figure 1. Delivery technology for distance courses at the University of Alaska Anchorage (UA), fall 2005

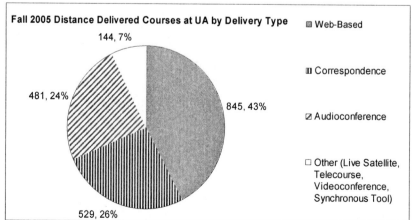

chronous communications comprise 1% of the course offerings, but the percentage is growing, with all major campuses in the state using either Macromedia Breeze™ or Elluminate Live™ for instruction.

Interestingly, the performance of the students enrolled in distance education seems to improve more over time as compared with the performance of their peers in traditional courses. While students in college preparatory classes had lower grades, students in introductory courses had results similar with the traditional students, and upper-division distance-delivered courses showed more student success than traditional courses (OPRA, 2005). Although the University of Alaska Anchorage has an open enrollment policy, more students in the distance-delivered courses were degree-seeking (75% vs. 65% among all undergraduates), indicating more focus and maturity among distance students.

The same study (OPRA, 2005) identifies that women outnumber men two-to-one in distance-delivered courses, even though the university distribution is almost even (57%:42%), possibly because women are more likely to suffer from scheduling constraints due to both work and family. Reyes and Bradley (2000) report a similar gender distribution, going back as far as 1983. They attribute the gender difference to the fact that men are more likely to be involved in subsistence-related activities.

An emphasis has been made at the University of Alaska Anchorage to offer health-related courses (nursing, counseling, etc.), many of which include media-rich content. Courses are delivered over a mix of old and new infrastructure, including channels with a wide range of bandwidth capabilities. Where bandwidth is limited, programs may require students to travel to a community meeting point where videoconference facilities are available, rather than attend class from home. This increases the community spirit of the students, who bond as a team with their local classmates, while also interacting with the larger

class population from all the locations where the course is videoconferenced. A particularly successful program is the Master of Science in Arctic Engineering, offered entirely online. The ability to take courses from any computer with Internet access is particularly important for engineers who often spend extended time in the field (sometimes working two weeks at a remote location alternating with two weeks in town). E-learning technologies are also widely used in the College of Education.

Implications for Professional and Continuing Education

Online continuing education is also available for several types of licensed professionals in the state. In particular those professionals that must live in the remote communities in which they work (e.g., teachers and health care workers) are most dependent on distance education to maintain their education.

The Alaska Staff Development Network (ASDN) offers distance-delivered professional development courses for educators (ASDN, n.d.). These courses are approved by the State of Alaska for teacher recertification and are offered in an ongoing manner. The course can be started at any time and must be completed within a year. This asynchronous nature is critical for rural teachers, who might not be able to connect due to seasonal weather extremes, local subsistence requirements or job-related time pressures.

The SchoolAccess product that links students across the state also allows teachers to share lesson plans and teaching tips (more details about this are provided below in the section on challenges). The Northwest Alaska Career and Technical Center allows teacher aides to participate in distance-delivered classes in the village.

Aside from these development programs, teachers also learn indirectly, in the course of coteaching with colleagues from across the state via distance education. In courses where a master teacher broadcasts the lectures to several village locations, local teachers or teacher aides assist with the classroom administration. As they participate in lectures, local teachers learn best teaching practices by example. By listening to the lecture, they also learn more about the subject matter. Even though courses were not intended for teachers' professional development, local administrators noted that some of the local teachers' performance improved after watching the remote teachers, in particular, for interdisciplinary courses (Yap, 1996).

There are federal requirements for teacher aides to have at least a two-year associate's degree to work in the classroom. Availability of distance education options makes it easier for Alaska Native teachers to become licensed without leaving their community. Historically, the lack of access to courses delayed Native teachers in acquiring licenses and in advancing in the profession. According to Reyes (2002) many Natives worked as teacher aides in villages. In fact they led the teaching, communication with the parents, trained the inexperienced, but licensed, white teachers, who came from outside the community (often from out of state) and had spent only a brief time teaching in the village. Many of the Native teachers ended up taking 10-15 years to complete their training, while already working in the position for which they were studying.

Another type of professional who benefits from distance-delivered continuing-education courses are health care workers. Currently, the state licenses osteopaths, paramedics, physicians, physician assistants, podiatrists, and nurses and nurse aids. Online refresher courses are approved, for example, for license reinstatement for nurses from providers as far as South Dakota and Washington (State of Alaska, n.d.). The Alaska Telemedicine Network (www.afhcan.org) is used primarily to provide remote health care to villages and to reduce expenses associated with medical evacuation, but also to deliver continuing education training. Among the health care-related distance-education offerings statewide, 63 of the 347 students enrolled in 2005 were taking professional-development courses (HDEP, 2005).

Implications for People with Disabilities

Because it already uses technology to mediate communications, distance education offers seamless options for dealing with disabilities. Captioning (speech to text and text to speech) allow visually and hearing impaired students to attend class. Asynchronous learning modules accommodate varied learning rates. This is particularly relevant in rural Alaska, where some disabilities tend to occur more frequently than in the urban population. According to a McDowell Group report (2001), Alaskan Natives comprise 31.5% of the students enrolled in special-education classes and 55% of Native students have specific learning disabilities.

As an example of distance-delivered special education, the Southeast Island School District, south of Juneau, is considering videoconferencing as a low cost way to bring speech pathologists to village children (Gaither, 2004).

Spillover Effects in the Community

The community at large also benefits from the increased access to education; Yap (1996) reported a decreased dropout rate, as well as increased stability of families, thanks to distance education. The increased stability is expected, given that students have access to educational offerings in their community or even from their homes. Franks (1996) cites results of a survey of student attitudes towards distance education in Alaska. The reasons these students favor distance education all have to do with family obligations ("cannot move to the city to take classes," "cannot attend on campus until my children are older" or "wouldn't have a chance for a teaching degree if not for distance education"). Once again, given the strong community ties and the large geographical distances separating Alaskan communities, moving to an urban center to study is a difficult proposition for many rural Native learners.

CHALLENGES AND NEGATIVE IMPLICATIONS OF E-LEARNING

The most obvious challenges of e-learning are the high costs (especially for disadvantaged populations described in this chapter), the learning curve and the reduced human interaction. The large financial expenses often require the pooling of resources to operate e-learning networks. Initial deployments in Alaska were operated by consortia and subsidized by state and federal funds. When government funding fell, such as during the 1986 collapse in oil prices, distance-education programs suffered. Historically, the most successful e-learning programs in Alaska have been those where an existing need was met by financial support from the legislature or the administration.

More recently, private organizations have entered the field. In particular, General Communications Incorporated (GCI), one of the competitive local carriers in Alaska, has developed a unique business model they apply to distance delivery of instructional materials across the state. The company has even expanded its School Access product to make it available to students in Arizona, Montana and New Mexico. The costs are $3,000 per month, but the federal government subsidizes up to 90% of the costs (Campbell, 2005). Often, Alaska Native Corporations subsidize costs in regions where they operate.

Two statewide consortia are currently operating in Alaska. The Alaska Distance Learning Partnership was started by GCI in partnership with six school districts, a vocational center, a marine research center and the Alaska Challenger Learning Center (The center is part of a network of 50 learning and discovery centers created fol-

lowing the Challenger shuttle disaster in 1986). The second consortium, Alaska Online, uses both synchronous and asynchronous teaching tools.

The second major challenge is related to technology adoption and perceived success. The learning curve for new technologies is often rather steep. Tenured faculty, especially those who have taught for a long time, may be reluctant to learn new technologies and to change the way they teach. As new technologies continue to arise, some faculty might not have the time and energy to keep up to date. Sometimes faculty members perceive technology-enabled courses as more successful than they really are. In a recent report (HDEP, 2005), faculty estimated the success of e-learning at much higher values than students did. Finally, students are not always ready to adopt new technologies, especially in a state where there is a gaping digital divide between technology haves and have-nots.

A major challenge for the pioneers of distance education in Alaska was trying to provide everything for everybody (K-12, university and community programs)—a goal that may have been too broad for the technology and available funds. Additionally, the lack of a single project leader, poor communications and lack of cooperation among the organizations led to slow resolution of problems. Such reasons tend to be common for failed distance-education projects, which all require consortia to operate the expensive, distributed and technologically complex networks. Sometimes even success stories failed in getting parties to cooperate. The very successful Health Distance Education Partnership (HDEP) was supposed to be a collaborative effort statewide. Instead, each University of Alaska campus has been operating relatively independent of each other (HDEP, 2005).

More subtle challenges are often hidden and may not be as apparent even to teachers and students. For example, new training opportunities may make some of the local students more prepared to leave the community and move on to places where they have a higher earning potential. It is not clear whether this brain drain may ultimately have a positive overall impact.

Deploying technology without a good understanding of the social implications can lead to a waste of resources. Sponder (1990) reports on the limitations of audioconferencing in western Alaska, where the Native population has a history of hearing problems. The technology was deployed because it was one of the few cost effective technologies available at the time.

Some of the potentially negative impacts of distance education are yet to be fully determined. Huang and Howley (1996) conclude that disadvantaged students perform better in small schools than in medium or large ones. This would indicate that the small school size in Alaskan villages mitigates some of the disadvantages faced by the local population. An interesting (but unanswered) question is whether the distance-delivered courses would change this dynamic and remove some of the advantages of small schools described in the study.

Additionally, sometimes technology can effect the community at a deeper level, for example, leading to unexpected role reversal between generations. Traditionally, Alaskan Natives have a high respect for "Elders," who are the repository of the community wisdom. Kushman and Barnhardt (2001) cites a case of the village of Quinhagak where the school is open two to three nights per week for parents to use computers. In technology matters, younger generations are savvier than their Elders and get to help them in these computer sessions. The social impact of such role reversals is not yet understood.

Finally, some challenges transcend technology and relate more to human nature. As technology evolves, cultural perceptions and prejudices sometimes lag. Creating appropriate role models for the community and for students and addressing cultural barriers are just as important for affecting change as is the availability of e-learning options. Even when Native teachers are available, racial

stereotypes may make it difficult for them to get hired, even by boards on which Alaskan Natives are in majority (Reyes, 2002). Reyes also cites Lipka (1998) on how such social pressures in turn forced Native teachers to teach in Western ways, rather than in more culturally sensitive ways they could have adopted.

CONCLUSION

For the state of Alaska, geography, climate and cultural diversity make distance education highly desirable to provide quality education options to all state residents. E-learning technologies provide multimedia-rich learning content, can adapt to a variety of bandwidth channels and allow for interactive but asynchronous interaction.

Among the positive social implications of distance education, in general, we have noted an increased access to a variety of education options, reduced travel expenses associated with study and flexible work/study schedules due to the asynchronous instruction. E-learning technologies offer these benefits at lower cost and higher reliability than the older distance education means. Given the isolation of some communities and the tightly knit cultural ties of village residents with the local community, another highly beneficial implication is the ability of rural residents to live in the local community while studying. The multimedia-rich nature of e-learning technologies has greatly expanded the range of training that can be delivered in remote locations.

Furthermore, given the cultural differences and the different learning styles of the various Native Alaskan cultures, the ability to share the relatively small number of culturally aware teachers among several communities is of considerable help. We discussed the difficulty of recruiting teachers from outside the community and the difficulty of retaining these teachers. E-learning technologies allow village residents to obtain new credentials, to renew existing ones and to become culturally-aware teachers. Teachers with strong roots in the community are likely to remain in the village long term and provide the stability needed in the school system.

Distance education has had more positive implications than negative implications for Alaskan residents, especially for Alaskan Natives living in remote communities. Among the potentially negative implications, we explored role reversals, where younger residents can be more technologically savvy than their elders, as well as cultural disruption caused by exposure to the outside world, which may accelerate the out-migration from small communities. Some of the potential negative impacts are not fully understood and may take much longer to emerge.

In the meantime, distance-education options continue to expand and to bring village residents in closer and more frequent contact with the world outside their village, outside their state and outside their continent. Although e-learning technologies are helping to train teachers and health workers among rural residents, many communities still have unmet needs for such professionals. It remains to be seen when and to what extent the promise of equal access to education via distance delivery will become a reality in rural Alaska.

REFERENCES

ADLP. (2005a). *Shared courses bring new opportunities* [Online]. Retrieved December 15, 2005, from http://www.alaskadistancelearning. org/modules.php?op=modload&name=News& file=article&sid=20&mode=thread&order=0& thold=0

ADLP. (2005b). *Learning crosses old boundaries* [Online]. Retrieved December 15, 2005, from http://www.alaskadistancelearning.org/ modules.php?op=modload&name=News&file =article&sid=21&mode=thread&order=0&tho ld=0

ADLP. (2005c). *Distance education enriches learning* [Online]. Retrieved December 15, 2005, from http://www.alaskadistancelearning. org/modules.php?op=modload&name=News& file=article&sid=22&mode=thread&order=0& thold=0

Alaska. (2000). *Census 2000: Alaska profile* [Online]. Retrieved December 15, 2005, from http://ftp2.census.gov/geo/maps/special/profile2k/ AK_2K_Profile.pdf

ASDN. (n.d.). Retrieved Dec. 15, 2005, from http://www.asdn.org/distance_education.html

Bartman, D. (1992). *Integrating academic and vocational education and thinking skills: An Alaskan model.* Paper presented at Work Now and in the Future Conference, Portland, OR (ERIC Document Reporduction Service No. ED357231). Retrieved December 15, 2005, from http://www. eric.ed.gov/

Cadigan, J. (1993). Report from Alaska. *Journal of Research in Rural Education, 9*(1), 32-34.

Campbell, M. (2005, February 20). Program takes the job fair to the Bush. *Alaska Journal of Commerce, 29*(8), 6. Retrieved Dec. 15, 2005, from http://www.alaskajournal.com/PalmPilot/ stories/022005/hom_20050220008.html

Cavanagh, S. (2003). Alaska correspondence school avoids threatened shutdown. *Education Week, 23*(15), 10.

Cavanagh, S. (2004). Alaska seeks to tighten rules on correspondence schools. *Education Week, 23*(31), 10.

Chu, L., & Culbertson, J. (1982). Rural Alaskan youth's attitudes towards education. *Research in Rural Education, 1*(1), 27-31.

Darnell, F. (1970). *Alaska's dual federal-state school system: A history and descriptive analysis.* Unpublished doctoral dissertation, Wayne State University, Detroit, MI.

Distance Education Report. (2004, March 15). University of Washington delivers Internet program to Bering Sea community. *Distance Education Report,* 8(6), 2.

Distance Learning. (n.d.). Distance learning service celebrates first-year success educational opportunities in Alaska expanded for 89 Schools. Retrieved Dec. 15, 2005, from http://www.schoolaccess.net/newsroom/pr030630.htm

Franks, K. (1996). Attitudes of Alaskan distance education students toward media and instruction. *American Journal of Distance Education, 10*(3), 60-71.

Gaither, C. (2004, November 11). No child left behind in the cold. *Los Angels Times.* Retrieved December 15, 2005, from http://www.aedcweb.com/content/docs/latimes.pdf

GCI/CEO. (n.d.). GCI *career exploration opportunities.* [Brochure]. Retrieved December 15, 2005, from http://ceo.schoolaccess.net/CEO%20brochure.pdf

HDEP. (2005). *An evaluation of first year activity of the Health Distance Education Partnership of the University of Alaska.* Retrieved April 20, 2005, from http://www.distance.uaf.edu/steeringboard/ett/docs/HDEPEvalReport.pdf

Holznagel, D. C. (1992). *Distance education resource directory for Northwest Schools.* Portland, OR: Northwest Regional Education Lab (ERIC Document Reproduction Service No. ED348937). Retrieved December 15, 2005, from http://www.eric.ed.gov/.

Huang G., & Howley, C. (1996). Mitigating disadvantage: Effects of small-scale schooling on student achievement in Alaska. *Journal of Research in Rural Education, 9*(3), 137-149.

Kleinfeld, J., & Williamson McDiarmid, G. (1986). The satisfaction of Alaska's isolated rural teachers with their work life. *Research in Rural Education, 3*(3), 117-120.

Kushman, J. W., & Barnhardt, R. (2001). Reforming education from the inside-out: A study of community engagement and education reform in rural Alaska. *Journal of Research in Rural Education, 17*(1), 12-26.

LearnAlaska Network. (1985). *Annual report 1984-1985.*

Lipka, J. (1998). *Transforming the culture of schools.* NJ: Lawrence Erlbaum Associates.

McDiarmid, G. W., Goldsmith, S., Hill, A., & Hull, T. (1998). *Current and future demand for distance education.* Institute of Social and Economic Research (ERIC Document Reproduction Service No. ED429628). Retrieved December 15, 2005, from http://www.eric.ed.gov/

McDowell Group. (2001). *Alaska Native education study: A statewide study of Alaska Native values and opinions regarding education in Alaska.* Retrieved December 15, 2005, from http://www.alaskool.org/native_ed/McDowell.pdf

Metzger, S. (2004). State profiles: Alaska. *Education Week on the Web,* [Online] May 6. Retrieved December 15, 2005, from http://counts.edweek.org/sreports/tc04/state_profile.cfm?slug=35ak.h23

Moore, G. M., & Kearsley, G. (1996). *Distance education: A systems view.* Wadsworth Publishing Company.

Office of Planning, Research and Assessment. (2005). *Cohort: DistanceeEducation students—undergraduate.* Anchorage: University of Alaska Anchorage, Office of Planning, Research and Assessment.

Reyes, M. E. (2002). Reaching out to the teachers of teachers: Distance education in rural Alaska (An Imperfect World: Resonance from the Nation's Violence. 2002 Monograph No.). In *Proceedings of the Annual Meeting of the National Association of African American Studies, the National*

Association of Hispanic and Latino Studies, the National Association of Native American Studies, and the International Association of Asian Studies, Houston, TX (pp. 648-665).

Reyes, M. E., & Bradley, C. (2000). Hello, out there: A look at distance education. *First Monday*, 5(10). Retrieved December 15, 2005, from http://firstmonday.org/issues/issue5_10/reyes/index.html

Rider, C. D. (1982). Folklore and educational administration in Alaska: An ethnographic study of rural school administration. *Research in Rural Education, 1*(1), 15-19.

SchoolAccess. (n.d.). *SchoolAccess case study 1: Alaska's Bering Strait School District—GCI SchoolAccess enhanced Internet service*. Retrieved December 15, 2005, from http://www.schoolaccess.net/experience/casestudy1.htm

Schnorr, J. M. (1992). Collaborative recruitment and retention of teachers: A joint responsibility. In *Proceedings of the Fifth Teacher Education Division Conference of the Council for Exceptional Children*, Cincinnati, OH (pp. 2-9).

Sponder, B. M. (1990). *Reaching the way-out student: A qualitative study of students enrolled in audioconference courses in western Alaska*. Doctoral dissertation, Utah State University, Logan.

State of Alaska. (n.d.). Retrieved December 15, 2005, from http://www.dced.state.ak.us/occ/pub/RefresherCourseInformation.pdf

Willis, B. (1992). Effective distance education: A primer for faculty and administrators. *Monograph Series in Distance Education 2*. Alaska University System, Fairbanks, AK.

Yap, K. O. (1996). Distance education in the Pacific Northwest: Program benefits and implementation barriers. In *Proceedings of the Annual Conference of the American Educational Research Association*, New York (pp. 1-16).

Chapter IV
Games–Based E–Learning:
Implications and Challenges for Higher Education and Training

Thomas Connolly
University of Paisley, UK

Mark Stansfield
University of Paisley, UK

ABSTRACT

This chapter introduces games-based e-learning as a means of providing enriching and stimulating learning experiences within higher education and training. It highlights how e-learning has evolved and the developments that have opened the way for games-based e-learning, giving examples of specific applications. The authors hope that through gaining a better understanding of the implications, challenges and barriers to games-based e-learning, educators, practitioners and developers will be able to make better use of and gain substantial benefit from these exciting learning technologies. Finally, the chapter will identify what the authors believe to be future trends in relation to e-learning and games-based e-learning.

INTRODUCTION

Over the last decade, e-learning has developed to a point where it now provides a credible alternative to more traditional forms of education and training, as well as providing new opportunities to both educators and learners. In recent years a new form of learning has been developing, namely games-based e-learning, which in many ways builds on the successes of e-learning, whilst providing a more stimulating and relevant learning environment for younger people who have been brought up in an environment of powerful home computers, graphic-rich multiplayer Internet gaming and mobile phones with ever increasing functionality. This is in contrast to many of today's educators and instructors whose learning experiences were largely underpinned by the use of more passive technologies (Prensky, 2001). This chapter explores the concepts of e-learning and games-based e-learning and examines their contribution to higher education and training. Games-based e-learning is an exciting phenomenon that draws upon many different areas that include learning theory, interactive technologies, computer-games theory and design, and specific subject matter expertise.

BACKGROUND

The term *e-learning* has been defined as, *"the use of digital technologies and media to deliver, support and enhance teaching, learning, assessment and evaluation"* (LTSN, 2003, p. 6). In this chapter we distinguish between "online learning" and "e-learning." We use the term *online learning* to represent any class that offers its entire curriculum via the Internet, thereby allowing learners to participate regardless of geographic location (place-independent) and theoretically 24 hours a day (time-independent). This is in contrast to the traditional classroom instruction, which is time and place bound, face-to-face (FtF), typically conducted in an educational setting and consisting primarily of a lecture/note-taking model, and *blended learning*, which is a combination of online learning and traditional classroom instruction. We use e-learning as a generic term to encompass both (fully) online learning and blended learning. The instructional media elements employed within the context of this definition of e-learning could consist of text, video, audio, graphics, animation or any combination thereof. A central component of most e-learning courses is some form of two-way interaction between learners and their instructor and between the learners themselves. Synchronous communication tools, such as real-time chat, and asynchronous tools, such as e-mail and discussion boards, are common.

Over the past decade, e-learning has evolved and developed at a rapid pace so much so that it is a commonly accepted and increasingly popular alternative to traditional FtF education (Gunawardena & McIsaac, 2004; Connolly, MacArthur, Stansfield, & McLellan, in press). Some faculty members are strong proponents of e-learning and believe online courses can provide educational opportunities to learners who would otherwise have to do without. They also believe that the quality of these courses can be comparable to traditional place-bound courses (Dutton, Dutton, & Perry, 2002).

According to Connolly and Stansfield (2006), there have been six generations of distance learning, the last three of which represent the first three generations of e-learning. This first generation of e-learning is based on mainly passive use of the Internet (circa 1994-99), primarily consisting of conversion of course material to an online format, basic mentoring using e-mail, and low-fidelity streamed audio/video. However, the educational philosophy still belongs to the pre-Internet era. The use of more advanced technologies consisting of high-bandwidth access, rich streaming media and virtual learning environments that provide access to course material, communication facilities and student services represents the second generation of e-learning (circa 2000-03). Asynchronous communications support a constructivist form of learning and allow learners to communicate in writing. This approach encourages more reflection and disciplined and rigorous thinking, which helps learners to make connections among ideas and to construct internal, coherent knowledge structures (Garrison, 1997). The most recent developments in e-learning (since 2003) are more collaborative learning environments based much more on the constructivist epistemology, promoting reflective practice through tools like e-portfolios, blogs, wikis, using games-based e-learning and highly interactive online simulations. We are also now starting to see the development of mobile learning (m-learning) through devices like personal digital assistants (PDAs), mobile phones and smartphones. M-learning is still at an early stage, but as these devices become more functional, we would expect to see significant developments in this area.

In terms of its contribution to higher education and training, the research literature cites many advantages of an e-learning environment, particularly the convenience and flexibility offered by the (asynchronous) "anytime, anywhere, any pace" education (McDonald, 2002). The asynchronous nature of the medium also allows learners time for research, internal reflection and "collective thinking" (Garrison, 1997). Moreover, the text-based nature of e-learning normally requires written communication from the learner, which along with reflection, encourage higher-level learning, such as analysis, synthesis, and evaluation, and encourage clearer and more precise thinking (Jonassen, 1996). McComb (1993) considers that e-learning also provides efficient access to information, which means that new resources and updates/corrections to course material can be posted relatively quickly, and at the same time learners have access to the wealth of related information available on the Internet. In addition, e-learning courses also have the capability to present multiple representations of a concept, which allows learners to store and retrieve information more effectively (Kozma, 1987). Most e-learning systems also provide an automatic paper trail of all discussions that instructors and learners can subsequently elaborate or reflect on.

Increased social distance provides a number of distinct advantages to online conferences (synchronous or asynchronous). In written communications, anonymity of characteristics such as gender, race, age, or social status can be preserved, which can reduce the feeling of discrimination, and provide equality of social interaction among participants. In turn, this can permit the expression of emotion and promote discussion that normally would be inhibited. However, there is some evidence that the social equality factor may

not extend to participants who are poor writers but who must communicate primarily in a text-based format (Gunawardena, 1993).

DEVELOPMENTS TOWARD GAMES-BASED E-LEARNING

During the past five years, there has been a significant amount of work carried out into the use of computer games-based technologies and concepts to enhance teaching and learning, both for higher education and training purposes. Connolly and Stansfield (2006) define games-based e-learning as, "the use of a computer games-based approach to deliver, support, and enhance teaching, learning, assessment, and evaluation" and can be differentiated from the more common term games-based learning, which tends to cover both computer and noncomputer games, such as card and board games. This is a research area that may be conceptualized as the intersection of learning theory, computer games theory and design, user interfaces, and subject matter expertise. In this conceptualization, learning theory serves as the foundation to ensure that technology does not become the dominant factor. In this section, we discuss some of the pedagogic underpinnings for games-based e-learning. The interested reader is referred to Connolly and Stansfield (2006) for a fuller discussion of the concepts of games-based e-learning.

Motivation, Engagement, and Challenge

Motivation is a key concept in many theories of learning. Katzeff (2000) stresses that motivation is a critical factor for instructional design and that for learning to occur the learner must be motivated to learn. Malone and Lepper (1987) present a theoretical framework of intrinsic motivation (doing something because it is inherently interesting or enjoyable) in the design of educational computer games. They suggest that intrinsic motivation is created by four individual factors—challenge, fantasy, curiosity and control—and three interpersonal factors—cooperation, competition and recognition. Computer games induce conditions within players that encourage them to continue involvement with the game. Such conditions include satisfaction, desire, anger, absorption, interest, excitement, enjoyment, pride in achievement and the (dis)approbation of peers and others. It is in provoking and harnessing some of these emotions and their consequences that computer games might benefit education (British Educational Communications and Technology Agency (Becta), 2001). This is borne out by a study cited in Garris, Ahlers, and Driskell (2002), which found that incorporating game features into instruction increased motivation and consequently produced greater attention and retention. An empirical study by Chen, Shen, Ou, and Liu (1998) demonstrated the positive effects of computer games on motivation and learning.

Prensky (2001) argues that learning today is unengaging compared to all the alternatives like television, computer games and even work. The current younger generation going through higher education, which Prensky terms *digital natives*, has grown up in a technologically sophisticated environment; an environment populated by home computers, the Internet, graphic-rich movies, multi-player Internet gaming, PlayStations, Xboxes, Game Boys, DVD players, mobile phones, interactive television, PDAs and iPods, which has led to a change in their experiences, attitudes. and expectations. Contrast this with the predigital generation (today's instructors) who grew up largely with the passive technologies of books, television and radio and who were "educated in the styles of the past" (Prensky, 2001). Table 1 highlights features that contribute to motivation.

Gee (2003) believes that challenge is crucial to sustain engagement but that this can be achieved by building into interactivity the same learning principles used in effective classrooms, namely:

Table 1. Features that contribute to motivation (Source: Becta, 2001)

What indicates motivation?	Independent work Self-directed problem posing Persistence Pleasure in learning
What generates motivation?	Active participation Intrinsic and prompt feedback Challenging but achievable goals Mix of uncertainty and open-endedness
What can motivation usefully support?	Collaborative interaction Peer scaffolding of learning Creative competition or cooperation Equal opportunities
What does sustained motivation rely on?	A version of reality Relevance to the user Recognizable and desirable roles for players
What are problems with motivation?	Motivation may lead to obsession Motivation may cause transfer of fantasy into reality Motivation may induce egotism

- **Active, critical learning principle:** All aspects of the learning environment are set up to encourage active and critical, not passive, learning.
- **Design principle:** Learning about and coming to appreciate design and design principles is core to the learning experience.
- **Semiotic principle:** Learning about and coming to appreciate interrelations within and across multiple sign systems (such as images, words actions and symbols) as a complex system is core to the learning experience.
- **Semiotic domains principle:** Learning involves mastering, at some level, semiotic domains and being able to participate, at some level, in the affinity group(s) connected to them.
- **Metalevel thinking:** About semiotic domains principle;
- Learning involves active and critical thinking about the relationships of the semiotic domain being learned to other semiotic domains.

Theories of Learning and Instruction

There is a growing body of research within the theories of learning and instruction that suggests computer games have highly desirable qualities that are worthy of further investigation. Connolly, McLellan, Stansfield, Ramsay, and Sutherland (2004) argue that computer games build on theories of:

- **Constructivism** is a philosophical, epistemological and pedagogical approach to learning, where learning is viewed as an active process in which learners construct new ideas or concepts based upon their current/past knowledge. The learner selects and transforms information, constructs hypotheses and makes decisions, relying on a cognitive structure to do so.

- **Situated learning** is a function of the activity, context and culture in which it occurs (Lave, 1988).
- **Cognitive apprenticeship** is an instructional strategy that models the processes experts use to handle complex tasks. The focus is on cognitive and metacognitive skills, requiring the externalization of processes that are usually carried out internally. Observing the processes by which an expert thinks and practices these skills teach students to learn on their own (Collins, Brown, & Newman, 1989).
- **Problem-based learning** is an instructional strategy for posing significant, contextualized, real world situations, and providing resources, guidance and instruction to learners as they develop content knowledge and problem-solving skills (Mayo, Donnelly, Nash, & Schwartz, 1993).

EXAMPLES OF GAMES-BASED E-LEARNING IN HIGHER EDUCATION AND THE WORKPLACE

In recent years an increasing number of games-based e-learning applications have been developed across a wide range of subject areas and disciplines, such as medicine, dentistry, health education, computing science, history, maths, physics, chemistry, construction, environmental science and languages. In this section, we provide examples of games-based e-learning for two areas, namely business and military training.

Business

SimuLearn's Virtual Leader (http://www.simu-learn.net) is an educational 3D-simulation training game that is part of its methodology known as 3-to-1 leadership, which is designed to provide accelerated learning in a wide range of areas related to effective leadership, such as communication, team building, fostering creativity, project management, group dynamics and personal effectiveness. The player joins a group of animated artificial intelligence (AI) characters as the leader and is tasked with having them work together toward a common business goal. The characters have personalities, points of view, allies and agendas. As their leader, it is the player's task to apply the principles of power and tension to get the group to focus on the correct work. The player's success or failure in this task can be seen by how individuals in the group respond verbally, how they adjust their body language, and in the (in)action that they may or may not take. This simulation is being used by a number of large organizations, such as Coca-Cola, Johnson & Johnson, United Technologies Corp. and the U.S. Army. Figure 1 provides a sample screenshot of the game with explanations of the main screen features.

KM Quest (http://www.kmquest.net) is a Web-based simulation game aimed at developing core knowledge-management skills. At the outset of the development, the goal of the project was to develop and evaluate a learning environment for *knowledge management,* based on a *learning game* with *situated problems* using *collaborative learning.* KM Quest is a team-based game in which up to three players are responsible for a fictitious company called Coltec, a product leadership organization. The general goal of the simulation game is to optimize the level of a set of general organizational effectiveness variables: market share, profit and the customer satisfaction index. Players play their roles as knowledge managers for three consecutive years in the life span of the company, with each year divided into quarters. During this time, they can inspect the status of business process indicators and knowledge process indicators, ask for additional information, and choose interventions in an attempt to change the behavior of the business simulation. Most indicators are characterized by a decay factor so that the value of an indicator decreases over time

Figure 1. Screenshot from Virtual Leader

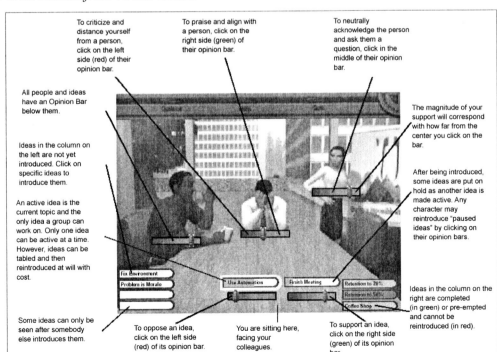

when no interventions are implemented. Players are given a budget at the start of the game, which they can use to implement interventions and buy information. At the start of each quarter players are confronted with an event that could affect the knowledge household of Coltec, and they have to decide if and how they want to react to these events. When they think they know enough to solve the problem, they indicate that they agree with the proposed interventions. The game proceeds to the end of the quarter and calculates new values for each of the business indicators.

Before the game proper starts, players are given an introduction to the basic concepts of knowledge management and how to play the game. The training consists of a limited form of the game with restricted choices and fixed events during which guidance, coaching and immediate feedback is given (based on the cognitive-appren-ticeship model). Leemkuil, de Jong, de Hoog, and Christoph (2003) provide a formative evaluation of this simulation. Figure 2 provides a sample screenshot from the game.

Military Training

A major user of games-based e-learning appli-cations for training purposes is the U.S. Army, which developed and published the tactical game America's Army. The game, released by the U.S. Army to aid its recruitment purposes, allows users to learn about a range of key skills that include teamwork, leadership and communication as they navigate challenges to achieve goals. The game contains two realistic simulations: Soldiers, a role-playing game in which players navigate various challenges to achieve goals, and Operations, a first-person action game. The Operations game allows up to 32 players to enter into "virtual service" with the U.S. Army on the same unit mission. Players begin their virtual experience as a recruit with an anonymous user name to experience challenging Army missions from a first-person perspective. The training missions, such as an obstacle course or parachute drop, build player capabilities. Mul-tiplayer missions are organized into assignment tours, which can only be joined once the player

Figure 2. Sample screenshot from KM Quest

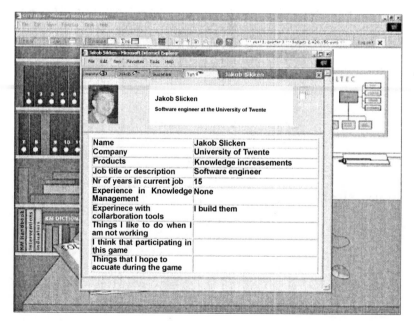

Figure 3 Sample screenshot from America's Army

has completed the appropriate training. Gamers use realistic equipment and authentic military hardware. As in any team effort, communication is key; gamers use different speech, whispers, shouts, radio messages and genuine military hand and arm signals. Statistics show that the game has had an average of roughly 3,000 to 6,000 players playing online at any one time between 2002 and 2005 (Computer and Video Games Survey, 2005). Figure 3 provides a screenshot from this game showing graphics approaching commercial games quality. The U.S. Army also has worked with a number of commercial game companies on other titles.

SOCIAL IMPLICATIONS AND CHALLENGES

Over recent years there has been an increase in the number of learners participating in e-learning courses. For example, according to Lawless and Allan (2004) the Open University in the UK has around 220,000 online students of which the business school has more than 30,000 students per year in more than 20 countries worldwide. However, associated with this growth has been the identification of a number of social implications and challenges that have been associated with e-learning. Over the past decade, there has been a shift in educational theory from behaviorist towards social constructivist models of learning. A behaviorist perspective views learning as being acquired through a series of linear steps to achieving a predefined goal in which periodic questions test progress and reinforcement of learned behavior. Social constructivist models affect all aspects of a learner's cognitive, emotional, social and cultural development in which learning is contextual. This shift presents a number of significant challenges to both tutors and learners in gaining a better understanding of social and cultural issues, as we discuss in this section.

Moore, Shattuck and Al-Harthi (2005) note that the growth in e-learning provision appears to be more focused within American and European universities, where many participants are from different social cultures, and suggest that this might cause conflict with values that underpin the culture of the students taking the e-learning courses. Brennan, McFadden and Law (2000) believe that cultural needs and differences should be taken into account at all stages in designing and developing e-learning materials and support. Moore et al. (2005) highlight a number of challenges and issues faced by students from cultural backgrounds that are different from those who develop and implement e-learning courses. For example, they found that Arab students studying in American distance education demonstrated anxiety and avoidance behavior due to not knowing what to expect from e-learning. They also identified situations where students found the lack of physical gestures and total dependence on a second language time consuming and difficult. Other issues include international students feeling marginalized within the e-learning environment as a result of their cultural experiences being different than the dominant educational cultures, such as the role of the teacher, expectations of how teaching and learning works, the type and amount of interaction required, and the imposition of another cultural framework on their own cultural expectations and traditions (Moore et al., 2005).

These issues and challenges are also highlighted by Timms (2001) who warns that, "e-learning is frequently promoted as a means for breaking-down barriers between cultures. The danger with this is that by ignoring cultural differences e-learning may become another potent form of cultural imperialism" (p. 4). Moore et al. (2005) found from their own studies that many international students avoid confrontation and suppress their frustrations if they feel neglected or doubt their abilities to learn within an e-learning environment.

Another challenge relates to how tutors and instructors facilitate and manage learning effectively within an e-learning environment and how to adopt new technical and quality standards. Technology is leading change at a rapid pace with the result that too little attention is being paid to exploring the new forms of pedagogy made possible by e-learning. The lack of effective use of technology to enhance interactions may be one of the key reasons why some people consider many current e-learning courses to be "boring and mindless" (Aldrich, 2003). Dutton, Cheong and Park (2004) suggest instructors generally teach the way they were taught, based on class lectures and discussion in a one-to-many relationship, a situation that is characteristic of higher-education culture throughout the world. As a result, it is believed that these traditional teaching paradigms are designed into many e-learning products. Ror example, Blackboard "uses the analogy of the 'chalk-and-talk' to convey its centrality to traditional conceptions of teaching" (Dutton et al., 2004, p. 77). Therefore, an important challenge is to provide effective staff development to e-learning tutors and thereby change the way they think about teaching and learning and how to employ emerging technologies to enhance learning.

In terms of educational values, Darking (2002) points out that one of the most cited concerns is the autonomy of teacher and university, which could be compromised by the use of e-learning. Darking (2002) notes that:

Theories of learning are often used to support the idea that for intellectual development to take place teachers need to have an open relationship with their students, one which is not constrained by the protocols of a software programme (p. 1432).

Thus, it is important to consider ways of ensuring that the technological constraints of a particular e-learning environment do not adversely affect the open relationship between student and tutor, nor constrain freedom of learning and intellectual expression and development.

Taylor, Rodden, Anderson, Sharples, Luckin, Conole and Siraj-Blatchford (2004) highlight a number of research issues and challenges that were identified during a consultation exercise with the UK research community when producing an e-learning research agenda. These related to areas such as interactivity and social inclusion in the blurring of organisational boundaries and functional groups as a result of new technologies. Also highlighted was the potential these new technologies have to enhance communication and interaction and to build new communities and networks. There were some political themes about different local agendas and competition as well as areas relating to change impacting on motivational issues and drivers and strategies for managing change.

In relation to games-based e-learning, there are a number of additional social implications that are often cited in the literature. The most frequently cited concern is the long term effects of violence on game players, although there is no agreed upon consensus. For example, Provenzo (1991) claims that computer games: (a) can lead to violent, aggressive behavior; (b) employ destructive gender stereotyping; (c) promote unhealthy "rugged individualist" attitudes, and stifle creative play. On the other hand, catharsis theory states that games playing may be a useful means of coping with, or releasing, pent-up aggression (Emes, 1997). Squire (2003, p. 55) suggests recent developments in computer-games design are beginning to change the ideas of a link between violent games and social maladjustment: "thematically, video games are increasing in complexity, incorporating story, character development, and collaboration in the game design."

Gender stereotyping has been identified as an issue with computer games for some time now (i.e., Cassell & Jenkins, 1998; Bryce & Rutter, 2002). Newman (2004) notes that female characters are extremely underrepresented in games and make up only 16% of all characters, and that 47% of male characters are portrayed as competitors, while 50% of female characters are depicted as props or bystanders. Even when games possess female characters, there is some doubt as to their identity. For example, Kennedy (2002) questions whether the Lara Croft character from the Tomb Raider series presents a positive role model or an unhelpful vision of the "perfect woman." Sandford and Williamson (2005) observe that representations of female characters in games are still overtly "sexy"; the majority of protagonists still tend to be represented as male, white and Western; and enemies, particularly in war games, are still Japanese, German, Vietnamese or Middle Eastern. They suggest that most games persist in representing the ideology of male-led, white Western capitalism that should have had its day back in the last century. The lack of female characters and the overtly sexual female characters has served to alienate some females (Jenkins, 1998). Bryce and Rutter (2002) believe that the gender stereotyping is a complex and rapidly evolving issue and needs to be researched within a wider social context than that of the gaming experience alone.

Another important social implication is the physical and mental effects that computer games present for players. For example, doctors have found that frequent gaming can cause eye strains, wrist and back pains, photosensitive epilepsy, headaches, hallucinations, nerve and muscle damage, and repetitive strain injury (i.e., Cleary, McKendrick, & Sills, 2002).

Beavis (2002) argues that computer games represent new cultural forms with which young people are increasingly familiar and fluent, and suggests that educational systems should not remain fixated on transferring the traditional elitist vision of culture and society that they have sustained for decades. Young people, she maintains, are learning skills and practices more suited to the 21st century than anything schools prepare them for.

BARRIERS TO E-LEARNING AND GAMES-BASED E-LEARNING

A number of key barriers have been identified relating to the implementation of e-learning and to the provision of effective access and interaction within e-learning environments. One of the major barriers is that of cost. Grant (2004) points out that many organizations still view e-learning within an old business paradigm and consider it to be costly because of the high purchasing costs of a virtual learning environment and its maintenance thereafter. Attwell (2005) notes that while return on investment (ROI) studies have been common, he considers this to be an inadequate way of measuring the costs and benefits of e-learning within public-education bodies. In addition, given the limited resources available to universities and other publicly funded educational organizations, the issue of how e-learning should be costed and funded is a major one.

Berge and Muilenburg (2005) consider access to be a perennial problem with access to newer forms of educational technology is still difficult for some students and faculty members. Related to cost is the lack of effective administrative structures and the struggle against the organization's existing culture which Berge and Mullenburg (2001, p. 43) consider make those people who are involved in distance education feel as though they are "swimming against a strong current". For example, many universities do not support online enrollment, allow online payment of fees, access to a wide range of online journals nor the ability to sit exams away from the institution.

The effectiveness of certain aspects relating to e-learning has been questioned by certain authors. For example, in relation to the Open University in the UK, Lawless and Allan (2004) point out that, "Annual surveys of thousands of OU students by the Institute of Educational Technology show that on-line activity is one of the least popular elements of OU courses" (p. 121). Muilenburg and Berge (2001) also note that participants can feel isolated due to a lack of person-to-person contact. At the same time, Rovai (2002) believes that noninvolvement in the virtual community may lead to feelings of loneliness, low self-esteem, isolation and low motivation to learn, which in turn can lead to low achievement and dropout. These issues may partially account for why dropout rates tend to be higher in e-learning programs than in traditional FtF programs, often 10 to 20 percentage points higher (Carr, 2000). According to Grant (2004), there is some considerable scepticism about whether e-learning delivers results, and it may be subject to increased scrutiny regarding its effectiveness as it begins to take up larger shares of training and teaching budgets within organizations.

If e-learning has developed a reputation for being "boring and mindless," games have developed the reputation for being engaging and challenging. However, the social implications cited in the previous section place an enormous stigma on this approach. At the same time, some researchers believe that learning should not be fun. For example, Stoll (1999) states:

What seems like a game to someone will feel like work to another. The intention should be enlightenment, not entertainment. Learning isn't about acquiring information, maximising efficiency, or enjoyment. Learning is about developing human capacity. To turn learning into fun is to denigrate the two most important things we can do as humans: To teach. To learn. (p. 22)

While we have noted that some faculty can be nervous of adopting e-learning, there is significant resistance from faculty to the use of games-based e-learning, and this presents a significant barrier to the uptake of games-based e-learning within higher education, although less so within training. Interestingly, the term "simulation" appears to be much more acceptable to faculty, so semantics may play a role in overcoming this particular barrier.

In addition, generally speaking, there is usually a high start-up cost associated with the planning, design and development of a games-based e-learning environment. This means that whilst certain corporate organizations may be able to afford such costs, they may be out of reach for higher-education institutions, which have limited budgets. Furthermore, many games-based e-learning environments are still at the early prototype stages because of the long development times, and fully functioning games-based environments may take years to create.

Shaffer, Squire, Halverson and Gee (in press) suggest most educational games have been produced in the absence of any coherent theory of learning or underlying body of research. There are concerns of a negative impact on learning as gamers may concentrate on scoring and winning, rather than the actual learning objectives, and concerns that games may be pitched at the wrong level of challenge and interest. There are also concerns that some games have a high-learning curve and take a significant amount of time to work through, which may make them unsuitable for short modular educational systems.

FUTURE TRENDS

In recent years there has been a sharp increase in the uptake and development of e-learning applications within the context of higher education and training in many parts of the world, and we expect this to continue during the next few years. Whilst we do not expect online courses to become the norm, we do expect blended learning to replace traditional teaching methods. Although not all aspects of e-learning applications can be considered to have enhanced teaching and learning, the use of interactive technologies can provide an interesting platform from which to engage students and provide more interactive and challenging learning experiences. It is accepted by most people that e-learning will not always be suitable for all learners and that there will always be people who prefer FtF interaction in preference to computer-mediated interaction. However, it can be considered that e-learning has provided people (e.g., those who live in remote areas, work full-time or have special needs) with access to learning resources and opportunities to study that may not have previously existed.

As e-learning applications embrace ever more sophisticated interactive games-based technologies, this does present a number of challenges to higher-education institutions. Such challenges include the very high cost for fully functional and sophisticated interactive technology platforms. Whilst the costs may be within the reach of some multinational organizations, there are very few higher-education institutions that could manage to raise such funds. Furthermore, there is the problem of continuing to make such learning platforms ex-

citing and stimulating for learners, many of whom have low boredom thresholds and want to try the next new technological experiences. Whatever the challenges that e-learning and games-based e-learning present, higher-education institutions will not be able to ignore their development and proliferation, particularly as they become incorporated into mobile technologies, such as PDAs and Smartphones, as seen in the developing area of m-learning. If these new developments and applications are to enhance teaching and learning it will be vital that pedagogic issues are at the forefront as opposed to merely focusing on technology alone.

There are clearly significant barriers to the uptake of both e-learning and games-based e-learning. Perhaps because government and funding bodies see e-learning as a cost-effective way to provide mass higher education and training, they are strong supporters of e-learning, and funding is being made available to help overcome many of the barriers cited above. Not unexpectedly, much less centralized funding is being provided for games-based e-learning, and the adoption of this approach will have to rely more on individuals within organizations to experiment and improve the approach. We believe this will inevitably keep it as a small, albeit important, portion of e-learning provision.

REFERENCES

Aldrich, C. (2003). *Simulations and the future of learning: An innovative (and perhaps revolutionary) approach to e-learning.* New York: Pfeiffer.

Attwell, G. (2005). *E-learning and sustainability.* Creative Commons, Retrieved October 23, 2005, from http://www.ossite.org/Members/GrahamAttwell/sustainibility/view

Beavis, C. (2002). Reading, writing and role-playing computer games. In I. Snyder (Ed.), *Silicon literacies; communication, innovation and education in the electronic era.* London: Routledge.

British Educational Communications and Technology Agency (Becta). (2001). *Computer games in education project,* Retrieved September 23, 2004, from http://www.becta.org.uk/research/research.cfm?section=1&id=2846

Berge, Z.L., & Muilenburg, L.Y. (2001). Obstacles faced at various stages of capability regarding distance education in institutions of higher education: survey results. *Tech Trends, 45*(4), 40-45.

Berge, Z. L., & Muilenburg, L. Y. (2005). Student barriers to online learning: A factor analytic study. *Distance Education, 26*(1), 29-48.

Brennan, R., McFadden, M., & Law, E. (2000). *All that glitters is not gold: Online delivery of education and training.* Retrieved from http://www.ncver.edu.au/research/proj/nr9008.pdf

Bryce, J., & Rutter, J. (2002). *Computer and video gaming: Academic perspectives, positions and research resources* (CRIC discussion paper). Manchester, UK: University of Manchester.

Carr, S. (2000). As distance education comes of age, the challenge in keeping students. *Chronicle of Higher Education, 46*(13), A39–A41.

Cassell, J., & Jenkins, H. (1998). *From Barbie to Mortal Kombat: Gender and computer games.* Cambridge, MA: MIT Press.

Chen, G. D., Shen, G. Y., Ou, K. L., & Liu, B. (1998). Promoting motivation and eliminating disorientation for web based courses by a multi-user game. In *Proceedings of the ED-MEDIA/ED-TELECOM 98 World Conference on Educational Multimedia and Hypermedia and World Conference on Educational Telecommunications.*

Cleary, A. G., McKendrick, H., & Sills, J.A. (2002). Hand–arm vibration syndrome may be associated with prolonged use of vibrating computer games. *British Medical Journal, 324*(7332). Retrieved April 14, 2004, from http://bmj.com/cgi/content/full/324/7332/301/a

Collins, A., Brown, J. S., & Newman, S. E. (1989). Cognitive apprenticeship: Teaching the craft of reading, writing, and mathematics. In L. Resnick (Ed.), *Knowing, learning, and instruction: Essays in honor of Robert Glaser.* Hillsdale, NJ: Lawrence Erlbaum.

Computer and Video Games Survey. (2005). Retrieved October 14, 2005, from http://www.video-games-survey.com/online_gamers.htm

Connolly, T. M., MacArthur, E., Stansfield, M. H., & McLellan, E. (in press). A quasi-experimental study of three online learning courses in computing. *Computers and Education.*

Connolly, T. M., McLellan, E., Stansfield, M. H., Ramsay, J., & Sutherland, J. (2004). Applying games concepts to teach database analysis and design. In *Proceedings of the International Conference on Computer Games: Artificial Intelligence, Design and Education,* 352-359.

Connolly, T. M., & Stansfield M. H. (2006). *From eLearning to games-based eLearning: Using interactive technologies in teaching information systems.* Manuscript submitted for publication.

Darking, M. (2002). Integrating pedagogical technologies into UK Higher Education: Conceptual foundations. In *Proceedings of the 10th European Conference on Information Systems* (Vol. 2, pp. 1430-1438).

Dutton, J., Dutton, M., & Perry, J. (2002). How do online students differ from lecture students? *Journal of Asynchronous Learning Networks, 6*(1), 1-20.

Dutton, W. H., Cheong, P. H., & Park, N. (2004). The social shaping of a virtual environment: The case of a university-wide course management system. *Electronic Journal of e-Learning, 2*(1), 69-80.

Emes, C. E. (1997). Is Mr. Pac Man eating our children? A review of the impact of video games on children. *Canadian Journal of Psychiatry, 42*(4), 409–414.

Garris, R., Ahlers, R., & Driskell, J. E. (2002). Games, motivation, and learning: A research and practice model. *Simulation and Gaming, 33*(4), 441-467.

Garrison, R. (1997). Computer conferencing: The post-industrial age of distance education. *Open Learning, 12*(2), 3-11.

Gee, J. P. (2003). *What video games have to teach us about learning and literacy.* New York: Palgrave Macmillan.

Grant, M. (2004). *Five key barriers facing organizations in eLearning* [white paper]. Retrieved April 14, 2005, from www.elearncampus.com

Gunawardena, C. N. (1993). The social context of online education. In *Proceedings of the Distance Education Conference.*

Gunawardena, C. N., & McIsaac, M. S. (2004). Distance education. In D. H. Jonassen (Ed.), *Handbook of research for educational communications and technology* (2nd ed., pp. 355-396). Mahwah, NJ: LEA.

Jenkins, H. (1998). Voices from the combat zone: Game grrlz talk back. In J. Cassell and Jenkins, (Eds.), *From Barbie to Mortal Combat: Gender and computer games.* Cambridge, MA: MIT Press.

Jonassen, D. H. (1996). Computer-mediated communication: Connecting communities of learners. *Computers in the classroom* (pp. 158-182). Edgewood Cliffs, NJ: Prentice-Hall Inc.

Katzeff, C. (2000). The design of interactive media for learners in an organisational setting—the state of the art. In *Proceedings for NordiCHI 2000.*

Kennedy, H. (2002). Lara Croft: Feminist icon or cyberbimbo? On the limits of textual analysis. *Game Studies, 2*(2), Retrieved April 14, 2004, from http://www.gamestudies.org/0202/kennedy/computer_games/

Kozma, R. (1987). The implications of cognitive psychology for computer-based learning tools. *Educational Technology, XXVII*(11), 20-25.

Lave, J. (1988). *Cognition in Practice: Mind, mathematics, and culture in everyday life.* Cambridge, UK: Cambridge University Press.

Lawless, N., & Allan, J. (2004). Understanding and reducing stress in collaborative e-Learning. *Electronic Journal of e-Learning, 2*(2).

Leemkuil, H., de Jong, T., de Hoog, R., & Christoph, N. (2003). KM QUEST: A collaborative Internet-based simulation game. *Simulation & Gaming, 34*(1), 89-111.

Learning and Teaching Support Network (LTSN). (2003). A guide for learning technologists. In, *LTSN Generic Centre, E-Learning Series 4.* : LTSN.

Malone, T. W., & Lepper, M. R. (1987). Making learning fun: A taxonomy of intrinsic motivations for learning. *Aptitude, learning and instruction. Conative and affective process analysis* (Vol. 3, pp. 223-253). Hillsdale, NJ: Lawrence Erlbaum.

Mayo, P., Donnelly, M. B., Nash, P. P., & Schwartz, R. W. (1993). Student perceptions of tutor effectiveness in problem based surgery clerkship. *Teaching and Learning in Medicine, 5*(4), 227-233.

McComb, M. (1993). Augmenting a group discussion course with computer-mediated communication in a small college setting. *Interpersonal Computing and Technology Journal, 1*(3).

McDonald, J. (2002). Is "as good as face-to-face" as good as it gets? *Journal of Asynchronous Learning Networks, 6*(2), 10-23.

Moore, M. G., Shattuck, K., & Al-Harthi, A. (2005). Cultures meeting cultures in online distance education. *Journal of e-Learning and Knowledge Society, 2*(2).

Muilenburg, L. Y., & Berge, Z. L. (2001). Barriers to distance education: A factor-analytic study. *The American Journal of Distance Education. 15*(2), 7-22.

Newman, J. (2004). *Videogames.* London: Routledge.

Prensky, M. (2001). *Digital game based learning.* McGraw-Hill.

Provenzo, E. F. (1991). *Video kids: Making sense of Nintendo.* Cambridge, MA: Harvard.

Rovai, A. P. (2002). Building sense of community at a distance. *International Review of Research in Open and Distance Learning.*

Sandford, R., & Williamson, B. (2005). *Games and learning.* NESTA Futurelab.

Shaffer, D. W., Squire, K. T., Halverson, R., & Gee, J. P. (in press). Video games and the future of learning. *Phi Delta Kappan.*

Squire, K. (2003). Video games in education. *International Journal of Intelligent Simulations and Gaming, 2*(1), 49-62.

Stoll, C. (1999). *High tech heretic—reflections of a computer contrarian.* New York: First Anchor Books.

Taylor, J., Rodden, T., Anderson, A., Sharples, M., Luckin, R., Conole, G., & Siraj-Blatchford, J. (2004). *An e-learning research agenda.* Engineering and Physical Sciences Research Council.

Timms, D. (2001). *eLearning—back to the future.* Lund Keynote. Retrieved November 14, 2005 from http://www.odeluce.stir.ac.uk/docs/Lund-Keynote.pdf

Chapter V
Designing a CRM–Based E–Government Usability Services Framework:
Integrating Internal and External Customers in Public Services

Chi-Chang Chang
YuanPei Institute of Science and Technology, Taiwan

Yi-Fen Chen
YuanPei Institute of Science and Technology, Taiwan

ABSTRACT

The "electronic government" movement has swept across most countries in the last decade. This movement represents a new paradigm for public services. As we know, traditional public services may be improved in many ways by the Internet. According to the literature reviewed, we found many studies were only focused on how to technically establish Web sites that allow citizens appropriate access to government information. However, few studies paid attention to the relationship management among the different e-government stakeholders. Therefore, the objective of this chapter is to integrate the relationship management among the three groups of stakeholders: the government itself, its citizens and employees. In this chapter, we will examine the literature regarding to the underlying rationale of a successful e-government. Also, an evaluation system for the usability of government Web sites that support relationship management among citizens, government employees and public services are developed and empirically tested.

INTRODUCTION

The pervasiveness of the World Wide Web (WWW) has created a tremendous opportunity for providing services over the Internet. In the last decade, e-government has become an important catchword (Organization for Economic Co-operation and Development (OECD), 1998). Researchers and practitioners from different fields have investigated various issues of public administration for virtual processes. Much of the current e-government research focuses on improving efficiency and increasing performance within public administration. But e-government is definitely more than just redesigning citizen services and using state-of-the-art information technology (IT). According to a recent survey by OECD (1998), it was found that around 80% of e-government projects are either never implemented or abandoned immediately after execution. Beyond these failures, a further 30% fail partially by falling short of major goals or causing significant undesirable outcomes, or both. A few projects incur sustainability failures, succeeding for only a year or so. Most failures result from the gap between the design and reality (OECD, 1998). For example, citizens showed little demand for such information and did not have the presumed level of skill, which further inhibited their involvement, and the heterogeneity of systems, processes and cultural background and so forth. (Minoo, 2000). Since e-government face serious challenges and the most challenging is offering two-way-communication services for transactions between administrations and their partners (citizens, companies and other administrations) (Richter, Cornford, & McLoughlin, 2004).

A successful implementation of e-government services requires a coordinated development of their internal reorganization and their external relations with customers. To provide the benefits of such transaction services, a customer-centered solution is necessary. Yet a comprehensive approach has not been found (Shaw et al., 1997;

Galbreath & Gogers, 1999; Davison et al., 2005). The purpose of this chapter is to present a framework for customer relationship management CRM-based online support for public services. In the background section, we will present a review of relevant literature. In the next section we will develop the measurement scales to identify the best indicators for assessing the quality of a government's Web site and to conduct the different procedures were employed in this chapter, respectively. Then an analysis of the results and a CRM-based e-government framework will be discussed. Finally, limitations and future research directions will be presented.

BACKGROUND

E-Government in Action

The definition of e-government by United Nations and American Society for Public Administration is:

E-government includes the use of all information and communication technologies, from fax machines to wireless palm pilots, in order to facilitate the daily administration of government. However, just like e-commerce, the popular interpretation of e-government is one that defines it exclusively as an internet driven activity ... to which it may be added that improves citizen access to government information, services and expertise to ensure citizen participation in, and satisfaction with the government process ... it is a permanent commitment by government to improving the relationship between the private citizen and the public sector through enhanced, cost-effective and efficient delivery of services, information and knowledge. It is the practical realization of the best that government has to offer.

Similarly, e-government is narrowly defined as the production and delivery of government services through IT applications, however it can be defined more broadly as any way IT is used to simplify and improve transactions between governments and other actors (Pitt, Watson, & Kavan, 1995; Robert, Davison, & Ma, 2005; Smith, 2001; Tan, Yen, & Fang, 2002).

The functionality and utility of Web technologies in public management can be broadly divided into two categories: internal and external. Internally, the Web and other technologies hold promise as effective and efficient managerial tools that collect, store, organize and manage an enormous volume of data and information (Abanumy, Al-Badi, & Mayhew, 2005). One government agency also can transfer funds electronically to other governmental agencies or provide information to employees through an intranet or Internet system. Thus, the government can do many routine tasks more easily and quickly. On the other hand, externally, Web technologies also facilitate governmental linkages with citizens and businesses. Information and data can easily be shared with and transferred to external stakeholders. In addition, some Web technologies enable the government to promote public participation in policy-making processes by posting public notices and exchanging messages and ideas with the public. According to recent e-government research (Gore, 1993; Hutto, 2001; Lytras, 2006; Marche & McNiven, 2003; Whitson & Davis, 2001), even with the use of advanced IT, e-government plans still had some key usability problems which will be discussed as follows:

- **The problem of heterogeneous systems:** The electronically delivered services assume that the public sector functions as an integrated environment. One of the major problems that governments encounter is that their data are usually hard to reach and distributed in disparate and inaccessible systems across various departments. The problem becomes more crtical when it is related to culture that

resists information dissemination. Adequate working environments must be established, so employees can access information easily, evaluate it and share their emerging knowledge with colleagues. Therefore, government employees should be able to make the most of document management, workflow and intranet tools to assist them.

- **The lack of citizens' viewpoint:** Web-based consumer services are generally perceived as being successful, but there has been little evaluation of how well the Web meets its users' primary information requirements (Churchill, 1979; Kreizman, 2001). The important point is what citizens expect, want and need, and the way they perceive, accept and judge the services the receive from the administration (Jeong & Lambert, 2001). As an example, citizens not familiar with the logic of administrative thinking will need active help in finding the information for which they are searching. Thus, the challenge of today's e-government is to carefully integrate the technological advancements based on citizens' feedback.

- **The lack of officials' viewpoint:** Before the Internet emerged in the late 1980s, governments were already actively pursuing ITs that would improve operating efficiency and enchance internal communication (Palkovits & Wimmer, 2003; Traunmuller & Wimmer, 2003; Wimmer, 2002). However, the focus of e-government in that era was primarily internal and managerial. The Internet gradually has matured into user-friendly platforms for officials to communicate directly with citizens and to deliver massive quantities of information to the public. While the lack of internal customer's perspective, it make hard to design, evolving official expectations and integrate interdependent networks coordinated by governance.

In regard to these problems, Churchill (1979), Coulthard (2004), Cronin and Taylor (1992) and Dabholkar and Overby (2005) have proposed that e-government can be seen from four perapectives: citizens and customers, process (reorganization), (tele)cooperation and knowledge. Gisler and Spahi (2001) have three views of e-government: the institution-based view, the services-based view and the relation-based view. Hiller and Bélanger (2001) have proposed a five-stage e-government, which reflects the degree of technical interaction with users.

In the Table 1, Stage 1 is the most basic form of e-government and uses IT for disseminating information, simply by posting information or data on the Web site for constituents to view. Stage 2 is two-way communication characterized as an interactive mode between government and constituents. In Stage 3, the government allows online services and financial transactions by replacing public employees with "Web-based self-service." In Stage 4, the government attempts to integrate various government services vertically (intergovernmental integration) and horizontally (intragovernmental integration) for efficiency, user friendliness and effectiveness. This stage is a highly challenging task for governments, because it requires a tremendous amount of time and resources to integrate online and back-office systems. Both vertical and horizontal integrations push information and data sharing among different functional units and levels of governments for better online public services (Cullen & Houghton, 2000). Stage 5 involves the promotion of Web-based political participation, in which government Web sites include online voting, online public forums and online opinion surveys for more direct and wider interaction with the public. While the previous four stages are related to Web-based public services in the administrative arena, the fifth stage highlights Web-based political activities by citizens.

However, this framework just simply provides an exploratory conceptual tool that helps one un-

derstand the evolutionary nature of e-government (Janssen & Veenstra, 2005; Montagna, 2005). A crucial problem, not yet completely addressed, is the challenge of developing an evolutionary architecture to integrate large heterogeneous systems and to meet the requirements of customers. Frequently, crafting such an architecture involves not only reengineering technological systems, according to the government's needs, but also reengineering the administrative and business processes that provide services to customers.

Customer Relationship Management

This section will briefly review the customer relationship management (CRM) literature and also examine approaches to strengthening administration-service relationships, while pursuing quality and performance improvement. Due to technological advancement and economic changes, policy makers have had further incentive to shift the focus of IT usage from internal managerial needs to external linkages with the public. The National Performance Review report suggests that e-government, "will allow citizens broader and more timely access to information and services through efficient, customer-responsive processes—thereby creating a fundamental revision in the relationship between the federal government and everyone served by it" (Gore, 1993).

In order to manage new content, coming from changes in standards or regulations, for example, one must keep in mind that users' require the information or knowledge that comes from this change. Within these changes, CRM is one of the fastest growing business technology initiatives (Walter, 1999; World Economic Forum, 2000). That growth rate will keep going up when organizations increasingly recognize that in order to achieve a sustainable competitive advantage. The core concept of CRM is an integration of technologies and business processes used to satisfy the needs of a customer during any given

Table 1. Five stages of e-government (Source: Hiller & Bélanger, 2001)

Administrative functions						Political functions
		Stage 1	**Stage 2**	**Stage 3**	**Stage 4**	**Stage 5**
	Types of government	Information: dissemination / catalogue	Two-way communication	Service and financial transactions	Vertical and horizontal integration	Political participation
Internal	Government to government	Agency filing requirements	Requests from local governments		Electronic funds transfers	N/A
	Government to public employees	Pay dates, holiday information	Requests for employment benefit statements	Electronic paychecks	One-stop job, grade, vacation time, retirement information and so forth	N/A
External	Government to individual– Services	Description of medical benefits	Request and receive individual benefit information	Pay taxes online	All services and entitlements	N/A
	Government to individual– political	Dates of elections	Receive election forms	Receive election funds and disbursements	Register and vote: federal, state and local (file)	Voting online
	Government to business–citizen	Regulations online	Security and Exchange Commission (SEC) filings	Pay taxes online, receive program funds (SB, etc.), agricultural allotments	All regulatory information on one site	Filing comments online
	Government to business– marketplace	Posting request for proposals	Request clarification or specs	Online vouchers and payments	Marketplace for vendors	N/A
Technol-ogies used		Basic Web technology, bulletin boards	Electronic data interchange, e-mail	Electronic data interchange, electronic filing system, digital signature, interoperable technology, public key infrastructure	Integration of the technologies required for Stages 1, 2, and 3.	Public key infrastructure, more sophisticated interface and interoperable technologies, chat rooms

interaction (Bradshaw & Brash, 2001; Walter, 1999; Yuan & Chang, 2001). More specifically, few studies have focused on the management of relationships between the organization and its employees from the perspective of employees as customers. Furthermore, with respect to IT, studies have focused on data integration and customer-support activities as a foundation for improving an organization's ability to serve customers effectively. Consequently, how to iden-

tify customers' demands is becoming the most important issue (Richter et al., 2004).

CRM is a strategy asset that is a critical resource of government's adaptation and survival. In order to avoid CRM failures, Zachman (2005) proposed a framework of six perspectives (what-how-where-who-when-why) to define what aspects of CRM need to be studied. DeLone and McLean (1992) conducted extensive research on the possible constructs that would affect the success of an IT (Berry, 1995). They suggested that quality measures, which included information quality and system quality, are important constructs related to the success of IT. In order to communicate with the potential customers through WWW electively, a well-designed Web page is needed (Choudrie, Ghinea, & Weerakkody, 2004). Yet, the factors that affect customer's perception of a Web site are unclear.

A CRM-BASED E-GOVERNMENT USABILITY EVALUATION FRAMEWORK

Based on the requirements discussed in the Background section, the challenge for the e-government is the need to integrate the technological advancements for the benefit of citizens and government administration. In order to develop a CRM-based evaluation framework, a systematic approach is used. In the following, we first propose a research framework, then develop measurement scales and finally conduct an empirical study. Figure 1

shows the triple-diamonds architecture, which consists of three functional orientations—IT strategy orientation, citizen orientation, administration orientation and offering transport, basic and cooperative services by way of CRM-based e-government with each other.

- **IT strategy orientation:** A study of five countries (DeLone & McLean, 1992) has shown that, "information technologies are indeed an instrument of public management reform." Basically, the central issue for e-government is applying IT to government activities that citizen's and governmental agencies and institutions do as they exchange information or ideas in order to improve existing and/or redefine public administrative services (by introducing new digital products and services). IT is used in a broad sense of information-resource configurations, which refers to IT handling techniques (storage, processing, transport, capturing and presentation) of data, including text, sound and visual images and knowledge. It

Figure 1. The triple diamonds usability measurement framework

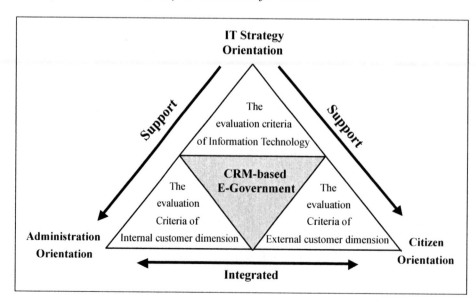

is an "intermediate technology" or "communication gateways," enabling electronic interaction between actors. Therefore, the public sector needs to understand the role of the new technology in policy making and service delivery (Steyaert, 2004; World Markets Research Centre, 2005), aiming at developing interorganizational cooperative information systems supporting e-government actions.

- **Citizen orientation:** Government support and assistance should be anywhere, anytime to aid citizens as valued customers, reflecting the fact that a government respects its citizens. According to the concept of the customer from management theory (Pitt et al., 1995; Richter et al., 2004), it is meaningful to call a user a customer only when this person can choose from at least two options. This is not the case with government services, which are by definition a monopoly. However, calling citizens customers reflects the attitude that a government must have when it interacts with its citizens. It is meant to acknowledge that issues, such as customer satisfaction, fulfillment of needs, quality of service and so forth, should be part of e-government's mentality and practice.

- **Administration orientation:** We suggest that governmental administrations face serious challenges and requirements in regards to their internal reorganization and their external relations with customers. A successful IT implementation of e-government services requires that the internal and external component be developed in a coordinated way. Therefore, tasks can be better structured, and officials can concentrate on improving the quality and performance facets of their workflows. For this purpose, the official-oriented design goes one step further by categorizing information and services on the Web according to the needs of different departments or work groups.

In response, governments have to rethink their existing services and possibly create new ones. These services must be developed in a way that is accessible to all citizens, easy to use and based on delivery channels assisted by technology, requiring a evaluation of most of the government's processes.

Development of Measurement Scales

According to a study by Galbreath and Gogers (1999), when customers decide to use a government's products and services the perceived quality of the information can be determined. When customers perceive that the information meets their needs and requirements, they are willing to criticize the value of each product or service based on their purchase-decision criteria. Thus determining customers' perception of information quality on the Web is a primary stage in assessing their potential behavior. In this chapter, customers' attitudes toward the government's Web site were constructed from a combined effect of three measurement scales: citizen, administration and IT (see Figure 1).

A citizen-focused performance evaluation scale was used for measuring the government's Web site and used 22 positively worded items from the e-g performance evaluation scale (Chen, Chang, & Wang, 2002). This scale was designed to measure the citizen-focused performance of a government's Web site. For a more complete list of these items, refer to Appendix B. In order to develop an official-focused performance evaluation scale for a government's Web site, we first came up with 12 dimensions of the government information service based on experts' opinions and a literature review (Coulthard (2004); Cronin & Taylor, 1992; Dabholkar & Overby, 2005; DeLone & McLean, 1992; Dyke, Kappelman, & Prybutok, 1997; Pitt et al., 1995). Then we developed 51 items for the 12 dimensions, which are named ease of use, ability, reliability, communication, safety, understanding, form, classification and frame, approachability, information quality, useable and maintainable. With growing interest in the evaluation of Internet information resources, many sets of criteria have been proposed for evaluation of Web sites (Cullen & Houghton, 2000; Marche & McNiven, 2003; Seilheimer, 2004; Smith, 2001; Whitson & Davis, 2001). In order to develop the criteria used for the evaluation of a government's Web site, we have adapted information from World Markets Research Centre (WMRC) and related literature and concluded with the IT measurement, which identified five dimensions (e.g., security, the constructional capacity of network, data processing, performance, database system) and 32 attributes(see Appendix A-1).

Study Procedures and Subjects

This study intended to provide a usability evaluation for the Web sites of Taiwan's local government. First, for the external customer, the authors organized a panel of coders composed of 98 college students to conduct a structured content evaluation of the Web sites of the Civil Affairs Department

Table 2. Citizen responses browser the average and variance of CADT Web site

Attribute	Average	Variance
Friendliness	2.60	0.65
Response	2.57*	0.67
Ability	2.92	0.44
Reliability	2.76	0.62
Communication	2.60	0.59
Safety	2.44*	0.65
Understanding	2.41*	0.57
Search	2.73	0.61
Channel	2.78	0.58
Information quality	2.88	0.50
Equitable	3.01	0.59
Total	2.60	0.65

Table 3. Official responses browser the average and variance of CADT Web site

Attribute	Average	Variance
Ease of use	2.91	0.57
Ability	2.72*	0.63
Reliability	2.94	0.56
Communication	2.71*	0.53
Safety	2.72*	0.59
Understanding	2.95	0.50
Form	2.97	0.52
Classification & frame	2.81*	0.58
Approachability	2.98	0.48
Information quality	2.86	0.46
Maintainable	2.63*	0.63
Total	2.84	0.55

Taipei City Government (CADT), in order to define the concepts as perceived from customers' perspectives. Subjects were given a 30-minute training session to familiarize them with using the Internet to locate and utilize the Web sites of CADT. Scales were developed for measuring each of the attributes as shown in Appendix B and C. For each scale, students were asked to express the degree to which they agreed with the statements on scale from 1-4 with "1" representing disagree completely and "4" representing agree completely. Ninety-eight students handed in their responses and all were valid.

Second, for the internal customer, we conducted 40 structured interviews with employees of CADT who were responsible for the management of administrative relationships with customers whose perception of the quality of the information is presumed to affect their intention to use and positive acceptance of it. In this study, attitude measures were developed by asking respondents to rate each attribute on 4-point semantic differential items was employed by anchoring from 'not at all agree' to 'very agree'. Third, IT quality is represented by five constructs: security, network capacity, data processing, operating performance and database system. In measuring IT with the intent to clarify how to discriminate among the different levels of each construct, we also adapted the same WMRC method of and marked each with "yes," "no" or "N/A" (not available), respectively (WMRC, 2005).

Results Analysis

For the external customer, there were 98 subjects, of whom 63 (64.3%) were males. Subjects in the 20-29 age category comprised 87.6% of the sample. As shown in Table 2, citizens' intention to use the e-government Web site was directly and positively affected by their perceptions of Web's "Understanding," "Safety," which received a lower average score, and followed by "Response," "Friendliness" and "Communication." For the internal customer, of the 40 respondents employed by institutions of higher education, 80% were government officials responsible for technical job and 20% were administrative position holders. The results are shown in Table 3. For IT quality, we studied the features that are available at the CADT government Web site; the results are shown in Appendix A-2.

Reliability and Validity of the Measurement Scales

The coefficient alpha estimation of the citizen-focused performance evaluation scale system for the government's Web site was 0.8988. The 22 items were divided into three dimensions, which were respectively named systemic ability, Web site design and government promotion (Chen, et al., 2002). In order to verify the official-focused performance evaluation scale for the government's Web site, we invited experts to examine the content validity and conducted a field study in the Taipei City government. Based on the results of the factor analysis, we found that three dimensions, which are respectively named usability, responsiveness

and reliability, can represent the proposed scale (see Table 4). Cronbach-α analysis revealed that each dimension and the scale have a high reliability range from 0.7567 to 0.8832 (see Table 5). The cumulative variance was 0.68717. Finally, a 14-item official-focused performance evaluation scale was developed to assess the government's Web site. The individual questionnaire items used to construct the scales in the analysis are shown in Appendix C.

The CRM-Based E-Government Usability Measurement Framework

As mentioned, CRM is a management concept that relies on technology and process automation to create its environment. In order to identify the success of an e-government action plan, we created a CRM-based e-government usability measurement framework as seen in Figure 2 and described below:

- **Citizen (external customer):** IT holds great potential to improve the interface between public organizations and citizens. The basic level of e-government public-services information is provided to the citizens, and such information may be comprised of simple where-to-go information, detailed information regarding public services, support for citizens participating in planning processes or even general everyday information. For example, citizens who are not familiar with the logic of administrative thinking will need active help in finding information. Therefore, by way of the external customer criteria for the evaluation of a government's Web site, the goal is to move constituents to this new channel while continuing to provide excellent service through the Internet.
- **Official (internal customer):** In the e-government domain, for information sharing over the network, the internal customer criteria for the evaluation of the

Table 4. Results of the exploratory factor analysis (internal customer)

Dimension	Items	Communality	Factor loadings	Cumulative variance explained
Usability	23	0.768	0.878	26.694%
	34	0.703	0.804	
	11	0.613	0.767	
	14	0.672	0.743	
	28	0.644	0.705	
	37	0.640	0.617	
Responsiveness	26	0.793	0.856	52.220%
	24	0.724	0.782	
	47	0.603	0.742	
	25	0.688	0.735	
	27	0.683	0.705	
Reliability	48	0.724	0.804	68.717%
	15	0.684	0.788	
	43	0.663	0.707	

government's Web site plays a crucial role for realizing the expected revolution. Similar to their citizen, officials do not only search and access information, but also complete administrative processes and communicate with others through the Web sites. The Web sites also provide on-demand support for officials as they work to accomplish their tasks.

- **E-government Web site (IT strategy):** For the purpose of cooperation, autonomous machine agents should be available to provide on-demand support to officials. These IT elements need to be tightly integrated and need effective analysis, using the IT criteria, for the evaluation of the government's Web site. In addition, the successful elements are highly dependent on the effectiveness of the other elements.

These elements must be integrated in a seamless fashion. While each of these IT elements has obvious advantages, it is the relationship among these elements that provides the potential to effectively interact with customers. When governments strategically link together with these key elements, it produces an atmosphere of customer interaction where the product is greater than sum of its parts. The problems that the CRM-based e-government system might face and the solutions to these problems have been stated previously. In summary, the transition of a government organization can be summarized in the following 11 critical success factors:

- New forms of delivering information and services
- New ways of making information widely available to citizens

Table 5. Results of the reliability test (internal customer)

Dimension	Reliability coefficients (alphas)	Total—scale reliability
Usability	0.8832	
Responsiveness	0.8686	0.8959
Reliability	0.7567	

- New ways of interacting with citizens (two-way communication), giving and receiving information to and from people, developing means for exchanging views and initiating dialogs
- New forms of linking communities locally and globally by creating online communitie
- New ways of creating conditions for communicating more freel
- New ways of tailoring services to individuals' need
- New forms of involving people in the process of government and policy making
- New ways of developing skills for active participation in e-government

- New forms of empowering citizens
- New ways of enhancing the representative role of government

Function Model for The CRM-Based E-Government System

As mentioned above, CRM is a new management concept that relies heavily on technology and process automation to create its environment; however, creation of such an environment entails change (Eddowes, 2004). Berry (1995) referred to technology's role in customer service as "high touch through high tech." IT can be used in both manual and automated customer interactions. Figure 3 shows the CRM-based e-government

Figure 2. The CRM-based e-government usability measurement framework

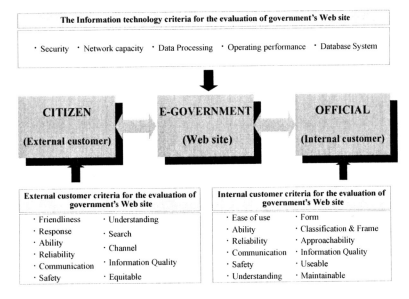

Figure 3. The CRM-based e-government system function model

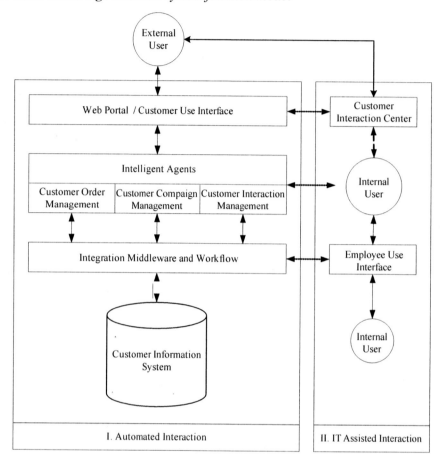

function architecture, which consists of two components offering transport, basic and cooperative services.

Automated Interaction

The key to the automated service encounter is to pass the control of the interaction process to the customer (see Figure 3, part I). The technical infrastructure is a key consideration when a government designs its automated-interaction strategy. This will consist of a telecommunication network and terminal equipment and can be internal or external to the government (Kreizman, 2001).

- **Citizen use interface (CUI):** IT has the potential to improve the interface between public organizations and citizens. E-government administrative information and information about public services may be provided through simple "where-to-go" information, detailed information regarding public services available, support for citizens or more general everyday information. As an example, citizens not familiar with the logic of administrative thinking will need active help in finding the information items for which they are searching. Therefore, the Web interface is well suited to creating new efficiencies for e-government services, but the goal is to move constituents to this new channel, while continuing to provide excellent service through Internet.

- **Intelligent agents (IAs):** IAs are a customer interface architectural sub layer, as are sets of customer-facing function logic that assist customers in conducting complex, multistage transactions or sets of transactions. Generally, these transactions represent events that have known, typical life cycles; IAs assist customers through the life cycle, over application boundaries, time (stop and start) and channels. IAs are the electronic equivalents of knowledgeable service clerks.

- **Integration middleware and intermediation hub (IM/IH):** A key function of this part is the ability to match customers to their records to ensure a unified customer history. Government organizations must develop metadata definitions for the customer's name and address, which are data elements that are used consistently across government databases. Ideally, updates, such as change of address, should be dealt with one time, with revisions made available to all systems that rely on this data, including shared services that provide functionality to multiple agencies or applications.

- **Customer information system (CIS):** Based on the MIS, marketing disciplines have studied IT's impact on customer sales and services. There have been those who have focused on how data integration and customer-support activities can be a foundation for improving a government's ability to serve customers effectively. Within this context, CIS is defined as the acquisition, storage and distribution of customer information. Besides, the desired end result is to increase profitability and customer satisfaction by getting the right campaign information, order information and interaction information to targeted customers. For a government, the goal is getting the right

information to the customer; the analytical focus is on improved service and more efficient internal operations.

IT-Assisted Interaction

IT-assisted interaction is predominantly a manual process that uses IT to enhance the relationship between the service provider (government) and the customer (citizens and officials) (see Figure 3, part II). It consists of a customer interaction center and an employee use interface.

- **Customer interaction center (CIC):** Providing customer service over the Web is common, but as expectations expand, customer demand for self-service options will cross to non-Internet channels. Therefore, anticipating and responding to customers with robust CICs is essential. CICs should concentrate on providing a framework for supporting applications that solve administrative issues, rather than satisfying the urge to deploy point solutions.

- **Employee use interface (EUI):** For information sharing over the network, the EUI play a crucial role for revolutionizing e-government. Similar to CUI, official do not only search and access information, but they also communicate and operate to fulfill the administrative process with others through the Web site. For this purpose, autonomous machine agents should be available that will support officials demands as they work on their tasks.

The previous discussion highlighted the fact that these IT elements need to be tightly integrated. The success of one element is highly dependent on the effectiveness of the other elements. It is our contention that for governments to maximize their ability to interact with customers, these elements must be integrated in a seamless fashion. While each IT element has obvious advantages, it is the relationship among these elements that provides governments with the potential to effectively interact with customers. When governments strategically link each of these key elements, it produces an atmosphere of customer interaction where the product is greater that the sum of its parts.

CONCLUSION

This chapter examined the emerging e-government in Web-based CRM framework. By investigating Taiwan's local government, the survey results showed that customers' needs are significant factors in the implementation and development of e-government. The data also raised a number of issues relevant to local e-government policymakers and practitioners. Among these is the question of whether the public-sector "customer" adequately encompasses the richness and complexity of the relationship between the government and its citizens. This chapter also proposed a framework to evaluate CRM-based online customer-service support. In this usability framework, there are obvious interrelationships that are necessary for governments to realize the benefits of CRM. However governments will fail if they develop an integrated view of the customer, but fail to modify the administrative procedures or provide customers with an effective interactive interface. Also to ensure that interactions with customers are successful, governments need to focus on the external transmission of customer information via interactive user-interface technology. Creating the optimal CRM-based e-government framework is and will increasingly become a critical government challenge. Therefore CRM will be a major strategic challenge in the 21st century.

We suggest that future research should assess the extent to which this model is validated by actual e-government, in particular the way in which e-government develops from initial rhetorical intentions through strategic planning, systems de-velopment, integration and finally transformation. Such innovations may well change governments as we know them today. In addition, the stages described can be used by public decision-makers as a guidance and direction for architecture development, to reduce the complexity of the progression of e-government initiatives, to communicate changes to the rest of the organization and to provide milestones to evaluate and control the cost of architecture development.

REFERENCES

Abanumy, A., Al-Badi, A., & Mayhew, P. (2005). E-Government Website accessibility: In-depth evaluation of Saudi Arabia and Oman. *The Electronic Journal of e-Government, 3,* 99-106.

Berry, L. L. (1995). *On great service: A framework for action.* New York: The Free Press.

Bradshaw, D., & Brash, C. (2001). Management customer relationships in the e-business world: How to personalize computer relationships for increased profitability. *International Journal of Retail & Distribution Management, 29,* 520-529.

Chen, C. K., Cheng, J. S., & Wang, K.M. (2002). Developing an e-government performance evaluation system—a study from citizen subjective aspects. *Journal of the Chinese Institute of Industrial Engineers, 19*(2), 39-52.

Choudrie, J., Ghinea, G., & Weerakkody, V. (2004). Evaluating global e-government sites: A view using Web diagnostic tools. *Electronic Journal of e-Government, 2,* 105-114.

Churchill, G. A. (1979). A paradigm for developing better measures of marketing constructs. *Journal of marketing research, 16,* 64-73.

Coulthard, L. J. M. (2004). Measuring service quality—A review and critique of research using SERVQUAL. *International Journal of Market Research, 46*(4), 479-497.

Cronin, J. J., & Taylor, S. A. (1992). Measuring service quality: A reexamination and extension. *Journal of Marketing, 56,* 55-68.

Cullen, R., & Houghton, C. (2000). Democracy online: An assessment of New Zealand government Web sites. *Government Information Quarterly, 17,* 243-267.

Dabholkar, P. A., & Overby, J. W. (2005). Linking process and outcome to service quality and customer satisfaction evaluations—an investigation of real estate agent service. *International Journal of Service Industry Management, 16*(1), 10-27.

Davison, R.M., Wagner C., & Ma, L.C.K. (2005). From government to e-government: A transition model. *Information Technology & People, 18*(3), 280-299.

DeLone, W. H., & McLean, E. R. (1992). Information system success: The quest for the dependent variable. *Information System Research, 6,* 60-95.

Drake, W. J. (2000, July 19). World economic forum: From the global digital divide to the global digital opportunity, proposals submitted to the G-8, Kyushu-Okinawa Tokyo, Japan.

Dyke, T. P., Kappelman, L. A., & Prybutok, V. R.(1997). Measuring information system service quality: Concerns on the use of the SERVQUAL questionnaire. *MIS Quarterly, 21,* 195-208.

Eddowes, L. A. (2004). The application of methodologies in e-Government. *Electronic Journal of e-Government, 2,* 115-126.

Galbreath, J., & Gogers, T. (1999). Customer relationship leadership: A leadership and motivation model for the twenty-first century business. *The TQM Magazine, 11,* 161-171.

Gisler, M. & Spahi, D. (2001). *E-government: Eine standortbestimmung.* Bern: Verlag Haupt Bern.

Gore, A. (1993). Reengineering through information technology. *Accompanying Report of the National Performance Review.* Retrieved April 21, 2005, from http://govinfo.library.unt.edu/npr/library/reports/it.html

Hiller, J., & Bélanger, F. (2001). *Privacy strategies for electronic government.* E-government series). Arlington, VA: PricewaterhouseCoopers Endowment for the Business of Government.

Hutto, D. H. (2001). Recent literature on government information. *Journal of Government Information, 28,* 185-240.

Janssen, M., & Veenstra, A. F. (2005). Stages of growth in e-Government: An architectural approach. *The Electronic Journal of e-Government, 3,* 193-200.

Jeong, M., & Lambert, C. U. (2001). Adaptation of an information quality framework to measure customers' behavioral intentions to use lodging Web sites. *Hospitality Management, 20,* 129-146.

Kreizman, G. (2001). *E-government architecture: CRM.* Garnter Research.

Lytras, M. D. (2006). The semantic electronic government: Knowledge management for citizen relationship and new assessment scenarios. *Electronic Government, 3,* 5-17.

Minoo, S. A. (2000). Information technologies: Challenges and opportunities for local government. *Journal of Government Information, 27,* 471-479.

Marche, S., & McNiven, J. D. (2003). E-government and e-governance: The future isn't what it used to be. *Canadian Journal of Administrative Sciences-Revue Canadienne des Sciences de l'Administration, 20*(1), 74-86.

Montagna, J. M. (2005). A framework for the assessment and analysis of electronic government proposals. *Electronic Commerce Research and Applications, 4,* 204-219.

Organization for Economic Co-operation and Development. (1998). *Information technology as an instrument of public management reform: A study of five OECD countries' Organization for Economic Co-operation and Development.* The Report of Public Management Service (PUMA) 14,3 December. Retrieved February 21, 2006, from http://www.olis.oecd.org/olis/1998doc. nsf/LinkTo/PUMA(98)14

Palkovits, S., & Wimmer, M. A. (2003). Processes in e-government—a holistic framework for modeling electronic public services. *Electronic Government, Proceedings* (LNCS 2739, pp. 213-219).

Pitt, L. F., Watson, R. T., & Kavan, C. B. (1995). Service quality: A measure of information systems effectiveness. *MIS Quarterly, 19,* 173-187.

Richter, P., Cornford, J., & McLoughlin, L. (2004). The e-citizen as talk, as text and as technology: CRM and e-government. *Electronic Journal of e-Government, 2,* 207-218.

Robert, M., Davison, C. W., & Ma, L. C. K. (2005). From government to e-government: A transition model. *Information Technology & People, 18,* 280-299.

Seilheimer, S. D. (2004). Productive development of World Wide Web sites intended for international use. *International Journal of Information Management, 24*(5), 363-373.

Shaw, M. J., Gardner, D. M., & Thomas, H. (1997). Research opportunities in electronic commerce. *Decision Support Systems, 21,* 149-156.

Sinnappan, S., & Carlson, J. (2004). An examination of website quality dimensions in Australian e-retailing: A confirmatory factor analysis approach. *Intelligent Information Technology, Proceedings* (LNCS 3356, pp. 410-418).

Smith, A. G. (2001). Appling evaluation criteria to New Zealand government websites. *International Journal of Information Management, 21,* 137-149.

Steyaert, J. C. (2004). Measuring the performance of electronic government services. *Information and Management, 41,* 369-375.

Tan, X., Yen, D. C., & Fang, X. (2002, Spring). Internet integrated customer relationship management. *Journal of Computer Information Systems, 42*(3), 77-86.

Traunmuller, R., & Wimmer, M. A. (2003). e-Government at a decisive moment: Sketching a roadmap to excellence. *Electronic Government, Proceedings* (LNCS 2739, pp. 1-14).

Walter, A. (1999). Relationship promoters-driving forces for successful customer relationships. *Industrial Marking Management, 28,* 537-551.

Well, J. D., Fuerst, W. L., & Choobineh, J. (1999). Managing information technology (IT) for one-to-one customer interaction. *Information & Management, 35,* 53-62.

Whitson, T. L., & Davis, L. (2001). Best practices in electronic government: Comprehensive electronic information dissemination for science and technology. *Government Information Quarterly, 18,* 79-91.

Wimmer, M. A. (2002). A European perspective towards online one-stop government: The eGOV project. *Electronic Commerce Research and Applications, 1,* 92-103.

World Economic Forum. (2000, July). *From the global digital divide to the global digital opportunity.*

World Markets Research Centre (2005). *Global E-government survey.* Retrieved February 18, 2005, from http://www.world Marketsanalysis.com

Yuan, S. T., & Chang, W. L. (2001). Mixed-initiative synthesized learning approach for web-based CRM. *Expert System with Applications, 20,* 187-200.

Zachman, A. (2005). *The framework for enterprise architecture.* Retrieved April 15, 2005, from http://www.intervista-institute.com/resources/zachman-poster.html

APPENDIX A

Appendix A-1. IT quality measure at CADT government Web site

Dimension	Attribute	Index	Result
Security	1 Firewall	Y/N	N/A
	2 Backup and load equation	Y/N	N/A
	3 Routine test and monitor	Y/N	N/A
	4 Standard operation procedure	Operating manual	N/A
		Obey communication protocol	N/A
	5 System monitor software	User access log analysis	YES
		User route log analysis	N/A
		User flow analysis	N/A
	6 Privacy	Selectivity	N/A
		Firewall function	N/A
		Privacy announcement	NO
		Accessible	NO
		Encryption	N/A
	7 Authority	Public key recognizes system	NO
		Independent supervises faculty	NO
		Copyright announcement	YES
	8 Completeness	Relief regulation	NO
		Data–guard supervisor system	NO
		Version declaration	YES
	9 Undeniable	Digital signature	NO
		Id/No. check	YES
Network capacity	1 Performance analysis	Low bandwidth support	YES
	2 Quality service	Proxy server provided	NO
Data processing	1 Reliable	Renew update	YES
		Full linkage executed	NO
	2 Rapid	Provide pure-text page	YES
		Download file within 15 seconds	YES
	3 Managerial efficiency	Show a message for wrong linkage	NO
		Backup function	N/A
	4 Free from suffering	Make a recovery plan	N/A
		24x7service	NO

continued on following page

Appendix A-1. continued

Dimension	Attribute	Index	Result
Operating performance	1 Speed	Reasonable average response time	22 Sec. second
		Fit in with three clicks	NO
		E-mail response within two days	N/A
	2 Consistence	Web page name in accord with content	YES
		Same format	YES
		Right information	YES
	3 Elasticity	Multiformat download files	NO
		Linkage to home page	YES
		Support Netscape browser	YES
	4 Malfunction service	Phone service	YES
		Linkage to Web master	NO
	5 Communication	Audio clip	NO
		Video clip	NO
		E-mail service	YES
		Chat	NO
		FAQ	NO
		E-newspaper support	YES
		Community or not	NO
	6 Effortless	Site map	NO
		Web site guild	NO
		URL in accord with content	YES
		No complex URL	YES
		Uses the ranking record	NO
		Content search function	NO
	7 Linkage portal	Y/N	YES
Database system	1 Usability	Click No. vs. Access No.	NO
		Several file formats for download	NO (word only)
	2 Expandable	FTP function support	NO
		Whether customizable or not	NO
	3 Multilanguage support	Y/N	NO
	4 English support	Y/N	YES
	5 Easy backup	Y/N	N/A
	6 Update function	Y/N	YES

Appendix A-2. The criteria of IT quality measure at CADT government Web site

1. Security criteria
1.1 Fir wall
1.2 Backup and load equation
1.3 Routine test andmMonitor
1.4 Standard operating procedure
1.5 System monitor software
1.6 Privacy
1.7 Authority
1.8 Completeness
1.9 Undeniable

2. Network capacity criteria
2.1 Performance analysis
2.2 Quality service

3. Data-processing criteria
3.1 Reliable
3.2 Rapid
3.3 Managerial efficiency
3.4 Free from suffering
3.5 Search

3.6 Publish
3.7 Related data linkage
3.8 Index

4. Operating-performance criteria
4.1 Speed
4.2 Consistency
4.3 Elasticity
4.4 Malfunction service
4.5 Communication
4.6 Effortless
4.7 Linkage portal

5. Database-system criteria
5.1 Usability
5.2 Expandability
5.3 Multilanguage support
5.4 English support
5.5 Easy backup
5.6 Update function

APPENDIX B

Appendix B-1. The criteria of citizen quality measure at CADT government Web site

1	I'm satisfied with the query system.
2	The government Web site informs me of the status of business processing.
3	I can find the information that meets my needs via the Web site anytime.
4	With my authorization, I can accomplish all the related applications to various offices. (For example, when moving, you will only have to change your residential information from the Web site of the residential office and it will actively update and transfer your residential information to all the related offices concerned, such as the gas company.)
5	All of the functions & service items can be operated normally.
6	The Web site is equipped with confidential service.
7	The Web site is equipped with the plan for identification.
8	There is no need to worry about personal information being used illegally by others.
9	There is no need to worry about government have not received my register.
10	The Q&A column answers to common questions.
11	Information offered by the government Web site meets my needs.
12	The image introduction of the government Web site is easy to find information.
13	Information provided by the government is organized.
14	The government Web site provides me with the latest news of the government.
15	The image introduction of the government Web site helps me to classify related business.
16	Information on the government Web site is easily understood.
17	The organization of the government Web site includes teaching activities to help me access the services I want.
18	The government Web site provides me with a way to express myself.
19	Through letters, ads, activities and so forth, the government informs me of the network service.
20	I know that I have as equal an opportunity as others to access to the service provided by the government Web site.
21	There is staff to respond to my opinions and questions on the Web site.
22	There is no difficulty finding the government Web site.

Note: Citizen-focused performance evaluation scale for government Web sites (Cronbach α=0.8988)

APPENDIX C

Appendix C-1. The criteria of official quality measure at CADT government Web site

1	This Web site improves the quality of my work.
2	This Web site saves me time.
3	I feel that this Web site can improve my efficiency.
4	The information provided by the Web site meets my working needs.
5	Through the Web site, I can respond to the questions and opinions from citizens.
6	Through the Web site, I can transfer and organize information from various organizations and citizens.
7	The e-government handles my problems correctly.
8	I can contact the Webmaster easily to inform him/her of Web site problems.
9	There is fast response from the customer service to my queries.
10	When I use the Web site, I have a clear idea of the steps and expected results.
11	The titles and content are consistent, and they are connected efficiently.
12	I don't see the wrong content and information.
13	All of the characters and illustrations can be presented normally when I access the Web site.
14	I trust the content provided by the Web site.

Note: Official-focused performance evaluation scale system for a government Web site (Cronbach $\alpha=0.8959$)

Chapter VI
Electronic Policing:
A Framework for Crime Control and Citizen Services

Roongrasamee Boondao
Ubon Rajathanee University, Thailand

Nitin Kumar Tripathi
Asian Institute of Technology, Thailand

ABSTRACT

This chapter examines electronic policing (e-policing), which has played an increasing role in government-management reform and has become an important area for e-government research. Firstly, the strategic framework and development of e-policing are reviewed. A framework of mobile policing is introduced that is derived from the system requirements of both police and citizens. We examine how an e-policing system is implementing this framework for improving the effectiveness and efficiency of crime control and also providing services to citizens. The system not only simplifies the collection, storage and retrieval of crime data but also uses Bayesian analysis to give constantly refined predictions of the risks of crime in different localities, along with the factors influencing the risk levels. Finally, evaluations of the system are discussed. User evaluations of the system allowed us to study the potential of the system for crime control and citizen services.

INTRODUCTION

Public administrative work has characteristics that distinguish it from business. The public sector provides a wide range of services to society that are different from those provided by business firms. The government uses information and communication technology to improve effectiveness and efficiency to meet the requirements of new forms of government management and accountability and to satisfy the demand of external agencies for information. E-government can facilitate more efficient and effective applications of e-business principles, which could provide citizens, employees, government agencies and businesses with more convenient access to government information and services (Hernon, Reylea, Dugan, & Cheverie, 2002). Police work can be viewed as being representative of government work as police officers must provide many critical services to citizens, ranging from policing duties (law enforcement, crime prevention, crime investigation, etc.) to nonpolicing duties (search and rescue, public relations, etc.). To modernize police work, a number of researchers and police agencies have emphasized the use of information and communication technology to improve effectiveness, efficiency and transparency, making police work more citizen centered and assisting in local problem-solving initiatives to reduce crime and ensure public safety (Lincolnshire Police, 2003; Liu & Hu, 2005; Pacific Council on International Policy (PCIP), 2002; Police Information Technology Organization (PITO), 2002; Spicer & Mines, 2002; Sussex Police, 2003; Woods, 2001). Crime control is one vital police task that is still problematic from a number of aspects. There is the problem of organizing the crime investigation process. Police have difficulties in crime investigation. They need support from witnesses. In order to motivate the public to interact with police agencies, police need to provide crime information and also convenient methods of communication. There have been a number of research studies and police projects relating to e-policing and crime control. E-policing strategic frameworks also have attracted the attention of police policy makers (Lincolnshire Police, 2003; Spicer & Mines, 2002; Sussex Police, 2003). A number of researchers have covered particular aspects of the application of information communication technology (ICT) to police work, such as information sharing and monitoring (Chen et al., 2003; Falcon, 1998; Zeng, Chen, Hsinchun, Daspit, Shan, Nandiraju, Chau, & Lin, 2003), forensic evidence (Smith, Puch, Wynn, Bates, Evett, & Champod, 2002), burglary

prediction (Oatley & Ewart, 2003), crime knowledge management (Pendharkar & Bhaskar, 2003) and geographic information systems (GIS) for crime analysis and monitoring (Bowers, Newton, & Nutter, 2001; Costello & Wiles, 2001; Gupta, 2001; Rich, 1999). However, in addition to crime control, police agencies also provide other services to citizens. Most of the studies and projects cited focus on only a particular aspect of police operations, without considering citizen services.

In this chapter, we report on our experience in designing and evaluating an integrated system for crime control and citizen services. This approach was implemented in a prototype system. The prototype system provides wireless GIS to support police work and also services to citizens. In addition, the research developed a Bayesian network model for analysis of the factors affecting crime risk. This chapter is organized into four sections: "Background" of e-policing is a review of e-policing systems development with research questions from this study outlined; "Mobile Policing Framework" provides insight into the development of the framework, the application scenarios of the system, system evaluation and implications for practice; "Future Trends" considers developments in technology and areas for further study; and the "Conclusion."

BACKGROUND

Defining E-Policing

Definitions of e-policing abound in the literature. The following definitions characterize e-policing in a variety of ways.

- E-policing refers to the use of the Internet to deliver police services to the public. A Web site, e-mail and fax are contact methods that the public can use in addition to the telephone and face-to-face channels. The ideal is to provide consistent citizen access irrespective of the access channel that is being used (Sussex Police, 2003).

- The use of the computer (including digital telephony) technologies to deliver police services (Lincolnshire Police, 2003).
- E-policing focuses on the needs of the frontline police officer and the public. The exploitation of new technology will support the provision of an infrastructure and communications network to facilitate getting information and services to the right person at the right time in the right place, whether to a citizen or police officer, as well as providing choice for the public (Spicer & Mines, 2002).
- E-policing is the use of ICT in police work to improve effectiveness and efficiency, support frontline officers and assist in local problem-solving initiatives to reduce crime and reassure the public (Woods, 2001).

In practice, police work covers a wide range of functions. Goldstein (1977) has categorized these as follows:

- To prevent and control conduct widely recognized as threatening to life and property
- To aid individuals who are in danger of physical harm, such as the victims of violent attacks
- To facilitate the movement of people and vehicles
- To assist those who cannot care for themselves—the intoxicated, the addicted, the mentally ill, the physically disabled, the old and the young
- To resolve conflict, whether it be among individuals, groups or individuals, or individuals and their government
- To identify problems that have the potential for becoming more serious problems
- To create and maintain a feeling of security in communities

The Working Group on E-Government in the Developing World, under the auspices of the Pacific Council on International Policy, listed the following as broad categories of goals for e-government (PCIP, 2002):

- Improving services to citizens
- Improving the productivity (and efficiency) of government agencies
- Strengthening the legal system and law enforcement
- Promoting priority economic sectors
- Improving the quality of life for disadvantaged communities
- Strengthening good governance and broadening public participation

It can be readily seen that a number of these goals can be effectively applied to e-policing. E-policing can employ numerous features of local e-government as the building blocks for service delivery, such as acknowledging that it is important to provide to the public appropriate services electronically 24 hours a day, 7 days a week (Spicer & Mines, 2002). ICT has played an important role in providing support for police functions. E-policing has huge potential in both developed and developing countries. Internet technology is expected to enhance police services in terms of convenience and cost efficiencies that will give the public increased choice when deciding how to use police services and help build a new police service that fits 21st century needs (Woods, 2001). A number of e-policing strategic frameworks have been proposed as ways of delivering e-policing.

In England, most e-policing strategic frameworks have been produced in response to the government's White Paper on Modernizing Government, which lists the objective: "By 2005 all services (with exclusions for policy or operational reasons) should be available electronically" (Lincolnshire Police, 2003; Spicer & Mines, 2002; Sussex Police, 2003). In addition, the police agencies follow the Police Information Technology Organization (PITO) national e-policing strategic framework. As an important part of the e-government initiative in the U.K., the e-policing program was introduced to revolutionize the police service and improve the effectiveness of crime prevention and detection by providing the following (PITO, 2002):

- Ready access for the public to police information and services through a variety of easy to use, safe and secure channels, including the use of intermediaries;
- Provision of information and services of relevance to the citizen, particularly victims of crime, in a timely and efficient manner;
- Support for cooperative working across police forces and with other criminal justice agencies and local authorities;
- Better use of information across all forces and with other criminal justice agencies to support the implementation of the National Intelligence Model and to make policing more effective in combating criminality;
- The collection, exchange and storage of information in a secure and trusted environment; and
- Flexibility to accommodate new business requirements and to take advantage of changes in technology.

Development of E-Policing

Most police agencies have developed their own information technology (IT) systems to support their work. Primarily, these IT systems can be grouped into categories based on the particular applications for which they were developed. Examples of each type from the literature are reviewed here under the following categories: information sharing and monitoring, intelligent crime analysis and GIS for crime analysis and monitoring.

Information sharing and monitoring. Information sharing and monitoring are especially important for crime analysis and investigation. Timely access to information is often critical. With rapid advancement of IT and the Internet, researchers and police agencies have paid special attention to developing such systems. Future Alert Contact Network (Falcon, 1998) is a community-based policing system. It offers the functionality of monitoring all incoming records relevant to a request and then notifies an officer by e-mail or pager when the request is met. COPLINK Connect system (Chen et al., 2003) enables law enforcement agencies to search for information more effectively by providing an interface that integrates data from various sources, including incident records, mug shots and gang information. COPLINK Agent (Zeng et al., 2003) is designed to provide automatic information filtering and monitoring functionalities. The system also supports knowledge sharing by proactively identifying officers who are working on the same or similar cases on a real-time basis.

Intelligent crime analysis. The adding of an intelligent component to crime analysis is one of the most attractive areas to researchers. Some intelligent techniques, such as Bayesian networks, and neuron networks have been applied to crime analysis. Smith et al. (2002) developed an inferential framework for a future custom-built decision support system to help forensic scientists perform their sometimes delicate and nonstandard tasks. A system would be particularly helpful for scientists who investigate forensic evidence arising from high-volume crime, such as the burglary of electronic equipment, which frequently occurs and shares many qualitative features. Oatley and Ewart (2003) undertook a study making use of both historical and contemporaneous information to generate a burglary prediction system. Their paper detailed how the final predictions on the likelihood of burglary were calculated by combining all of the varying sources of evidence into a Bayesian belief network and the issues surrounding the construction of such a model. Pendharkar and Bhaskar (2003) proposed an approach for building a hybrid Bayesian network based on a multiagent system for drug crime knowledge management. They used distributed artificial intelligence architecture to create a multiagent information system that integrated distributed knowledge sources and information to aid decision making.

GIS for crime analysis and monitoring. GIS have been adopted by police forces for use in several areas, such as crime pattern analysis, repeat victimization and crime monitoring. Bowers et al. (2001) developed a GIS-based database application to assist in the identification of vulnerable targets for a domestic-dwelling, target-hardening scheme. Their system used defined criteria to prioritize recent victims of burglary. This prioritization system produced targeting information on a daily basis. Costello and Wiles (2001) used geocoded crime data to look at the patterns produced by analyzing the location of offenses and the residential addresses of offenders and victims, and the relationships between the locations linked by offenses. Gupta (2001) developed a GIS routine to help police to correlate, visualize and analyze crime data. The crime picture becomes crystal clear, thereby improving police management. Rich (1999) illustrated that mapping can be used for tracking drug flow into the United States and law enforcement areas. However, in these cases, GIS was used in applications suitable for office work without wireless access for police in the field.

Research Questions

Each of the above systems focuses on only certain aspects of police operations but does not consider services to citizens. The goal of the system developed here is to provide an integrated solution to crime control and the provision of services to citizens. Effective crime control requires the collection, organization and retrieval of a variety of data. Multiple types of data, such as text (criminal data, property data, gang information, case information), graphic (photographs of criminals, pictures of crime scenes) and geographic data (crime locations, details of the area), need to be accessed when and where they are needed, especially in time-critical situations. A new trend in technology, wireless access devices like personal digital assistants (PDAs) and mobile telephones are among the most important technologies to support e-policing initiatives. Since people tend to carry their mobile devices with them wherever they go, they remain linked to the Internet at all times, not only when sitting at a desk in front of a computer. Therefore, police agencies need to plan for a massive change in the way many of the public use the Internet and interact with each other and with agencies. A police agency also needs to look for ways to utilize wireless technology to improve the effectiveness and efficiency of the delivery of core operations and in doing so help the public. Police officers spend a lot of their time patrolling the streets and investigating crimes. To accommodate this mobility, wireless access is important. Geographical locations play an important role in crime control. It would be of value to the police officers to access geo-mapping data anywhere and at anytime. For this research a Bayesian network model was developed to analyze the factors affecting crime risk. The objective of this study was to answer these three important research questions:

- How can e-policing services be integrated to serve communities better?
- How will such a system support police officers in their crime control and investigative work?
- How will the system support citizens in obtaining services from police agencies?

MOBILE POLICING FRAMEWORK

Architecture of a Mobile Police System

Here we propose a framework for an integrated wireless GIS to support crime control and provide services to citizens. The design of the framework was guided by user requirements from both police and citizens that were obtained through structured questionnaires and interviews. The proposed architecture of the system is illustrated in Figure 1. The system consists of a user interface, a database management system (DBMS), which contains spatial and nonspatial database and five functional modules, namely the wireless GIS module, crime factor analysis module, reporting and searching module, location-based system (LBS) module and security module. The functionality of each module is described below.

Wireless GIS module. The wireless GIS module is used to develop real-time crime data access to help the police to be more effective and efficient in crime control and also provide services to citizens. The wireless GIS with integration of technologies, such as global positioning systems (GPS), digital photography, digital videography and databases, is used for developing the functions of crime recording, updating and representing

crime-map data. The system consists of mobile devices capable of accessing the Internet with proper extensions for a GPS receiver and compact flash camera. Data can be simply logged from the crime scenes and uploaded to a geo-database server. OpenGIS enables spatial data sharing and system interoperability, leading to data integrity and timeliness and reduced data replication. Open source software and freeware packages, such as Minnesota MapServer, PostgreSQL and PostGIS, were used to develop the system (Boondao, Esichaikul, & Tripathi, 2004a).

Crime factor analysis module. The crime factor analysis module (Boondao, Esichaikul, & Tripathi, 2004b) was developed based on the crime pattern analysis of Brantingham and Brantingham (1991) and theory of crime control through environmental design (Jeffery, 1971; Rhodes & Conly, 1991). Pattern theory focuses attention and research on the environment and crime and insists that crime locations, characteristics of such locations, the movement paths that bring offenders and victims together at such locations and people's perceptions of crime locations are significant objects for studies. Pattern theory synthesizes its attempt to explain how changing spatial and temporal ecological structures influence crime trends and patterns. This research analyzes the factors affecting crime risk in the

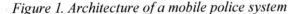

Figure 1. Architecture of a mobile police system

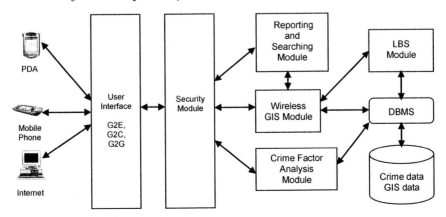

Bangkok metropolitan area, Thailand, using a Bayesian network. The factors considered in this study are classified into five main groups: variables describing population, variables describing crime location factors, variables describing types of crimes, variables describing traffic and variables describing the environment. Due to the uncertainty and incomplete nature of the variables, Bayesian network theory is used to analyze the data, since it is well suited to dealing with noisy and incomplete crime data. The Bayesian network model was developed by expert elicitation and crime theory, and it learned using the machine learning software, HUGIN Researcher 6.3 (Hugin, 2003).

Reporting and searching module. The reporting and searching module accepts crime reports and queries from both police officers and citizens. This module allows police in the field to access crime cases and search for details of a suspected criminal. In addition, it also accepts crime reports from citizens and forwards them to the police officers. Citizens can track the status of cases whenever they wish.

LBS module. The LBS module involves the ability to find the geographic location of a person who reports a crime and needs help. This information is required by wireless GIS to determine the locations of mobile devices and to transmit location-specific information to the police officers.

Security module. Security is a critically important issue in an e-policing system. Therefore, the security module is separated from other modules to handle all security and confidentiality issues on the importing and exporting of data.

Database Preparation

The data, consisting of crime occurrence, population, streets, buildings, landmark data and so forth, were collected from the National Statistical Office of Thailand, the Royal Thai Police, the Bangkok Metropolitan Administration and the Ministry of Transportation. The data are divided into two formats: spatial data, which consists of data in map format, and nonspatial data, which consists of tabular data relating to crime, criminals and population.

Spatial data. Police departments need large amounts of detailed location data, including crime type, site of crime, perpetrator address, victim address and the exact nature of the crime. GIS software is used to create the data in map format. It represents data on a map using points, lines and polygons. Features that can be represented as points include crime events, police stations, hospitals and schools. Bus routes, streets and rivers are usually represented using lines; districts, provinces and police precincts are depicted using polygons. By using GIS, users can analyze multiple layers of crime information.

Nonspatial data. The preparation of nonspatial data, such as crime details, criminal details, police station addresses, street names, buildings, landmarks and population data, are essential for linking the data with the corresponding spatial database. The nonspatial data is implemented through a table processing technique (PostgresSQL).

Application Scenarios

Crime monitoring. Crime monitoring provides data for different types of crime, such as murder, robbery and gang robbery. This feature can help the police in crime control. Police can view which crimes are most common in certain areas. Moreover, the police can view which crimes are frequently linked. For example, murder is often linked with robbery and drug addiction with burglary. The police can query when and where each particular crime occurred. Citizens also can view crime data and may see for themselves that certain crimes are much more common in some districts than in others. This could encourage them to take precautions to protect themselves from crime.

Crime investigation and crime reporting. Due to the difficulty of crime investigation, police need support from witnesses. It is easier for the witnesses to tell the police where, when and how a crime occurred if they do have to go to a police station. Using online crime reporting, citizens can submit information about the type of crime, location, date and time and also provide their personal details so that the police can contact them to give help and ask for more information.

This type of online crime reporting is new and may reduce a lot of problems faced by the general public in visiting police stations and reporting crimes. It could save time and make the process well documented, while reducing the police workload.

Find a police station, track a case and find information on criminal laws. Citizens can use the online system to find a police station, track the case, find important information related to their safety and information on criminal laws.

Real-time crime case/criminal records. The police can enter real-time crime data or record criminal/suspect data using online crime and criminal/suspect recording. When they go to the crime scene, they can record data, such as crime ID, crime case, crime type, complainant, criminal, latitude, longitude, picture of the crime scene, behavior of the criminal, date, time and place where the crime occurred. This system will help the police to record crime data more accurately by using the GPS connected to the system to record the crime point. For online criminal records, the police can record data about a criminal/suspect, for example, ID card number, name, nickname, gang name, date of birth, picture of the criminal, nationality, race, religion, education, occupation, address, phone number, scars, weapon used, vehicle used, behavior, places regularly frequented, height, weight, hair and eye color, and known associates and accomplices.

Searching for criminals. Police in the field can access details of a criminal using the mobile police system. The system provides the criminal's record, for example, ID card number, name, nickname, gang name, date of birth, picture of the criminal/ suspect, nationality, race, religion, education, occupation, address, phone number, scars, weapon used, vehicle used, behaviour, places frequented regularly, height, weight, and hair and eye color. The search function is important when the police have only limited data. For example, if police are informed by witnesses that the criminal is about 40 years old with a scar on his left cheek, the police can use these data to query the database, which will provide them with a list of criminals who fit the description. The police can then review the list obtained to select the most likely suspects.

Searching for a case and a criminal's record. Police also can retrieve data about a case and a criminal's record whenever and wherever they need it. This will help police in searching for criminal's crime history. The police will know how many cases in which the criminal has been involved. Police can select any case that interests them from the list to see more details.

Crime risk factors analysis. The system can be used for analysis of the factors affecting crime risk. The analysis is accomplished using a Bayesian network. The results from this analysis can be used to help in crime-control planning and environmental design to prevent crime. The government can apply the model to a specific area to analyze the crime problems. For instance, if we know that an area in the district has high crime rate as a result of environmental factors, the government can solve the problem by increasing the number of patrol officers or increasing the degree of lighting on the streets in that area.

System Evaluation

The prototype system was evaluated by both police and citizens. The details of the evaluation method and analysis are described next.

Evaluation methodology. A stratified-sampling method was used to choose two groups of participants. The first group consisted of police officers of the Command, Control, Communication & Information Center, Metropolitan Police Bureau, Royal Thai Police. The second group consisted of Thai citizens. For the police sample group, the officers had worked on 191 calls and were experienced in using a digital map in their work, and the citizens chosen had experience in using computers and the Internet and were likely to use advanced communication technology in the future.

Members of each sample group were given the opportunity to use the system and then asked to complete questionnaires—a specific questionnaire for each group—designed to determine the usability of the system. Usability is the extent to which a computer system can be operated by users to achieve specified goals effectively and efficiently, while promoting feelings of satisfaction in a given context of use (International Standards Organization, 1999). The questionnaires were designed to assess the police and citizen attitudes with special attention to their acceptance of the system.

The series of items that comprised the usability questionnaire were based on a number of widely used measures (Hartson, Andre, & Williges, 2003; Lewis, 1995; Park & Lim, 1999). Items on the questionnaire used to assess the system were based upon user perceptions of such standard measures of usability as: system usefulness (impact of system on job performance, productivity and effectiveness of information); information quality (information provided by the system is clear and easy to find, and the messages that inform the

Table 1. Police participant demographic

Police sample characteristics	Percentage
Level of education	vocational certificate 45%, bachelor's degree 50%, master's degree 4%, higher than master's degree 1%
Computer/Internet experience	inexperienced 12%, somewhat experienced 54%, very experienced 32%, expert 2%
Age	18-24 years old 23%, 25-34 years old 49%, 35-44 years old 22%, 45-54 years old 6%
Gender	male 100%

Table 2. Citizen participant demographic

Citizen sample characteristics	Percentage
Level of education	bachelor's degree 54%, master's degree 44%, higher than master's degree 2%
Computer/Internet experienced	somewhat experienced 44%, very experienced 48%, expert 8%
Age	18-24 years old 36%, 25-34 years old 46%, 35-44 years old 14%, 45-54 years old 4%
Gender	male 42%, female 58%

user of errors are understandable); and interface quality (measures of organization of the information on the screens, ability to find information and the interface design and satisfaction with the interaction). Tests of validity and reliability were carried out on the questionnaire.

The validity of each of the questionnaires was controlled using the content-analysis method (Henerson, 1978). Items for the questionnaires were selected and adapted from the IBM computer usability satisfaction questionnaires: psychometric evaluation and instructions for use (Lewis, 1995). Items for the police questionnaire were reviewed and tested by 20 police officers at the Command, Control, Communication & Information Center, Metropolitan Police Bureau, Royal Thai Police. Items for the citizen questionnaire were reviewed and tested by 20 Thai citizens. Items were deleted, added or modified based on the information obtained from these critiques.

Reliability means that the set of latent construct indicators (scale items) are consistent in their measurements. It is the degree to which two or more indicators "share" in their measurement of a construct (Hair, Anderson, Tatham, & Black, 1992). Cronbach's alpha (Cronbach, 1951) was used to measure reliability as it does not require multiple administration of the survey instrument and avoids the weakness inherent in the split-half method resulting from the variety of possible combinations that exist (Flynn et al., 1994). Cronbach's alpha was computed using SPSS (Norušis, 1991) for each set of construct indicators.

Participants. The prototype system was tested by 90 police officers of the Command, Control, Communication & Information Center, Metropolitan Police Bureau, Royal Thai Police and 50 Thai citizens, selected as mentioned above. The participant profiles are shown in Table 1 and 2.

Summary of evaluation results. The IBM computer usability satisfaction questionnaire scale was used to interpret the level of acceptance with "1" as the highest level of acceptance and "7" as the lowest level of acceptance. This research considers a level of acceptance lower than 3.5 as a positive response as pointed out by Henerson (1978). The results are shown in Table 3.

Evaluation results from the police participants. As the results in Table 3 show, police participants on average rated system usefulness, information quality and interface quality ratings of the system 2.02, 2.40 and 2.22, respectively. Since we used a 7-point scale (with 1 indicating the strongest agreement), a rating average of <2.5 suggests relatively high user satisfaction. However, there were some suggestions from respondents. The two main functions, recording and searching for case and criminal/suspect data, in the prototype were well accepted. By contrast, the features of the prototype that needed improvement were the details of the map, which needed a smaller scale giving details of small lane names. The factor in this prototype that gained the highest acceptance rate was the ease of access at any time and at

Table 3. Mean for the system usability ratings

Variables	Police M(SD)	Citizens M(SD)
System usefulness	2.02 (1.1)	2.17 (1.2)
Information quality	2.40 (1.2)	2.50 (1.3)
Interface quality	2.22 (1.1)	2.36 (1.1)

any place. One popular feature was the ease of searching for a case and criminal data. In addition, the police were able to efficiently complete the case and criminal data recording, searching and updating using the prototype.

Evaluation results from the citizen participants. Based on the responses of the citizen participants, system usefulness, information quality and interface quality ratings of the system averaged 2.17, 2.50 and 2.36, respectively, on the 7-point scale. This sample indicated had a high acceptance rate and suggested a strong endorsement for using the prototype in a crime control environment. Additional comments were made regarding improvements, including the need for more help in entering text in dialog boxes and the need for minimal typing when reporting a crime case. The very positive response from this sample indicates the full implementation of the prototype will be highly accepted as a support crime control tool in the real environment.

Implications for Practice

The findings reported in this study have a number of important implications for consideration by both senior police administrators and academics.

Police officer preparation and development. The user evaluation results suggested that police officers need more training in the use of computers and modern electronic communications. If the system developed and tested in this research was to be implemented, officers would need training to familiarize them with the system. Education and training related to the new equipment and software would need to be provided to all police officers including top- and middle-level commanders, not only prior to and concurrent with its adoption, but also after the implementation stage.

Top commander commitment. It is very important that the top- and middle-level police command-

ers are highly motivated and committed to the implementation of the new system. This commitment can be shown in many ways, for example, by establishing a policy and long-range plan with regard to operation and service improvement, providing sufficient financial support for training, establishing a personal involvement in the projects and supporting continuous involvement activities for staff. Convincing older, very senior staff of the desirability of change is often the most difficult and most important step in innovation.

Public training. Implementing the system also will provide services to citizens. Therefore, there is a need for training and providing information about the system to the public. This may be done through local police stations. This also will lead to a better relationship between the police and the citizens. The citizens can cooperate with the police in their fight against crime and help keep the area where they live safer.

System security management. The system is intended to support the police in their work and also provide services to the public. Therefore, there will be many people involved with the system. To achieve these aims, users will need access to the system via the Internet. A consequence of providing such access is increased security risks. In order to protect the system from unauthorized access, an effective security system must be implemented.

Open-source software adoption. New software implementation generally requires considerable investment of both time and money. By using open-source software in the implementation of this system costs can be minimized with no loss in effectiveness or reliability. This could serve as an example to the Royal Thai Police force and to other government departments of the effectiveness and economy of the implementation of open-source solutions to problems arising in e-government. One implication of using open source is that some effort may be needed to convince senior management that such a seemingly radical approach is a wise decision.

FUTURE TRENDS

The use of broadband Internet is becoming more widespread in Thailand as costs decrease, making it more affordable. More sophisticated mobile telephones are becoming popular. It is only a matter of time before mobile telephones with satellite navigation capabilities become commonplace. The development of the European Galileo satellite navigation system will provide greater accuracy and reliability, enabling the measurement of a location to within a few meters. Receiver manufacturers are already gearing up to make full use of the opportunities generated by this new system (European Space Agency, 2005). As telephone and computer technologies converge, there will be an ever-growing proportion of the public with mobile equipment capable of accessing a system developed along the lines of the prototype described in this chapter. One of the great promises of e-policing is what is known as 24-7 availability, meaning that police services would be available 24 hours a day, seven days a week. The availability of faster Internet connections, increased functionality of wireless equipment and greater accuracy of the satellite navigation system will make this promise possible. Without doubt, e-policing will play an important role in government-management reform in the next few years and that poses an important challenge for e-government research. In addition, the development of police intelligence systems is becoming more popular for crime analysis.

For future work, the Bayesian network for crime risk prediction, which was tested only for the crime of murder in the prototype, may, with further research, be extended to cover the full range of criminal activities and further refined to improve its performance. With some modi-

fication it also could be applied to the study of road accidents, which are a major cause of death and injury in Thailand, eventually enabling the police to adopt a proactive approach to accident prevention.

The functionality of the system should be improved by standardizing the crime data collection, implementing Web Map Services so that the system can be used in a distributed (peer-to-peer) database environment and incorporating metadata search capabilities.

CONCLUSION

In this chapter, we highlighted some of our experiences in designing, developing and evaluating the mobile police system. The prototype system was developed based on a comprehensive design framework that combined the necessary functions that a modern police system should have. The wireless GIS was developed for real-time crime recording, updating, and representing crime and criminal data, eliminating the current tendency for time-consuming duplication of effort between police departments. The system also provided services to the public for crime reporting, case tracking, crime-map monitoring, finding the nearest police station and obtaining important information related to safety. These features are quite unique among police systems. There was a challenge in applying a Bayesian network for crime risk factors analysis, for which no research work had been done before. The Bayesian network has been adopted for inference and analysis of the crime risk factors. A key feature of this approach was the use of existing data to set up the initial model and the continuing enhancement of the model's predictive capabilities as new data was added. The Bayesian network could provide useful information for crime risk factors analysis. The Bayesian technology proved very flexible and suitable to the requirements of this research project.

The HUGIN software used with the EM algorithm made the creation of a sophisticated network relatively straightforward. In this research, some factors that affected the crime risk in the Bangkok Metropolitan Area, Thailand, were analyzed. The factors considered were classified into five groups. These groups were population, crime location, crime type, traffic and environment. The results of the model indicated that the factors affecting crime risk in the Bangkok Metropolitan Area were environment, types of crimes, crime location, traffic and population, in that order. Of the environmental factors, the number of drug-sale areas in a district had the most powerful influence on the expected increase in the murder rate. The receiver operating characteristic (ROC) analysis was used to test the accuracy of the model. The area under the ROC curve for the model was 0.77, which indicated a good performance of the model in terms of its predictive accuracy. This accuracy suggested that this machine-learning technique can be used to analyze crime data and help in crime-control planning.

From the evaluation study involving both police and citizens, it was found that wireless GIS allowed the users to access records in order to retrieve spatial and nonspatial crime data in an efficient way. Ninety-two percent of police officers responding to the survey indicated a positive attitude to the ability of the system to assist them to efficiently complete the tasks involved in a case and criminal data recording, searching and updating. The citizens' responses to the survey indicated that 92% of them felt that they could use the system to efficiently report crimes and search for information.

The prototype system provided a great opportunity for time saving. Mobile access to databases, allowed both police and citizens to easily access crime data in near real time at any time or place, thus allowing police to take quicker action in investigating and solving crimes. The survey results showed that the police and citizen participants agreed that it was easy to access the system at anytime and any place with 93% of police and 70% of citizens responding positively. In addition, the prototype system enabled spatial data sharing and support for crime control. The survey results showed that both police and citizens agreed that the system was a good tool to support crime control at 81% and 80% respectively.

From the police point of view, the prototype system could greatly reduce the paperwork involved in crime recording; it fed crime scene data directly into the system. According to the police survey result, 93% of the officers strongly agreed that the system could assist them to record cases and criminal data at the crime scene. Moreover, the prototype system could save time and money, fostering faster police action in crime investigation and decision making. The police responses to the survey showed that 82% agreed that the system could support them in crime-control decision making.

One limitation of the system was that the speed of Internet access for wireless GIS was slower than for the wired GIS. We look forward to 3G availability in Thailand to make data transmission faster for better efficiency. Also, in order to harness the full potential of the prototype system, a more detailed, smaller scale map will be required. Moreover to maintain the effectiveness of the system, the map database must be frequently updated. Citizens indicated that they needed more help when required to enter text into fields in dialog boxes and would like the system to minimize the typing required to report a crime. We were able to use the feedback from the user evaluations to create a list of system enhancements that we plan to implement in the next phase of the system development. Another important issue that affected the effectiveness and efficiency of the prototype was training and familiarity with the prototype. Some participants who were familiar with computer and Internet technologies felt that the system was easy to learn and were able to use the system better than users who were less familiar with the technology. This issue could have been dealt with by proper training. An additional evaluation of the system will be conducted based on the real usage situation of the system.

ACKNOWLEDGMENTS

The authors would like to thank the HUGIN expert for providing HUGIN Software for Bayesian network analysis. Sincere thanks to T. J. King for his assistance in preparing this manuscript. The authors are grateful to all the participants of the user evaluation study.

REFERENCES

Boondao, R., Esichaikul, V., & Tripathi, N. K. (2004a). TELOCATE: A wireless GIS for crime control in e-policing. *WSEAS Transactions on Information Science and Applications, 5*(1), 1365-1370.

Boondao, R., Esichaikul, V., & Tripathi, N. K. (2004b). A Bayesian network model for analysis of the factors affecting crime risk. *WSEAS Transactions on Circuits and Systems, 9*(3), 1895-1900.

Bowers, K., Newton, M., & Nutter, R. (2001). A GIS-linked database for monitoring repeat domestic burglary. In A. Hirschfield & K. Bowers (Eds.), *Mapping and analysing crime data: Lessons from research and practice* (pp. 120-136). New York: Taylor & Francis.

Brantingham, P. L., & Brantingham, P. L. (1991). Notes on the geometry of crime. In P. L. Brantingham (Ed.), *Environmental criminology* (pp. 5-15). Wavelend Press Inc.

Chen, H., Schroeder, J., Hauck, R. V., Ridgeway, L., Atabakhsh, H., Gupta, H., Boarman, C., Rasmussen, K., & Clements, A. W. (2003). COPLINK Connect: Information and knowledge management for law enforcement. *Decision Support Systems, 34*, 271-285.

Costello, A., & Wiles, P. (2001). GIS and the journey to crime: An analysis of patterns in South Yorkshire. In A. Hirschfield & K. Bowers (Eds.), *Mapping and analysing crime data: Lessons from research and practice* (pp. 27-60). New York: Taylor & Francis.

Cronbach, L. J. (1951). Coefficient alpha and the internal structure of tests. *Psychometrika, 16,* 297-334.

D'Angelo, P. (2003). *Hugin manual.* Retrieved October 23, 2003, from http://hugin.sourceforge.net/docs/manual

European Space Agency. (2005). *Galileo: The European programme for global navigation services.* Noordwijk, The Netherlands: ESA Publications Division.

Falcon. (1998). *Future alert contact network: Reducing crime via early notification.* North Carolina: University of North Carolina at Charlotte (UNCC); Charlotte-Mecklenburg Police Department (CMPD). Retrieved February 10, 2002, from http://pti.nw.dc.us/solutions/solutions98/public_safety/charlotte.html

Flynn, B. B., Schroeder, R. G., & Sakakibara, S. (1994). A framework for quality management research and associated instrument. *Journal of Operations Management, 11,* 339-366.

Goldstein, H. (1977). *Policing a free society.* Cambridge, MA: Ballinger.

Gupta, V. K. (2001). Monitoring crime. *GIS@ development, 5*(4), 33-35.

Hair, J. F., Anderson, R. E., Tatham, R. L., & Black, W. C. (1992). *Multivariate data analysis with readings.* Macmillan Publishing.

Hartson, H. R., Andre, T. S., & Williges, R. C. (2003). Criteria for evaluating usability evaluation methods. *International Journal of Human-Computer Interaction, 15*(1), 145-181.

Henerson, M. E. (1978). *How to measure attitudes.* Beverly Hills, CA: Sage Publications.

Hernon, P., Reylea, H. C., Dugan, R. E., & Cheverie, J. F. (2002). *United States government information: Policies and sources.* Westport, CT: Libraries Unlimited.

International Standards Organization (ISO). (1999). *ISO9241: Ergonomic requirements for office work with visual display terminals, part 11: Guidance on usability.* Retrieved February 5, 2004, from http://www.iso.ch/iso/en/CatalogueDetailPage.CatalogueDetail? CSNUMBER= 16883&ICS1=13&ICS2=180&IC53

Jeffery, C. R. (1971). *Crime prevention through environmental design.* Beverly Hills, CA: Sage Publications.

Lewis, J. R. (1995). Computer usability satisfaction questionnaires: Psychometric evaluation and instructions for use. *International Journal of Human-Computer Interaction, 7*(1), 57-78.

Lincolnshire Police. (2003). *A strategic framework for the delivery of e-policing* [Strategy statement]. Retrieved April 12, 2004, from www.lincs.police.uk/getFile.asp?FC_ID=261&docID=262

Liu, K., & Hu, M. (2005). Semiotic analysis of e-policing strategies in the United Kingdom. In W. Huang, K. Siau & K. K. Wei (Eds.), *Digital government: Strategies and implementations in developed and developing countries* (pp. 373-393). Hershey, PA: Idea Group Publishing.

Norušis, N. M. (1991). *SPSS/PC+ Studentware Plusä.* Chicago: SPSS Inc.

Oatley, G. C., & Ewart, B. W. (2003). Crime analysis software: 'Pins in maps', clustering and Bayes net prediction. *Expert Systems with Applications, 25,* 569-588.

Pacific Council on International Policy (PCIP). (2002). *Roadmap for e-government in the developing world.* The Work Group on E-Government in the Developing World, Pacific Council on International Policy. Retrieved February 15, 2004, from http://www.pacificouncil.org/pdfs/e-gov.paper.f.pdf

Park, K. S., & Lim, C. H. (1999). A structured methodology for comparative evaluation of user interface designs using usability criteria and measures. *International Journal of Industrial Ergonomics, 23,* 379-389.

Pendharkar, C., & Bhaskar, R. (2003). A hybrid Bayesian network-based multi-agent system and a distributed systems architecture for the drug crime knowledge management. *International Journal of Information Technology and Decision Making, 2*(4), 557-576.

Police Information Technology Organization (PITO). (2002). *E-policing strategic framework.* London: PITO.

Rhodes, W. M., & Conly, C. (1991). *The criminal commute: A theoretical perspective in environmental criminology.* Wavelend Press Inc.

Rich, T. (1999). Mapping the path to problem solving. *National Institute of Justice Journal,* 55-63. Retrieved February 15, 2003, from http://www.ncjrs.gov/pdffiles1/jr000241b.pdf

Smith, J. Q., Puch, R. O., Wynn, H. P., Bates, R., Evett, W. I., & Champod, C. (2002). *A Bayesian decision support system for forensic inference.* Department of Statistics, University of Warwick. Retrieved May 24, 2002, from http://icfs5.eco.uniroma3.it/ Vsmith_puch_et%20al.doc

Spicer, R., & Mines, B. (2002). *E-policing vision statement.* Retrieved April 11, 2004, from http://www.devon-cornwall.police.uk/v3/ShowPDF.cfm?PDFName=epolvis.pdf

Sussex Police. (2003). *IT strategy 2003/2008.* Retrieved April 12, 2004, from http://www.sussexpoliceauthority.gov.uk/meetings/1003/agenda12a.pdf

Woods, P. (2001). *E-policing.* Retrieved September 15, 2003, from http://www.e-policingreport.com

Zeng, D., Chen, Hsinchun, C., Daspit, D., Shan, F., Nandiraju, S., Chau, M., & Lin, C. (2003). *COPLINK agent: An architecture for information monitoring and sharing in law enforcement* (LNCS 2665, pp. 281-295). Germany: Springer-Verlag.

Chapter VII
Benchmarking the Usability and Content Usefulness of Web Sites:
Developing a Structured Evaluation Framework

Shahizan Hassan
Northern University of Malaysia, Malaysia

Feng Li
University of Newcastle upon Tyne, UK

ABSTRACT

Although the benchmarking technique has been widely used in various aspects of organizations and businesses, there is no clear framework on how the technique can be applied for Web evaluation. This article presents a framework for measuring the usability and content usefulness of Web sites by using the benchmarking approach. It describes the purpose of evaluation, metrics to be used and processes through which Web benchmarking can be performed. Several methods were used in the development of the framework, which include content analysis of literature and expert review. A total of 46 criteria were identified to be used as the benchmarking metrics. The framework was tested for its applicability by evaluating four political Web sites in Malaysia. The results proved that the framework is easy to follow and implement, and would be particularly useful for those who intend to benchmark the overall usability and content usefulness of Web sites against competitors.

INTRODUCTION

Benchmarking is a measuring method widely used by companies to improve many areas of activities, including human resource management, information systems, customer processes, quality management, purchasin, and supplier management (Elmuti, 1998). The common goal of this approach is to identify the "best practices" of other organizations so that it can be implemented in one's own operation. In Web evaluation, benchmarking could be used to measure the performance of one's Web site against others, particularly competitors'. By doing this, strengths and weaknesses of one's Web site can be identified, and the quality and usefulness of the Web site could be improved accordingly. For many years, the benchmarking technique has proven its success and widely been used in business (The Government Centre for Information Systems, 1995; Reider, 2000) and various aspects of organizations. However, very little information is available on how this approach can successfully be implemented in Web-site evaluation.

With this in mind, a framework was developed on applying the benchmark technique to measuring Web sites in terms of usability and content usefulness. This framework is aimed at both technical and nontechnical people involved in Web site design and evaluation. Some empirical work was conducted to test the applicability of the framework, which will be presented in this chapter.

This chapter will first describe some existing Web evaluation methods, followed by the definition of the concept of Web usability and content usefulness. Then methods used in this study will be explained briefly. The findings and the proposed benchmarking framework are then discussed in detail. Finally, this chapter ends with some suggestions for future studies.

EXISTING WEB SITE EVALUATION METHODS

Despite the lack of Web evaluation studies that use the benchmarking technique, many studies on Web evaluation have been carried out for many years that employed conventional methods, including usability testing (e.g., Nielsen, 1993; Zimmerman, Muraski, Palmquist, Estes, Mc-Clintoch, & Bilsing, 1998), expert review (e.g., Shneiderman, 1998; Zhang & Dran, 2000), case study (e.g., Smith, Newman, & Parks, 1997) and automated assessment (e.g., Tausher & Greenberg, 1997; NetMechanic, 2000).

However, several attempts were made to measuring Web sites using the benchmarking approach. Simeon (1999), for example, performed a study on how benchmarking techniques can be used to compare the attracting, informing, positioning and delivering (AIPD) strategies of commercial Web sites in order to clarify strategic opportunities and advantages. In this study, he used the AIPD approach to compare Web site strategies of 68 American and 54 Japanese banks. Nonetheless, this approach has its limitations in that there was no clear explanation on how the AIPD elements was identified and grouped into the four (AIPD) categories. In addition, the AIPD model is only applicable to banking Web sites and no attempts as of yet have been made to test it on other types of Web sites. Other research was carried out by Misic and Johnson (1999), where four factors of Web site effectiveness (functions, navigation, content and contact information) were used to benchmark the Web site of the College of Business at Northern Illinois University against 45 other business schools. The main limitation of this study is the lack of items used in the metrics. It only covered limited aspects of functional/navigational issues, content and style, and contact information. Other important aspects of Web evaluation, such as proper use of multimedia elements and issues of accessibility, were not included.

A more recent example is a study by White (2004) on the usability of library Web pages. This study employed a benchmarking approach to compare the levels of usability of four library Web sites in the United Kingdom—University of Derby, Huddersfield, Staffordshire and Leeds Metropolitan. Despite its contribution to the usability research, this study tackled only two main usability areas, namely visual appearance and ease of use. Other important elements, such as content, interactivity, and accessibility, were not covered.

There also are attempts to design methodologies for benchmarking and assessing the quality of Web sites. A good example is WebQual—a method for measuring the quality of an organization's e-commerce site (Barnes & Vidgen, 2002). WebQual uses an index that gives an overall rating of a Web site based solely on customer perceptions of quality weighted by importance. The index was designed according to three dimensions: usability, information quality and service interaction quality. Although the creators claim that the measures are valid and reliable, the main limitation of WebQual is that the results heavily rely on the Internet users' perceptions. Other actors, for example, designers, business partners, suppliers and related governmental organizations are not considered. In addition, the method has, so far, been applied only to business firms, for example, the Internet bookshops, raising the question of whether the criteria used also can be applied to noncommercial Web sites. WebTango is another Web evaluation methodology worth mentioning. It is an automated tool developed specifically for assessing Web usability and accessibility (Ivory-Ndiaye, 2003). This tool is very useful in the sense that it can be used by designers to measure their Web sites automatically. However, the tool focuses more on design aspects rather than content.

From this information, it is clear that although the benchmarking approach has been successfully used to analyze many business functions, the applicability of this approach in Web site usability and content evaluation requires further research.

THE CONCEPT OF USABILITY

Usability is a very broad concept in system design and is defined differently by different human-computer interaction (HCI) scholars. Because of this, approaches to measuring usability also differs. Shakel (1991), Nielsen (1993), and Lu and Yeong (1998) defined usability as an attribute of a product or system acceptance. Therefore, their model of usability is explained in terms of its relationship with the concept of acceptability of a system.

According to Shakel (1991), a user would compare four properties of a system to the sacrifices needed to use it. The properties are utility (the match between users' needs and functions of a product), usability (users' ability to utilize the functions), likeability (users' affective evaluations) and costs (both financial and social consequences). In view of this, Shakel defines a product or system's acceptance as a function of perceived utility, usability, likeability and costs. Nielsen (1993), on the other hand, presents a slightly different concept by suggesting that both usability and utility together form usefulness. Utility refers to whether the functionality of a system can do what is needed, while usability relates to the question of how well users can use the functionality. Usefulness and other perceived system attributes like cost, compatibility and reliability will lead to practical acceptability of a system. In defining usability, Nielsen outlines five operational criteria: learnability (the novices' ability to reach a reasonable level of performance), efficiency (expert users' level of performance), errors (number of errors by users), satisfaction (users' subjective assessment of a system) and memorability (users' ability to remember how to use a system). Nielsen's view is supported by Lu and Yeong (1998) who also propose the concept of usefulness as one of the attributes for system acceptability. Their model divides usefulness into two aspects—functionality (which is similar to utility in Nielsen's model) and usability. Lu and Yeong's perception on usability is slightly different, since their model is developed specifically for Web environments. Usability in their model refers to users' ease-of-browsing, ease-of-reading and satisfaction.

The usability models described here highlight the need for researchers to understand the underlying concept of usability as a measurement. Although the approaches to defining the concept of usability are slightly different, all models tend to have agreement on the dimensions of usability that cover aspects of effectiveness, efficiency, learnability and user satisfaction. One important issue with regard to usability definition is the question of whether the content of a system should be included as one of the elements of usability. To date, there is no clear discussion on this in the usability literature. However, most models of usability (Shakel, 1991; Nielsen, 1993; Lu & Yeong, 1998) include "user satisfaction" as one of the usability criteria. This element has an indirect relationship with the need for quality content in a particular system. User satisfaction is related to users' subjective assessment of a particular system in terms of ease-of-use and usefulness. Thus, it can be said that both user interface and content determine users' level of satisfaction.

METHODOLOGY

There are five phases of this study: the identification of the metrics for benchmarking and Web usability and content usefulness from the literature; the verification of the metrics from the usability experts; the classification of the objective and subjective criteria; the development of the benchmarking framework; and the application of the framework on selected political Web sites in Malaysia as an example to test the framework.

Content analysis used in phase one was to analyze various literature on Web usability. The main objective was to gather the key Web usability criteria proposed in the selected literature. These criteria will then be used as the metrics for benchmarking the usability of Web sites. Several guides, articles and textbooks were selected based on the recommendation from the HCI scholars, such as Jakob Nielsen (Useit.com, 2002), Keith Instone (Usableweb.com, 2002) and Gary Perlman (Perlman, 2001). At least 30 guides were selected, including IBM Web Design Guide (IBM, 2000), Yale Web Style Guide (Lynch & Horton, 1999), Microsoft Web Workshop (Web Workshop, 1999), Designing Information-abundant Web sites: Issues and Recommendations (Shneiderman, 1997), Writing For the Web Guide (Sun Microsystems, 1999), Web Content Accessibility Guidelines 1.0 (W3C, 2002), Web Graphics Design (Benjamin, 1996), and Web Design: the Complete Reference (Powell, 2000).

All these guides were analyzed to extract generic criteria of Web usability. Each criterion identified was recorded in a standard form. During the analysis, all criteria and elements of usability that were considered too technical were rephrased or in some cases, excluded to cater to both technical and nontechnical people. Both concept existence and frequency were used for coding the data (i.e., any usability criterion identified from the selected literature was not only coded for its existence but also for the frequency it was mentioned—see example in Table 1). Once all the criteria were recorded, they were revised and refined to remove duplication. Then, the criteria were grouped into seven categories based on suitability and context of use, which will be discussed further in the next section. The outcome from phase one was a revised list of Web usability criteria grouped into seven categories.

During the second phase, the expert review method was utilized to verify the key criteria identified from the literature in phase one. A list of the identified criteria was sent to 36 experts

Table 1. An example of data analysis summary for Web criteria elicitation

No.	Criteria	Guide 1 (Benjamin, 1996)	Guide 2 (IBM, 2000)	Guide 3 (Web Workshop, 1999)	Guide 4 (MIT et al., 1999)	Total
1	Clear title for each pages	X	X	X	X	4
2	Compatible content for all main browsers	X	X	-	-	2
3	Labelling of all static media	-	X	X	-	2

Note: X means that the criterion was mentioned in the guide.

for review and verification of whom 15 replied with their comments and review. These experts are those who have more than five years experience in HCI and usability areas. The selection of experts involved two processes—identifying the experts from the proceedings of past conferences on human factors in computing systems (CHI) and sending invitations to participate in the CHIWeB e-mail list. The main objective of the review was to get verifications and suggestions from the experts with regard to generic Web usability criteria. Additionally, they also were requested to comment on the suitability of the criteria groupings. The experts were allowed to edit (add, delete and rephrase) all the criteria derived from the literature in a review form (see example in Table 2). Their feedback was analyzed and used to further refine the usability list.

During phase three, all criteria were analyzed and classified into objective or subjective measures. A two-hour brainstorming session involving three evaluators was carried out for this purpose. Since Web design environment are closely related to multimedia, information retrieval and net-working areas (Powell, 2000), the three selected evaluators were those who have strong knowledge in each of these disciplines. The card-sorting technique was used during the brainstorming session to classify the criteria. Using the criteria derived from phase three, a benchmarking framework was developed in phase four. Several general models for benchmarking were referred to including Anderson and Petersen(1996), Bramham (1997), Chang and Kelly (1995), and Codling (1992).

Finally in phase five, the framework was tested on all major political Web sites in Malaysia for applicability and practicality. Political Web sites were selected for this study as they are noncommercial Web sites that deal with the government and general public (customers). Studies on commercial Web sites are plentiful (business-to-customers) but only a few focus on noncommercial ones, particularly political Web sites (government-to-consumers). Furthermore, at the time of testing in phase five (late 2002), Malaysia was about to have a general election. During this time, most political parties heavily utilized Web sites as one of their political communication media.

Table 2. An example of the expert review form

Criteria for Navigation	Reviewer's Comment	
Objective	*About Criteria*	*About Grouping*
1. Menus are fit on screen (no scrolling)	OK	OK
2. Accurate/ unbroken links	OK	OK
3. Menus are positioned on the left side of screen	Not a recommended criterion—a disadvantage for a lefthanded users.	-
4. Use of text within text link (where applicable)	OK	OK
5. Labelling of all static media used as menu	OK	Should be moved to 'Media Use' group

WEB USABILITY AND CONTENT USEFULNESS: MAIN FINDINGS

Content analysis of the literature and expert review had resulted in the identification of 57 key Web usability criteria, which were clustered into seven main groups based on their suitability and context as shown in Table 3.

Screen Appearance

Screen appearance, or layout, can be divided into four categories: space provision, choice of color, and readability and scannability (Lynch & Horton, 1999; Seminerio, 1998). All experts agree that these are four very important areas of usability. More space should be allocated for content, and the variety of different screen types (palm tops, television, etc.) should be taken into consideration. Additionally, proper use of color not only attracts users to a Web site but also improves learnability and ease of use. Equally important is the issue of readability.

Almost all experts agree that a readable content is associated with choice of color, fonts and the color used for text and the background. Designers should not only design for readability but also for scannability, for example, the use of typography and skimming layout. The proposed list of Web usability criteria for screen appearance is presented in Table 4.

Accessibility

One of the goals of having a Web site is to attract as many visitors as possible from various loca-

Table 3. The seven categories of Web usability criteria

Grouping of Web Criteria	No. of Criteria		
	Objective	*Subjective*	*Total*
Screen Appearance	8	2	10
Content	16	2	18
Accessibility	3	1	4
Navigation	8	3	11
Media use	5	3	8
Interactivity	3	0	3
Consistency	3	0	3
Total	46	11	57

Table 4. List of Web usability criteria for screen appearance

Sub-category	Objective	Subjective
Space allocation	-NA-	• More space for contents than to other display elements
Choice of colour	• Non excessive use of colour for text • Sharp colour contrast between text and its background • Use of colour to differentiate between functional area (e.g., tool bar and menu bar) with content display	-NA-
Readability	• Different text sizes to differentiate between titles, headings and texts • Avoidance of background images in the content display area	• Use of fonts that are easy to read
Scannability	• Clear titles for each pages • Clear headings, sub headings for text/ document • Use of typography and skimming layout (e.g., bold fonts and highlighted words)	-NA-

tions. The basic way to achieve this is to ensure that the site is accessible to the target users. In this study, three elements of accessibility are identified: loading time, browser compatibility and search facility. Generally users could not tolerate long loading times (Morkes & Nielsen, 1998), so designing for speed should be a priority. The Yale Style Manual (Lynch & Horton, 1999) ranks "design for speed" as a top priority by stating that the threshold of frustration for most computing tasks is around 10 seconds. All experts agree that users should not be kept waiting too long while a Web page loads. However, they failed to agree on the exact length of waiting time that would be considered acceptable by the users. Apart from loading time, designers also should consider different browsers with different versions used by Internet users across the world. Additionally, the experts also agree on the need to provide effective local search facility because it will speed up users search for information on a particular Web site. One of Nielsen's studies found that search facility is highly recommended by participants (Nielsen, 1997a). The proposed accessibility elements of the Web are shown in Table 5.

Navigation

Some people believe that the best site contains lots of graphics, animation and colors but often neglect a basic element of an effective Web site: its navigability. Good navigation in a Web site is comparable to a good road map. Our findings from the expert review show that with good navigation, such as logical tree-like structure, proper grouping of contents and use of navigational tools on all pages, users know where they are, where they have been and where they can go from their current position. In short, navigation is the key to making the experience enjoyable and efficient. The usability criteria proposed by the experts are listed in Table 6.

Media Use

The main multimedia elements are sound, graphics, images, audio and video (Shirley, 1999). Some Web sites embed audio as background music, downloadable audio files or on-the-fly audio clips. Sound also may be used in conjunction

Table 5. List of Web usability criteria for accessibility

Sub-category	Objective	Subjective
Loading speed	-NA-	• Acceptable loading time
Browser compatibility	• Compatible contents for all main browsers • Compatible contents between different versions of the same browser • Compatible display for different screen types (e.g., black and white, palm top and digital TV)	-NA-
Search facility	• The use of local search facility	-NA-

Table 6. List of Web usability criteria for navigation

Objective	Subjective
• *MENU/ LIST OF KEY CONTENT IN THE MAIN PAGE* • *MENU/ LIST OF KEY CONTENT IN ALL SUB-PAGES** • Links to the main page in all sub pages* • Accurate/unbroken links • Use of sitemap • Menus are fit on screen (no scrolling) • Use of text within text link(where applicable) • No/ short page scrolling	• The wording for each category of contents is meaningful to users • Contents should be grouped into a small number of key categories • Small number of steps/ links to arrive at a particular information (rule of thumb is 3)

Note: * These criteria are not applicable to Web sites that use frames/separate windows for sub-pages.

with animation or video. As with color, sound can help improve or degrade usability. There are things that cannot be described by words and thus the use of graphics and images is very helpful. Furthermore, in certain cases, graphics could be used to emphasize text. In our study, all experts emphasize the need for providing alternative access to information whenever audio, animation and video elements are used to allow accessibility for those with browsers that do not support these elements. Table 7 presents the list of the proposed usability criteria for proper use of media.

Interactivity

Interactivity is a broad concept. In this study, it refers to features in a Web site that facilitate a two-way communication between users and site owners or other preassigned personnel. Additionally, the features allow users to give feedback and comments on issues raised by the Web site. The introduction of interactivity features, such as e-mail, guest books, and Net forums, may enhance

a Web site's worthiness. While agreeing that these elements are important, some of the experts say that making them available are insufficient. Designers should take into consideration whether the elements are effective and easy to use, especially when dealing with multiple forms. Three criteria are proposed and were agreed upon by the experts as presented in Table 8.

Consistency

This study also found that design consistency is important to speed up user's learning. All experts agree to the fact that designers need to provide consistent layout for title, subtitle, page footers, background, and navigation links and icons in terms of color, size, space and fonts used. However, one of the experts suggests that minor changes should be made to the structure of the screen appearance every now so that users will not get bored and "banner blind." Details on the proposed usability criteria for consistency are shown is Table 9.

Table 7. List of Web usability criteria for media use

Sub-category	Objective	Subjective
Continuos/time-based media (audio, animation and video)	• Control features for continuous media where appropriate (e.g., replay/turn off) • Alternative access (e.g., text version) to any information in continuous media • Avoidance of looping animation to prevent users' distraction	• Use of continuous media to suit content (e.g., demonstration, instruction, speeches, and speeches)
Static media (graphics, images, pictures)	• Labelling of all static media especially those used for menus and icons • Use of thumbnails to display photos	• Use of static media to enhance the information being presented • Non excessive use of static media

Table 8. List of Web usability criteria for interactivity

Objective	Subjective
• Availability of features for users' feedback about the site (e.g., Web master's e-mail address and online form) • Availability of features for sharing views and discussions (e.g., e-forum, Net conference and Net chatting) • Availability of entertainment features (e.g., online games and puzzles)	-NA-

Content

Apart from user interface, content is undoubtedly a very important Web siteelement. It is the content that attracts people to visit a particular Web site. Among the suggested criteria by the experts are suitable language for the audience, high quality writing with no grammatical and typographical errors, passages that are easy to read and understand, and clear information about cited authors and references, where applicable. In addition, several experts suggest that merely having a section for press releases and publications is not enough. Instead, Web developers should ensure that these publications are up-to-date and

archived accordingly. Another suggestion is that users should be informed about the difference between internal and external links. Providing a printer friendly environment within Web pages that offer long document also could boost usability. The result of the expert review pertaining to the generic criteria of content usefulness is shown in Table 10.

EVALUATION: THE BENCHMARKING APPROACH

This section explains our framework for benchmarking the usability and content usefulness of Web sites. As presented earlier, the identified

Table 9. List of Web usability criteria for consistency

Objective	Subjective
• Consistent page layout (e.g., screen size for content display, banners, and menu bar). • Consistent use of text in terms of its type, font size and colour. • Consistent use of navigational aids (e.g., menu bar, buttons and links in terms of graphics metaphor, size and colour).	-NA-

Table 10. List of generic criteria for content usefulness

Sub-category	Objective	Subjective
Scope	• Suitable language for audience • Up-to-date publication (e.g., news and articles) • Archive of previously published materials	• Contents provided meet the expectation of target users
Accuracy	•	• High quality writing (e.g., good grammar)
Authority & Reliability	• Information on authors of text/documents (e.g., names) • References or sources of text and other documents • Background information of institution/ organisation/ owner of the site (i.e., logo, name, address, phone number)	-NA-
Currency	• Up-to-date contents	-NA-
Uniqueness	• Options for output/ print format when appropriate • Choices of language for multi-ethnic audience • Choices of media type for particular information (e.g. text only, audio or video) • Information/ warnings on file type and size for downloading	-NA-
Linkages	• Clear distinctions between internal and external links • Links to other relevant sites (e.g. state & local branches)	-NA-
Text Quality	• News/articles/documents/stories with pictures • Summary of news/articles/documents/stories with links to full versions • Divide news/articles/documents/stories according to scope (e.g. local & international)	-NA-

evaluation list was grouped into objective and subjective criteria. In this framework, only the objective criteria will be used as the benchmarking metrics because they are absolute criteria that can be measured easily, even by the laypersons. In contrast, the subjective criteria are mostly relative measures that can only be evaluated qualitatively. Furthermore, these criteria depend on the perception of users towards a particular Web site.

The main purpose of this framework is to assist individuals or teams who intend to measure the usability of their Web sites against those of their competitors or of similar types. It provides guidance to technical and nontechnical people who are involved in Web-evaluation projects on what, who and how to benchmark Web sites. This framework also can be used by those who want to know the generic usability criteria that need to be taken into account in determining the level of Web usability.

What is Benchmarking?

Benchmark is a standard or point of reference from which measurements can be performed (Merriam Webster, 2006). Benchmarking, however, is comparing one's current performance and practice with others in the same area of interest or business (Codling, 1992; Bramham, 1997). The result of

benchmarking is normally used for bridging the gap with competitors and for moving from where one is to where one wants to be (Chang & Kelly, 1995). There are many advantages that an organization could gain from benchmarking, including an awareness of changing consumer needs and an improvements made by learning from others who are better. Benchmarking also can be performed on Web sites and can be divided into two types (Anderson & Pettersen, 1996; Bendell, Boulter, & Kelly, 1993): internal benchmarking (comparisons among Web sites of units/departments/branches) and competitive or external benchmarking (direct comparisons against competitors' Web sites outside an organization).

Eight Steps to Web Benchmarking

Web benchmarking is a continuous process of measuring and comparing one's Web site with others, which involves at least, eight steps (Anderson & Pettersen, 1996; Bramham, 1997; Chang & Kelly, 1995; and Codling, 1992) as shown in Figure 1.

- **Step 1. Identify what to benchmark:** There are many aspects of Web sites that can be evaluated in order to improve their effectiveness and usefulness. One of them is

Figure 1. Eight steps to Web benchmarking

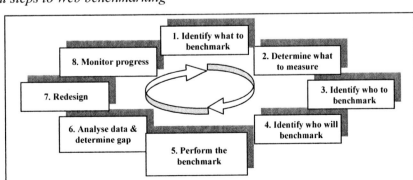

usability—the main focus of this framework. As explained earlier, Web usability is a broad concept covering at least seven major factors: screen appearance, consistency, accessibility, navigation, media use, interactivity and content. Considering this, those who intend to benchmark their Web sites need to decide whether to benchmark all seven factors or concentrate on certain factors. This decision depends on the purpose of the evaluation, time constraints and the number of people involved.

- **Step 2. Determine what to measure:** Once it has been decided which Web usability factors to benchmark, one needs to determine what measures to use for each factor. Table 3 presented provides the information on the number of measures (objective criteria) to be used in the benchmarking for all factors. Although Web sites can be measured quantitatively or qualitatively, this framework only focuses on the quantitative measures by using the 46 objective criteria as listed in Tables 4 through 10.

- **Step 3. Identify benchmarking sites:** The identification of Web sites to benchmark depends on the type of benchmark to be performed (i.e., internal or external benchmarking). When performing an internal benchmarking, one should select Web sites from other departments or branches within the same organization. On the other hand, for an external benchmarking, one should select a number of Web sites (at least three) of the closest competitors. In the case of too many Web sites to benchmark, ones can employ a suitable sampling technique.

- **Step 4. Select evaluators:** Selecting evaluators will not be difficult because they do not have to be experts in HCI or Web usability. The metrics used in the benchmarking are based on Web usability criteria that are easily understood by general Internet users. Evaluators could be any individuals who are competent and frequent Internet users, and who are familiar with Web site environment and terminology. They should be independent (not members of the design team) so that the issue of potential bias can be avoided. The number of evaluators to be used in the benchmarking will depend on the time frame and budget provided for Web evaluation project. However, for quick and better results, at least two evaluators should be selected.

- **Step 5. Perform the benchmark:** Once one has identified what to benchmark (Step 1), what measures to use (Step 2), the benchmarking sites and the evaluators (Steps 3 and 4), the benchmarking process can be conducted. First, prepare the necessary equipment and a suitable room for the benchmarking. A minimum of two computers should be used with the specifications described in Table 11.

Table 11. Computer specifications for Web benchmarking

Computer	Processor	Random Access Memory (RAM)	Internet access	Internet browser	Screen resolution
1	Low speed (e.g., Pentium 1)	Low Memory (e.g., 32 Megabytes)	Low speed (e.g. 33Kbps modem)	Lower versions of Netscape/Internet Explorer	Low screen resolution (e.g., 640 × 480 pixels)
2	Medium/high speed (e.g., Pentium 3)	Medium/ high Memory (e.g., 128 Megabytes)	Medium/high speed (e.g. 56Kbps modem)	Higher versions of Netscape/Internet Explorer	Medium/ higher screen resolution (e.g., 1024 × 768 pixels)

Table 12. Sample benchmarking form Web usability benchmarking

	Web Usability Benchmarking		
URL: _____ Date: _____ Time: _____			
Evaluator's Name: _____ Category: Screen Appearance			
Subcategory	**Criteria**	**YES**	**NO**
Choice of colour	1. Non excessive use of colour for text 2. Sharp colour contrast between text and its background (e.g., black and white) 3. Use of colour to differentiate functional area with content display area	( ) ( ) ( )	( ) ( ) ( )
Readability	4. Different text sizes to differentiate between titles, headings and texts (e.g., 14pt. for headings and 12pt. for sub headings) 5. Avoidance of background images in the content display area as it will greatly affect readability	( ) ( )	( ) ( )
Scannability	6. Clear titles for each pages 7. Clear headings, sub headings for text/ document 8. Use of typography and skimming layout (e.g., bold fonts and highlighted words)	( ) ( ) ( )	( ) ( ) ( )
Total		(/8)	(/8)

Table 13. Summary form for the number of usability criteria in all SCANMIC categories

	Web Site A			Web Site B			Web Site C		
	YES	NO	NA	YES	NO	NA	YES	NO	NA
<u>Screen Appearance (F1)</u> *Choice of colour (/3)* *Readability (/2)* *Scannability (/3)*			░			░			░
Total (/8)			░			░			░
<u>Consistency (F2) (/3)</u>			░			░			░
<u>Accessibility (F3)</u> *Display Compatibility (/2)* *Search facility (/1)*			░			░			░
Total (/3)			░			░			░
<u>Navigation (F4)</u> (/8)			░			░			░
<u>Media use (F5)</u> *Static Media (/3)* *Continuous Media (/2)*									
Total (/5)									
<u>Interactivity (F6)</u> (/3)			░			░			░
<u>Content (for general Web sites -F7)</u> *Scope (/3)* *Authority & Reliability (/3)* *Currency (/1)* *Uniqueness (/4)* *Linkages (/2)* *Text Quality (/3)*			░			░			░
Total (/16)			░			░			░
Grand Total (/46)									

To assess different usability aspects of Web sites particularly those related to display compatibility, computers with different specifications, network connection capabilities, Internet browser versions and screen resolutions as described above are necessary. Furthermore, not all Internet users are using the latest computer technology with high specifications. When the necessary equipment is ready, a briefing session on the purpose of the benchmarking and how to carry it out should be given to the evaluators. Each evaluator should be provided with a set of benchmarking forms (for each Web site), which contains the list of Web usability criteria as listed in Tables 4 through 10 (only objective criteria). The evaluators will then fill in the form (see a sample form in Table 12) while assessing the selected Web sites. They will tick "YES" for criteria existence and "NO" for nonexistence. For the media use category, an additional column should be provided for "N/A" (not applicable) because not all Web sites fully utilize all media elements.

- **Step 6. Analyze data and determine the gap:** The next step is to analyze the data derived from Step 5. First, the data can be summarized by counting the number of criteria were existence (YES) and nonexistence (NO) for each SCANMIC category. An example of a form that can be used for this is shown in Table 13. Then, the data can be further analyzed to identify the usability level of the Web sites that are being benchmarked as exemplified in Table 14.

From the analysis, the gaps that exist between the Web sites can be determined. If UB > UA and UB > UC, then Web site B shows a higher usability level than Web site A and C. To see the gaps more clearly, plotting charts, such as bar charts based on the results, can be used.

- **Step 7. Redesign:** The results derived from steps 5 and 6 will help identify weaknesses and strengths of one's Web site against others

Table 14. An example of calculation for percentage Web usability index for three general Web sites

SCANMIC Factors	Web Site A			Web Site B			Web Site C		
	YES	NO	NA	YES	NO	NA	YES	NO	NA
F1 (/8)	a_A	h_A	▨	a_B	h_B	▨	a_C	h_C	▨
F2 (/3)	b_A	i_A	▨	b_B	i_B	▨	b_C	i_C	▨
F3 (/3)	c_A	j_A	▨	c_B	j_B	▨	c_C	j_C	▨
F4 (/8)	d_A	k_A	▨	d_B	k_B	▨	d_C	k_C	▨
F5 (/5)	e_A	l_A	o_A	e_B	l_B	o_B	e_C	l_C	o_C
F6 (/3)	f_A	m_A	▨	f_B	m_B	▨	f_C	m_C	▨
F7 (/16)	g_A	n_A		g_B	n_B		g_C	n_C	
Total (/46)	$\sum a_A + ... + g_A$	$\sum h_A + ... + n_A$	$\sum o_A$	$\sum a_B + ... + g_B$	$\sum h_B + ... + n_B$	$\sum o_B$	$\sum a_C + ... + g_C$	$\sum h_C + ... + n_C$	$\sum o_C$
	YES_A	NO_A	NA_A	YES_B	NO_B	NA_B	YES_C	NO_C	NA_C

% Usability Index for Web Site A
$$= U_A = \left(\frac{YES_A}{46 - NA_A} \right) \times 100 \quad \text{or} \quad = U_A = \left(\frac{46 - NO_A}{46 - NA_A} \right) \times 100$$

% Usability Index for Web Site B
$$= U_B = \left(\frac{YES_B}{46 - NA_B} \right) \times 100 \quad \text{or} \quad = U_B = \left(\frac{46 - NO_B}{46 - NA_B} \right) \times 100$$

% Usability Index for Web Site C
$$= U_C = \left(\frac{YES_C}{46 - NA_C} \right) \times 100 \quad \text{or} \quad = U_C = \left(\frac{46 - NO_C}{46 - NA_C} \right) \times 100$$

in terms of usability. In particular, areas of concern that need to be modified and enhanced can be located. Due to the dynamic nature of Web sites and Internet technology, redesigning Web sites has become a continuous process. As such, the result from the benchmarking also should be of help for Web developers in their Web redesign process. In some cases, Web redesign and enhancements would require more money and manpower. Thus, the benchmarking results also can be used to justify the need for more funding for Web projects.

- **Step 8. Monitor progress:** After the redesign process (if necessary), the next step is to monitor the progress of the new version of the Web site. Several measures can be used for this, such as counting page hits, tracking

Figure 2. Sample Web pages of four selected political Web sites used in the benchmarking—The National Front Party (http://www.bn.org.my), The Malaysian Pan Islamic Party (http://www.parti-pas.org), The Democratic Action Party (http://www.malaysia.net/dap) and The Islamic Youth Movement (http://www.abim.org.my)

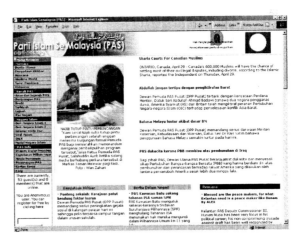

user logs and identifying the level of sales volume (in case of e-commerce sites). After several months, Web benchmarking should be repeated to track progress as compared to others in similar fields or businesses.

FRAMEWORK TESTING

Once completed, the benchmarking framework was tested for its applicability and practicality. The main purposes of the benchmarking are threefold: to test the suitability of the criteria in terms of wording and terminology used, to test the practicality of the eight benchmarking steps and proposed calculation methods, and to identify the level of usability of major political Web sites in Malaysia. The benchmark only focused on the benchmarking of Web usability in seven key areas of screen appearance, consistency, navigation, media use, interactivity and content. The list of the objective criteria used as the benchmarking metrics is shown in Tables 4 through 10. This benchmark could be considered as an external benchmarking because it involved comparisons between different political Web sites in Malaysia. Four major political Web sites were selected: National Front Party (BN), Malaysian Pan Islamic Party (PAS), Democratic Action Party (DAP) and Islamic Youth Movement (ABIM) (see screenshots in Figure 2).

Two evaluators (expert Internet users) were invited to participate. They conducted the evaluation in a room with two computers with the specifications as presented in Table 15.

The evaluators were briefed on the purposes of the benchmarking and what they were supposed to do. Benchmarking forms were supplied to the evaluators before they started the benchmarking. Using the forms, the evaluators then performed the benchmarking for about 3 hours on the selected Web sites. After the benchmarking, the forms were collected from the evaluators. The number of criteria that were existence and nonexistence were calculated and summarized as presented in Table 16. The percentage usability index for all four Web sites with a bar chart also are presented.

The results show that all four political Web sites had very good design in terms of screen appearance. In general, designers of these sites utilized proper color, text, titles, headings and layout. In terms of consistency, Web sites belonging to PAS and DAP were very consistent in all three aspects of page layout, use of text and navigational aids. The other two Web sites—BN and ABIM—however, suffer from page layout inconsistency, such as the placement of content and banners. Apart from page layout, BN's Web site also has inconsistent use of text in terms of its types, font size and color. Three Web sites, BN, PAS, and DAP, were highly accessible in both aspects of display compatibility and searching facility. ABIM's Web site, however, did not provide any search function for better accessibility.

DAP's Web site has the highest level of usability in the navigation category. BN and PAS also rate well in this category. However, ABIM's Web site ha major navigation problems, including a few broken links, long page scrolling and unavailability of a site map. In the media use category, most Web sites did not utilize continuous media in presenting information. All sites also failed to properly use static media where graphics, logos and pictures were not labeled. However,

Table 15. Computer specifications for Web benchmarking

	Processor	RAM	Internet access	Internet browser	Screen resolution
Computer 1	Pentium 1	32 Mb	33 Kbps Modem	Netscape 4.5 & Explorer 5.0	640 × 480 pixels
Computer 2	Pentium 2	128 Mb	56 Kbps Modem	Netscape 6.2 & Explorer 6.0	800 × 600 pixels

Table 16.(a) The benchmarking score and percentage Web usability index for the selected Web sites; (b) bar chart of the benchmarking score (in %) for the four selected Web sites

Factors	BN			PAS			DAP			ABIM		
	YES	NO	NA	YES	NO	NA	YES	NO	NA	YES	NO	NA
F1 (/8)	7	1		6	2		7	1		7	1	
F2 (/3)	1	2		3	0		3	0		2	1	
F3 (/3)	3	0		3	0		3	0		2	1	
F4 (/8)	6	2		5	3		7	1		3	5	
F5 (/5)	1	1	3	2	2	1	0	2	3	1	1	3
F6 (/3)	0	3		2	1		2	1		2	1	
F7 (/16)	7	9		10	6		7	9		6	10	
Total(/46)	25	18	3	31	12	1	29	14	3	23	20	3

Note: % Usability Index for: BN=25/(46- 3)×100=58.14%, PAS=31/(46-1)×100=68.89%, DAP=29/(46-3)×100=67.44%, ABIM=27(46-3)×100=53.49%

(a)

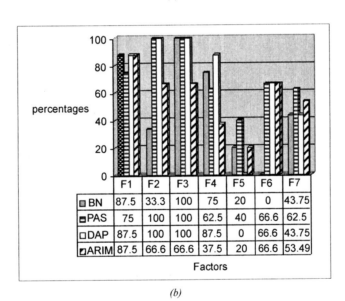

	F1	F2	F3	F4	F5	F6	F7
BN	87.5	33.3	100	75	20	0	43.75
PAS	75	100	100	62.5	40	66.6	62.5
DAP	87.5	100	100	87.5	0	66.6	43.75
ARIM	87.5	66.6	66.6	37.5	20	66.6	53.49

Factors

(b)

most Web sites were rated better in terms of interactivity. Although features for entertainment were not available, Web sites belonging to PAS, DAP and ABIM provided all features for user feedback and discussions. BN's Web site, on the other hand, had very severe interactivity problems, where all three criteria were absent. When benchmarking content criteria, PAS and ABIM performed better than BN and DAP. Both had contents that were wider in scope, especially material related to content authority and linkages.

Despite performing slightly worse than the others in most aspects, BN's Web site scored highly for content in terms of authority and reliability. On the other hand, DAP's Web site suffered severe linkage and text-quality problems.

In practice, Web benchmarking is normally performed by an organization by comparing its Web site with its competitors. The result can be used to make changes for better Web sites in terms of usability. However, the benchmarking in this research was used only to test the applicability of the framework and was not being performed on behalf of any particular organization. Hence, Step 7 and 8 are not contextually applicable. Nonetheless, the results of the benchmarking revealed some usability problems faced by all organizations as described in Step 6. In general, the usability level of the Web site belonging to PAS had the highest level of usability with 68.89%, followed by DAP, BN and ABIM with 67.44%, 58.14% and 53.49%, respectively. The results also provided ideas for designers of all the Web sites, particularly BN and DAP, on areas that they need to concentrate on in the redesign of their sites.

Outcomes of the Framework Testing

The benchmarking was conducted successfully with satisfactory results. The benchmarking processes, or steps, were followed and executed easily. Good feedback was obtained from the evaluators. The criteria used were understood and evaluated easily. The number of criteria for all categories also was considered adequate. Nonetheless after the testing, several issues were noted to improve the applicability of the framework.

1. The whole process of performing the benchmarking in Step 5 was very time consuming, particularly when the evaluators had to go through every Web page in the site to assess a criterion (e.g,. clear title for each Web page). Two solutions were recommended to minimize this problem:
    *   during Step 4, select more evaluators (e.g., one evaluator for each SCANMIC category) and
    *   during Step 5 (perform the benchmark), instead of evaluating all Web pages, allow evaluators to test parts of the Web site (e.g., if the site has five subcategories, evaluating at least two pages for each category is adequate).
2. The outcome of the testing also suggests that the benchmarking evaluation method

needs to be expanded particularly for Step 7 (redesign). In addition to relying on the results of Step 6 (analyze data and determine the gap) to redesign the Web site, other evaluation methods (e.g., expert reviews) also could be used particularly those that deal with the assessment of the subjective criteria. Therefore, it should be mentioned in Step 7 that the results of the benchmarking, together with the results of other assessment methods (e.g., expert review, interview and user observation), should be utilized in the redesign process.

The testing also revealed the need for individuals, organizations and the government, which were involved in political Web site design and content development, to put extra effort in raising the usability level of their Web sites. The results from the testing showed that all major political Web sites in Malaysia still suffered some severe usability flaws that needed to be tackled immediately. This type of Web sites plays a very important role in bridging the relationship between the government, business and the public at large (consumers).

CONCLUSION AND SUGGESTIONS FOR FUTURE STUDIES

There are many ways that companies can assess their Web presence, including usability testing, questionnaire survey, interview and expert review. Each method has its advantages and is being used to achieve certain objectives. Using only one method is not adequate to assess the quality of one's Web site. Thus, combining several approaches in Web evaluation would produce better results. This study provides an alternative approach to Web evaluation through the benchmarking approach. It highlights the need for Web developers to benchmark the usability and content usefulness of their sites against their competitors'. Apart from being able to identify their sites' weaknesses, the main advantage of this method is that Web developers also would be able to find out their competitors' strengths and then redesign their own Web sites for better usability.

The metrics used for our benchmarking are derived from rigorous analysis of the literature and expert verification. The groupings also are refined based on comments and recommendation from experts. Only key generic criteria are used so that they are applicable to all type of Web sites. Furthermore, only objective criteria are used for this framework. Based on our empirical study, the proposed framework can be applied to real-world situations. In addition, the outcome of the framework testing allows for a refinement to the framework. Most importantly, the cyclical nature of the benchmarking processes, as proposed in the framework, is very suitable for Web evaluation, due to the changing nature of Web technology and user requirements. The proposed benchmarking approach also has some advantages compared to other methodologies, such as those developed by Barnes and Vidgen (2002), Ivory-Ndiaye (2003), and Misic and Johnson (1999). Its main advantage is in term of coverage; our approach covers wider usability issues, including media use, accessibility and content. Additionally, the proposed approach does not require many Web users or experts to benchmark a particular site, which would certainly speed up the benchmarking process. The ease of use of the calculation steps is an added advantage.

However, there are a few points that are worth mentioning for further research. First, the framework only was tested on political Web sites. Further efforts should be made by testing the framework on other type of Web sites, including e-commerce sites. The results then could be used to strengthen the framework. Second, this study only deals with objective Web criteria. Although subjective criteria were identified during the early stage, no suggestion was given on how to tackle these criteria. Further studies are needed on how these criteria could be used in Web evaluation. Third, since the proposed framework only considers the objective measures, further work can be performed including automating the benchmarking process. Fourth, further study also is needed to identify the relative importance of each criterion within the same category or factor. Finally, this study only deals with the issue of Web usability and content usefulness. Many other factors, including technological, cultural, social, economic and legal factors also should be considered in future work.

REFERENCES

Anderson, B., & Pettersen, P. G. (1996). *The benchmarking book, step-by-step instruction.* UK: Chapman and Hall.

Barnes, S., & Vidgen, R. (2002). An integrative approach to the assessment of e-commerce quality. *Journal of Electronic Commerce Research, 3*(3), 114-127.

Bendell, T., Boulter, L., & Kelly, J. (1993). *Benchmarking for competitive advantage.* UK: Pitman Publishing.

Bramham, J. (1997). *Benchmarking for people managers.* UK: Cromwell Press.

Chang, R. Y., & Kelly, P. K. (1995). *Improving through benchmarking.* London: Kogan Page Ltd.

Codling, S. (1992). *Best practice benchmarking, the management guide to successful implementation.* UK: Industrial Newsletters Ltd.

Elmuti, D. (1998). The perceived impact of the benchmarking process on organizational effectiveness. *Production and Inventory Management Journal, 3ʳᵈ Quarter, 39.*

IBM. (2000). *IBM Web design guideline.* Retrieved January 3, 2000, from http://www-3.ibm.com/ibm/easy/eou_ext.nsf/publish/572

Ivory-Ndiaye, Y. M. (2003). An automated approach to web evaluation. *Journal of Digital Information Management, 1*(3), 75-102.

Lu, M., & Yeong, W. (1998). A framework for effective commercial Web application development. *Internet Research Journal, 8*(2), 166-173.

Lynch, P. J., & Horton, S. (1999). *Interface design for WWW Web style guide.* Yale Style Manual. Retrieved December 25, 1999, from http://info.med.yale.edu/caim/manual/interface.html.

Merriam Webster online dictionary. (2006). *Merriam Webster [online].* Retrieved July 9, 2006, from http://www.m-w.com

Misic, M. M. & Johnson, K. (1999). Benchmarking: A toll for web site evaluation and improvement. *Internet Research: Electronic Networking Applications and Policy, 9*(5), 383-392.

Morkes, J., & Nielsen, J. (1998). *Applying writing guidelines to web pages.* Retrieved November 25, 1999, from http://www.useit.com

NetMechanic. (2000). Retrieved July 20, 2000, from http://www.netmechanic.com

Nielsen, J. (1993). *Usability engineering.* San Diego: Academic Press.

Nielsen, J. (1997a). *Changes in web usability since 1994.* Jacob Nielsen's Alertbox. Retrieved December 23, 1999, from http://www.useit.com/alertbox/9712a.html

Nielsen, J. (1997b). *Report from 1994 web usability study.* Papers and Essays. Retrieved January 15, 2000, from http://www.useit.com/papers/1994_web_usability_report.html

Perlman, G. (2001). *Suggested readings in human-computer interaction (HCI), user interface (UI) development, & human factors (HF).* Retrieved June 14, 2002, from http://www.hcibib.org/readings.html

Powell, A. T. (2000). *Web design, the complete reference.* Osbourne/ McGraw-Hill.

Reider, R. (2000). *Benchmarking strategies: A tool for profit improvement.* Wiley.

Seminerio, M. (1998). *Study: One in three experienced surfers find online shopping difficult.* ZDNet. Retrieved June 8, 2000, from http://www.zdnet.com/intweek/quickpoll/981007/981007b.html

Shackel, B. (1991). Usability—context, framework, design and evaluation. In B. Shackel & S. Richardson (Eds.), *Human factors for informatics usability* (pp. 21-38). Cambridge: Cambridge University Press

Shirley, H. (1999). *Effective electronic training. Designing electronic materials: Articles and papers.* Retrieved November 9, 1999, from http://www.rockley.com/designin.htm

Shneiderman, B. (1997). Designing information-abundant Web sites:I issues and recommendations. *International Journal of Human Computer Studies, 47,* 5-29.

Shneiderman, B. (1998). *Designing the user interface: Strategies for effective human-computer interaction* (3rd ed.). London: Addison Wesley Longman Inc.

Simeon, R. (1999). Evaluating domestic and international Web-site strategies. *Internet Research: Electronic Networking and Policy, 9*(4), 297-308.

Smith, P. A., Newman, I. A., & Parks, L. M. (1997). Virtual hierarchy and virtual networks: Some lessons from hypermedia usability research applied to WWW. *International Journal of Human-Computer Studies, 47*(1), 67-95.

Sun Microsystems. (1999). Writing for the Web guide. Retrieved November 10, 1999, from http://www.sun.com

Tauscher, L., & Greenberg, S. (1997). How people revisit web pages. *International Journal of Human-Computer Studies, 47*(1), 97-137.

The Government Centre for Information Systems. (1995). *Improving for money from IS/IT service provision*. Benchmarking IS/IT. Norwich: HMSO Publications.

Usableweb.com. (2002). Keith Instone's Web site. Retrieved July 10, 2002, from http://usableweb.com

Useit.com. (2002). Jacob Nielsen's useit. Retrieved July 10, 2002, from http://ww.useit.com

W3C. (2002). *Web content accessibility guidelines* 1.0. Retrieved November 14, 2003, from http://www.w3.org/WAI/EO/Drafts/impl/eval/Overview.htm/

Web Workshop. (1999). Improving web site usability and appeal. Retrieved December 12, 1999, from http://msdn.microsoft.com/workshop/management/planning/improvingsiteuser.asp

White, S. (2004). Accessing library web page usability: How benchmarking can help. *Library and Information Research, 28*(88), 47-52.

Zhang, P., & Dran G. M. (2000). Satisfiers and dissatisfiers: A two-factor model for Website design and evaluation. *Journal of the American Society for Information Science, 51*(14), 1253-1268.

Zimmerman, E. D., Muraski, M., Palmquist, M., Estes, M., McClintoch, C., & Bilsing, L. (1998). *Examining WWW designs: Lessons from pilot studies*. Retrieved October 24, 1999, from http://www.miscrosoft.com/usability/webconf/zimmerman.htm

Section II
Social Shaping, Construction, and Consequences of E-Business

Chapter VIII
The Influence of the Internet on Relationships Between Consumers and Vendors

Horst Treiblmaier
Vienna University of Economics and Business Administration, Austria

ABSTRACT

In recent years a plethora of scholarly literature from the marketing and the information systems (IS) domain has dealt with the phenomenon of relationships. While during the precomputer era relationships always implied a social dimension, modern technology tries to mimic this interaction process by learning about customers' needs and addressing them individually. Interestingly, the central definition of a relationship remains vague in both marketing and IS. Finding the major constituents, therefore, could shed light on the question of whether technology actually could replace "social interactions." In this chapter, we show how relationships are defined in scholarly literature. Subsequently, consumers define what they perceive to be the crucial attributes of a relationship in general and with an online organization. The results indicate that the notion of relationship has to be redefined for online communication and interaction and offer practical implications for designing the interaction process with online users.

INTRODUCTION

For many years, electronic customer relationship management (e-CRM) stood out as one of the major research topics in the literature of IS and juxtaposed disciplines, such as relationship marketing (Romano & Fjermestad, 2002). From the company side, it can be seen as a great opportunity to use modern technology to learn more about individual customers' preferences, while they, in turn, should benefit from improved service. In order to be able to target their customers precisely, companies need to know many personal details, such as previous buying behavior and psychographic attributes. This increased need for information by companies somehow blurs the borders between private and public information. Today companies gather and process details about users' personal preferences that were previously inaccessible to them, and they refer to this as the management of customer relationships. By doing so, they significantly have changed their typical interaction patterns by personalizing their communication style in order to address customers efficiently.

Given the multifaceted dimensions of how humans can interact with organizations, different research interests within this context have emerged. The term "relationship" can be used equally for business-to-business (B2B) and business-to-consumer (B2C) relationships. For the purpose of this chapter, only the latter will be considered. In addition to that, our focus lies on computer-mediated relations. IS researchers deal mostly with the underlying technology, business models and the interaction between humans and computers (Ganapathy, Ranganathan, & Sankaranarayanan, 2004; Goodhue, Wixom, & Watson, 2002; Romano & Fjermestad, 2003), while the theoretical foundation has been built by marketers since the term "relationship marketing" was first coined by Berry (1983b). Figure 1 shows a framework that follows the argument of Gummesson (2002), who states that eCRM can be seen as computerized CRM, which itself represents the values and strategies of relationship marketing turned into practical application.

Since the notion of relationship stands out as the central term, further investigation of what exactly can be considered as the essential attributes of a social relationship appears to be crucial for clarifying and operationalizing the goals of e-CRM initiatives. Therefore it seems to be useful to use relationship marketing literature as a starting point.

As can be seen from Table 1, most definitions of relationship marketing are circular, that is they use the term relationship in both explanans and explanandum, which can be perceived as an indicator that a relationship is considered to be something that is common knowledge and does not have to be explained. A different approach is followed, for example, by Morgan and Hunt (1994) who circumscribe the key elements of relationship marketing by stating that "commitment and trust lead directly to cooperative behaviors that are conducive to relationship marketing." Both constructs have been discussed extensively in scholarly literature in recent years. Salam, Iyer, Palvia, and Singh (2005) show how external factors may influence trusting beliefs, which in turn affect the perceived trustworthiness of the Web vendor and may lead to the development of a relationship.

A tentative definition of relationship can be found in the work of Hakansson and Snehota

Figure 1. A derivation of eCRM

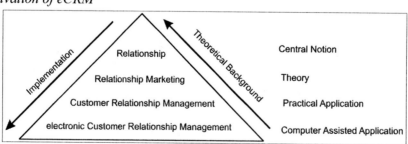

116

(1995), who describe a relationship as a "mutually oriented interaction between two reciprocally committed parties." However, the question that remains unanswered is the amount of "emotional proximity" or "social contact" that is actually perceived in a B2C interaction process. At the same time it could be asked whether "interactivity" would be a more appropriate term instead of relationship. Being aware that a plethora of definitions exist, for the purpose of this chapter, we follow Liu and Shrum (2002) and define interactivity as "the degree to which two or more communication parties can act on each other, on the communication medium, and on the messages and on the degree to which such influences are synchronized." The need for a clear distinction between relationship and ongoing interaction is postulated by Zolkiewski (2004), for example.

In summary, it can be ascertained that, while the importance of customer relationships remains unquestioned, the problem still persists as how to adequately describe the online interaction processes between a customer and a company. In the following sections we will briefly describe how the Internet has changed those processes. By addressing the question as to how the customers themselves perceive a relationship with an organization, both scholars and practitioners might gain some knowledge as to why customers react as they do, and whether the Internet can be used for creating social bonds. Furthermore, the issue of whether online data transfers can substitute for interpersonal relationships will be examined.

Table 1. Selected definitions of relationship marketing

#	Definition
1	Relationship marketing (RM) is attracting, maintaining, and—in multiservice organizations—enhancing customer *relationships* (Berry, 1983a).
2	... marketing oriented toward strong, lasting *relationships* with individual accounts (Jackson, 1985).
3	... marketing can be viewed as the building, maintenance and liquidation of networks and interactive *relationships* between the supplier and the customer, often with long-term implications (Gummesson, 1990).
4	... relates marketing to the development of long-term *relationships* with customers and other parties ... (Grönroos, 1990).
5	RM ... is not directly aimed at immediate transactions but is based on building, supporting and extending customer *relationships* (Matthyssens & Van Den Bulte, 1994).
6	RM is marketing seen as *relationships*, networks and interaction (Gummesson, 1994).
7	Consumer RM seeks to establish long-term committed, trusting and cooperative *relationships* with customers ... (Bennett, 1996).
8	Consumer RM is the organizational development and maintenance of mutually rewarding *relationships* with customers achieved via the total integration of information and quality management systems, service support, business strategy and organizational mission in order to delight the customer and secure profitable lasting business (Bennett, 1996).
9	The core of RM is *relations*, a maintenance of *relations* between the company and the actors in its microenvironment ... The idea is first and foremost to create customer loyalty so that a stable, mutually profitable and long-term *relationship* is enhanced (Ravald & Grönroos, 1996).
10	RM is to establish, nurture and enhance ... *relationships* with customers and other partners, at a profit, so that the objectives of the partners involved are met (Grönroos, 1996).
11	RM is an emergent disciplinary framework for creating, developing and sustaining exchanges of value between the parties involved, whereby exchange *relationships* evolve to provide continuous and stable links in the supply chain (Ballantyne, 1997).
12	... the ongoing process of engaging in cooperative and collaborative activities and programs with immediate and end-user customers to create or enhance mutual economic value at reduced cost (Parvatiyar & Sheth, 2000).
13	RM is marketing based on interaction within networks of *relationships* (Gummesson, 2002).

THE IMPORTANCE OF THE INTERNET FOR BUILDING CUSTOMER RELATIONSHIPS

Ever since the idea of one-to-one marketing emerged in the early '90s (Peppers & Rogers, 1993), the Internet has been regarded as being the ideal medium for the individualization of mass customer communication (Gillenson, Sherrell, & Chen, 1999; Mulvenna, Anand, & Büchner, 2000; Tan, Yen, & Fang, 2002). With consumers increasingly gaining access to the Internet, many companies realized that large customer databases and efficient methods of analysis allowed them to target consumers according to their individual preferences. Interactive marketing and database marketing began to challenge the existing paradigm of transaction marketing (Zahay & Griffin, 2003).

The Internet supports interaction processes between customers and organizations by facilitating the collection of customer-related data, which can be gathered with or without users being aware of or explicitly approving it (e.g., by log-file analysis or cookies) (Berghel, 2002; Munro, 1997). In addition during recent years, the methods of data mining have been vastly improved and, in combination with more powerful hardware, allow the extraction of information out of large amount of data (Adomavicius & Tuzhilin, 2001). Algorithms, such as collaborative filtering, even permit a prediction of a customer's potential interests (Konstan, Miller, Maltz, Herlocker, Gordon, & Reidl, 1997).

Besides enabling the individualization of communication, the Internet supports the whole transaction process. In the case of digital goods, all phases of the buying process, including the distribution, are conducted online without a direct interaction between human beings. Companies that supply digital goods and use the Internet as a medium for immediate delivery especially can gain significant advantages (Subramani & Walden, 2001). From a transaction-cost perspective, it can be argued that the ex ante costs of drafting, negotiating and safeguarding an agreement and ex post costs, such as maladaption costs, haggling costs, setup and running costs, and bonding costs of effecting secure commitments (Williamson, 1985), will decrease by the use of the Internet. This cost cutting leads, in turn, to a reduction of interpersonal social interactions, since no contacts with human beings during the entire buying cycle are needed. In order to compensate for the loss of social interactions, personal data, which is available in a company's database, may be used to simulate a close relationship and interest. The range of individualization strategies varies from letting users customize Web site features (Lam & Lim, 2004) to personalized birthday greetings or electronic recommendation agents (Rowley & Slack, 2001). Previous research has confirmed that customizing the content based on characteristics, behaviors and preferences of users may lead to an increase in the Web site's overall performance (Albert, Goes, & Gupta, 2004).

INTERACTION PATTERNS

In order to define the term relationship, different interaction patterns between humans or humans and organizations have to be taken into account. As was mentioned before, we perceive interaction as a process of two-way communication and exchange (Haeckel, 1998; Pavlik, 1998), including any kind of online transactions. Information technology (IT)-enabled interaction between customers and an enterprise can be differentiated into IT-assisted interaction and automated interaction, whereby the first is predominately a manual process and in the second the complete control is given to the customer (Wells, Fuerst, & Choobineh, 1999).

As can be seen in Figure 2, we differentiate between three types of interaction processes. "Private" interpersonal interaction takes place between two human beings (scenario a). During a sales process, the interaction between a buyer and a vendor (representing an organization), who are both confined to specific roles, becomes more formalized (scenario b). When transactions are completed online, the physical contact is lacking completely (scenario c). Users who are shopping offline experience social interactions with sales personnel, whereas in the case of buying online, no interpersonal interaction exists at all.

By using the framework depicted in Figure 2 as a starting point, three major research questions arise, which will be elaborated upon in more detail in the following sections.

Research question 1: What are the major attributes that constitute a relationship in general? By taking into account which features are to be considered essential for defining a relationship, we strive to analyze what may be called the "core attributes" or "defining attributes" of a relationship in general. This allows us at least to circumscribe the perceived semantic meaning of a relationship from a consumer's point of view. This research question is equally important for all interaction processes in Figure 2.

Research question 2: When does a relationship with an organization exist? In contrast to defining a relationship in general, it is essential to know what the main attributes of a relationship with

an organization are. As was indicated above, the interaction process with a human being may differ from the one with an organization as an abstract entity. This research question explicitly concentrates on scenario b in Figure 2.

Research question 3: What kinds of aspects are important to an online relationship with an organization? By hypothesizing that the online interaction process with an organization may be called a relationship, we asked users what they perceive to be the most important attributes to this situation. Most of the items were derived from the literature on CRM and focus on the specific abilities of the Internet to foster individualized communication and, thereby, allow for social interaction with a multitude of anonymous users. This situation is depicted as scenario c in Figure 2.

SURVEY DESIGN

We used Austrian Internet users as our universe to assess the importance of online relationships. The survey was supported by one of the major Austrian newspapers, der Standard, which included a link to our questionnaire in two weekly newsletters that were sent to 85,500 registered recipients. No incentive was given for filling

Figure 2. Interaction patterns

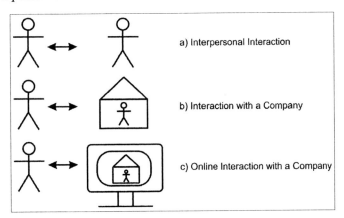

out the questionnaire. The online survey was conducted between August 25, 2004 (the day the first newsletter was sent out) and September 16, 2004. We used slider bars with a range from 1 (strongly disagree) to 100 (strongly agree). In total, we gathered 385 usable results. Besides asking for demographic characteristics, we included three major sections in our questionnaire, where we assessed the importance of online relationships and which will be discussed subsequently. Basically, in all sections, a general question was given (e.g., "In general, which meaning do you associate with the term 'relationship'?"), and the respondents were asked to assess individually the relevance of the respective items (e.g., friendship). The original questionnaire was in German. Since we did not use scales from existing literature, no translation-retranslation process was necessary. Instead, the results were translated by the authors and double-checked by a native speaker.

RESULTS

The respondents are 30.4% male and 69.6% female, with 71.1% between 21 and 35 years old and 84.6% possess at least a high school degree. The largest group, as far as the current employment situation is concerned, works as administrative or technical employees (45.2%), while the second largest group consists of students (20.7%). Most of the users possess considerable experience with the Internet, with only 9.1% indicating that they have been online for fewer than four years. The weekly frequency of Internet usage shows a wide range of answers with approximately one-fourth of the users (25.9%) being online for up to five hours a week. About the same number of respondents (22.6%) state that they use the Internet for 6 to 10 hours a week. Included in the sample is also a large number of "heavy users" with more than 30 hours of weekly usage (12.7%).

Table 2. Characteristics of respondents (n = 385)

Sex		Occupation		Experience on the Internet	
Male	30.4%	Management, civil servant	13%	less than 4 years	9.1%
Female	69.6%	Administrative/technical employee	45.2%	4-5 years	29.9%
		Self-employed	4.9%	6-7 years	24.4%
		Housewife or -husband	2.6%	8-9 years	17.9%
		Retired		more than 9 years	17.1%
		Student	20.7%	n/a	1,6%
		Other	11.9%		
Age		Education		Frequency of Internet use	
- 20 years	2.4%	Secondary school	2.9%	less than 5h/week	25.9%
21 – 25 years	24.9%	Vocational school	10.1%	6-10 h/week	22.6%
26 – 30 years	27%	High school graduation	57.5%	11-15 h/week	11.2%
31 – 35 years	19.2%	Technical college	5.5%	16-20 h/week	14%
36 – 40 years	10%	University	21.6%	21-25 h/week	4.2%
41 – 45 years	6%	Other	2.6%	26-30 h/week	7.8%
46 – 50 years	6%			30+ h/week	12.7%
50+	4.5%			n/a	1.6%

Note: Figures may not add up to 100% due to rounding differences.

For the following analyses the items, which were gained by literature research in IS and marketing publications dealing with relationships and e-CRM and related topics, are clustered into three main sections. The first category includes attributes that could be used to describe a relationship in general, while the second category focuses on the interaction between an individual and an organization. The third pool of items concentrates on those activities that a company can conduct only online, such as individualizing mass communication and production (Dewan, Jing, & Seidmann, 2000), or at least can be considerably supported by the use of the Internet, as is the case when offering customized pricing, such as discounts or rebates based on former purchases (Simon & Dolan, 1998).

In the first step, all three analyses will be discussed individually and then be integrated into a more comprehensive framework. For all three cases we used a principal axis factoring with Promax as the method of rotation. In contrast to the most commonly used principal component analysis, the results from principal axis factoring more accurately represent the population loadings (Widaman, 1993). Furthermore, we strive to understand the latent structure of a set of variables instead of simply reducing them without interpreting the resulting variables in terms of constructs (cf., Conway & Huffcutt, 2003, p. 150f.). An oblique rotation is chosen instead of an orthogonal rotation, since we expect a correlation between the constructs. The Promax procedure first conducts an orthogonal Varimax rotation and attempts to improve the fit to the data by allowing correlations (Russell, 2002). Fabrigar, Wegener, MacCallum, and Strahan (1999) write that besides getting "cleaner" solutions by using oblique rotation, simply "relying on an orthogonal rotation would also forfeit any knowledge of the existing correlations among factors" (p. 287). In all cases the number of factors is determined by using the scree test instead of retaining all factors with eigenvalues greater than 1.0, since the latter,

albeit commonly used, is perceived as being less accurate and leading to overextraction (Velicer & Jackson, 1990).

In order to find out what constitutes a good relationship in general, the respondents were asked to assess the perceived importance of several items for constituting a relationship (see Table 3). All items were scrambled within the respective categories (i.e., "constitutive attributes of a relationship," "relationship with a company," "online relationship with a company") and an exploratory factor analysis was used to detect underlying structures. The results of all three analyses will be discussed in the next section. The respondents were asked to assess separately the importance of a number of attributes in regard to the research questions elaborated above.

It is essential to mention that this chapter concentrates explicitly on so-called "good relationships." With the exception of the existence of a monopoly where no choice between suppliers exists, consumers will tend to change suppliers rather than maintain an unsatisfactory relationship.

The Kaiser-Meyer-Olkin measure of sampling adequacy (MSA) provides a measure of the extent to which the variables belong together and, therefore, are appropriate for factor analysis (Kaiser & Rice, 1974). A MSA value of 0.89 (meritorious) for the items used to measure the attributes that constitute a relationship indicates a good eligibility of the data for factor analysis. The three-factor solution shown in Table 3, with the items being grouped by their highest primary factor loading, turned out to be the best one, according to their interpretability. Based on the analysis and conceptual congruence, we labeled the three components as emotion, communication/transparency and ties to indicate that the first one mainly includes items that emphasize feelings, such as solidarity, familiarity, friendship and partnership, whereas the second one focuses on the exchange of information and communication. The third component describes the existence of invisible ties, as can be seen from items such as dependence and bondage.

In order to estimate the absolute valuation of the items, the means are shown in the second column of Table 3. Generally speaking, the emotional and communicational components are considered to be of greater importance than the perceived existence of ties. Interestingly, of all items "Interpersonal contact" achieved the highest level of agreement (84.29), which indicates the high importance of social interaction in a relationship. On the other hand, items such as trust (83.78) or satisfaction (73.60), which are also valued quite highly, do not necessarily call for human contact.

In the next step we look at the most important attributes of a relationship between an individual and an organization (see Table 4). The MSA value is 0.828 and can be interpreted as "meritorious."

As can be seen from the high level of agreement, indicated by the value of the means, service-related activities, such as the handling of personal requests (84.82) or complaints (81.15) and the provision of competent advice (82.70), are regarded as being highly important for a relationship with an organization. In addition to that, customers show a high level of agreement that regular (83.96) or frequent (76.87) purchases from a company may be called a relationship. Given the strict classifications in marketing literature, for example the differentiation into transaction marketing and relationship marketing (including

Table 3. Constitutive attributes of a relationship

	Mean	Item	F1	F2	F3
		In general, which meaning do you associate with the term "relationship"?			
Emotion	72.66	Friendship	0.909		
	76.73	Solidarity	0.891		
	80.57	Familiarity	0.830		
	76.57	Partnership	0.802		
	62.78	Intensity	0.682		
	70.22	Emotion	0.660		
	83.78	Trust	0.540		
	71.52	Long-term orientation	0.482		
	84.29	Interpersonal contact	0.476		
Communication/	68.03	Exchange of information		0.696	
transparency	61.34	Transparency		0.580	
	80.96	Communication		0.578	
	77.78	Concern		0.443	
Ties	30.67	Dependence			0.708
	47.28	Bondage			0.535
	36.71	Selflessness			0.431
Eigenvalue			6.10	1.95	0.97
Variance explained			0.32	0.10	0.5

Note: Factor loadings <0.4 are omitted for better readability.

Table 4. Relationship with a company

	Mean	Item	F1	F2	F3
		A relationship with an organization exists, if			
Service and	84.82	... personal requests are treated individually.	0.712		
transactions	81.15	... my complaints are handled satisfactorily.	0.637		
	82.70	... I get competent advice.	0.560		
	82.50	... I already have positive experiences with the company.	0.712		
	83.96	... I buy regularly from this company.	0.816		
	76.87	... I buy frequently from this company.	0.725		
	66.57	... I am already a customer of this company.	0.431		
	77.49	... I am so committed to this company that I won't buy anywhere else.	0.404		
Value for money	59.82	... the company offers high-quality products.		0.766	
	42.65	... the company offers brand products I know.		0.632	
	42.79	... prices are low.		0.609	
	51.87	... friends and acquaintances recommended this company to me.		0.511	
	65.52	... additional services exist.		0.478	
	63.29	... the corporate philosophy appeals to me.		0.409	
Information exchange	46.35	... I inform myself actively about the company.			0.761
	48.28	... I already have provided a lot of personal information.			.549
Eigenvalue			4.79	1.59	1.38
Variance explained			0.24	0.80	0.70

Note: Factor loadings <0.4 are omitted for better readability.

database marketing, interaction marketing and network marketing) (Zineldin, 2000), it seems remarkable that many customers perceive existing transactions as being de facto relationships, thereby blurring those distinctions. The other components that resulted from the factor analysis were labeled "Value for money," including the offer of high-quality products (59.82) and low prices (42.79), and "Information exchange". In general, these items are valued less important than service or existing transactions.

The third factor analysis is intended to include the Internet as an important communication and transaction channel. Again, a MSA value of 0.855 (meritorious) indicates a good eligibility of the data for factor analysis.

Service is the most important factor in the relationship with an organization. In addition to that, in the online world, transparency becomes a major criterion, which is reflected by items such as "I can inspect my personal data at any time" (85.74) or "the general terms and conditions are clearly defined" (73.34). Since the factor analysis allowed no clear distinction between items pertaining to service and those belonging to transparency, all items were combined and the factor label contains both constructs. The second most important factor, as indicated by the absolute means, includes the offering of presents or discounts (69.66) or aggregated rebates (75.16) and, therefore, is refered to as "Extended benefits." Interestingly, the items that reflect the potential advantages of

Table 5. Online relationship with a company

	Mean	Item	F1	F2	F3	F4
		In an online relationship, it is important for me that				
Service and	90.91	... I receive the ordered products and services on time.	0.825			
transparency	85.74	... I can inspect my personal data at any time.	0.778			
	82.84	... the Web site is clearly arranged.	0.764			
	88.82	... I get answers for my requests quickly.	0.719			
	80.18	... data can be encoded transmitted.	0.676			
	84.58	... I can find a contact person at anytime.	0.619			
	73.34	... the general terms and conditions are clearly defined.	0.557			
	78.82	... I can check my delivery status at anytime.	0.545			
	71.56	... I have the opportunity to give feedback.	0.477	0.448		
Individualization	55.64	... I regularly receive individualized newsletters.		0.788		
	62.30	... I receive individualized offers.		0.607		
	38.01	... I receive congratulations on important dates (e.g., birthday).		0.569		
	44.40	... I am personally welcomed.		0.536		
	56.27	... I can express my opinions in forums.		0.441		
Online	17.40	... the Web site offers online games.			.650	
entertainment	37.08	... I can download software.			.587	
	43.89	... I find the Web site entertaining.			.559	
	41.08	... I can send SMS free of charge.			.546	
	38.54	... I can participate in sweepstakes.			.501	
	63.14	... I like the Web site.			.422	
Extended	69.66	... I get presents or discounts.				0.805
Benefits	75.16	... I get aggregated rebates.				0.753
Eigenvalue			6.39	2.68	1.16	1.06
Variance explained			0.26	0.11	0.50	0.40

Note: Factor loadings <0.4 are omitted for better readability.

the Internet and were subsumed into the factors "Individualization" and "Online entertainment," tend to get lower levels of agreement. Personalized communication, such as congratulations on important dates (38.01) or welcome greetings (44.40), receive below-average acceptance. The same holds true for most items included in "Online entertainment," such as the valuation of online games (17.40), the download of software (37.08) or the participation in sweepstakes (38.54).

In a last step, the combined results are visualized in Figure 3. The ordinate represents the unweighted mean of all items loading on a single factor, while on the abscissa the different types of relationships are depicted.

Starting with the definition of a relationship in general, it can be seen that involuntary interactions usually are not perceived as being a relationship, as indicated by the position of the factor "Ties" in the lower left corner of the framework. On the

Figure 3. A framework for categorizing the constituents of relationships

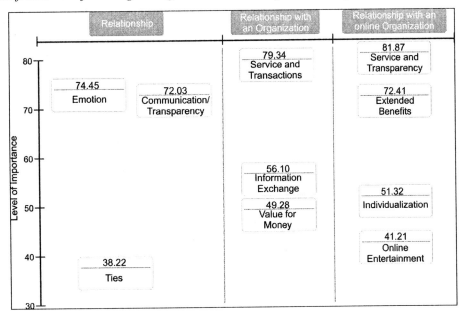

other hand, those items that refer to "Emotion" and "Communication/transparency" are, from a consumer's point of view, much better suited to characterizing the essence of a relationship. By having a look at the relationship with an organization, one can see that especially good service and existing transactions are associated with a relationship. In contrast, "Information exchange" or "Value for money" are rated much lower. The last section describes the relationship with an online organization and again good service is seen as being essential. In addition to that, transparency is considered being quite important. Measures of individualization or online entertainment are regarded as being of comparatively less importance for building relationships online. While in interpersonal interactions hedonic or social motives (e.g., familiarity or emotion) are seen as being very important for constituting a relationship, the opposite holds true for online organizations. For the majority of users of an entertaining Web site,

the ability to customize it or the participation in sweepstakes are not adequate instruments for producing a perceived relationship, as indicated by the below average grading for the latter.

CONCLUSION AND FURTHER RESEARCH

When RM emerged, the Internet was seen by many researchers as the ideal medium for creating and maintaining long-lasting relationships with customers. Due to the increased capacity to gather, store and process vast amounts of information about customers' attributes, behaviors, needs and wishes, companies hoped to be able to mimic social relationships. In this chapter, we took a closer look at how customers themselves would define a relationship either off- or online. The findings suggest that the term relationship (in the sense of a social relationship) might be misleading, since customers tend to emphasize different focuses, depending on the situation and their interaction partner (human vs. organization and online vs. offline). While in a noncommercial interpersonal interaction, emotional values are still of preeminent importance; in a selling situation, the level of service determines the perceived existence of a relationship. In addition, transparency is considered to be important when conducting business online. Our results indicate that in a business context, especially when conducting business online, customers prefer service and "tangible" benefits, such as discounts and rebates, to individualization measures. Therefore it comes as no surprise that items such as "In an online relationship it is important for me that I receive congratulations on important dates" (e.g., birthday) or "it is important for me that I am personally welcomed," were considered to be of minor importance for most respondents. Simply mimicking human behavior with technological means does not seem to be enough to create emotional bonds. However, this emotional component seems to be quite important for characterizing relationships, as indicated by the prevalent importance of items like trust or interpersonal contact for describing general relationships.

However, certain limitations must be taken into account when interpreting the results of this survey. First and foremost, it should be mentioned that some factors include a multitude of items, which makes it hard to find a common name. Further research has to concentrate on the validation of the factors. The low response rate, which is typical for e-mail surveys, requires further research in order to ensure the generalizability of the results. Nonetheless, even imperfect samples allow for important insights (Blair & Zinkhan, 2006), especially when they are confirmed by replication studies.

Furthermore, the factor loadings of some items fall below the commonly accepted threshold of 0.5 (Kaiser & Rice, 1974). For the sake of completeness, we included them in this exploratory study but recommend follow-up studies to improve the validity. While we did not explicitly concentrate on the development of scales for measuring antecedents of relationships, this chapter could nonetheless be used as a starting point for the development of a measurement instrument. Practitioners especially might find it useful to see how customers perceive ongoing interaction processes with a company.

ACKNOWLEDGMENTS

The author wishes to thank Martina Lausmann for her support in collecting the empirical data. An earlier version of this research was presented at the Fourth Annual Workshop on Human Computer Interaction Research in MIS, December 10, 2005, Las Vegas, USA.

REFERENCES

Adomavicius, G., & Tuzhilin, A. (2001). Using data mining methods to build customer profiles. *IEEE Computer, 34*(2), 74-82.

Albert, T. C., Goes, P. B., & Gupta, A. (2004). GIST: A model for design and management of content and interactivity of customer-centric Web sites. *MIS Quarterly, 28*(2), 161-182.

Ballantyne, D. (1997). Internal networks for internal marketing. *Journal of Marketing Management, 13*(5), 343-366.

Bennett, R. (1996). Relationship formation and governance in consumer markets: Transactional analysis versus the behaviourist approach. *Journal of Marketing Management, 12*(5), 417-436.

Berghel, H. (2002). Hijacking the Web. *Communications of the ACM, 45*(4), 23-27.

Berry, L. L. (1983a). Relationship marketing. In L. L. Berry, L. G. Shostack & G. D. Upah (Eds.), *Emerging perspectives on services marketing,* (pp. 25-28). Chicago: American Marketing Association.

Berry, L. L. (1983b) Relationship marketing of services: Growing interest, emerging perspectives. *Journal of the Academy of Marketing Science, 23*(4), 236-245.

Blair, E., & Zinkhan, G. M. (2006). Nonresponse and generalizability in academic research. *Journal of the Academy of Marketing Science, 34*(1), 4-7.

Conway, J. M., & Huffcutt, A. I. (2003). A review and evaluation of exploratory factor analysis practices in organizational research. *Organizational Research Methods, 6*(2), 147-168.

Dewan, R., Jing, B., & Seidmann, A. (2000). Adoption of Internet-based product customization and pricing strategies. *Journal of Management Information Systems, 17*(2), 9-28.

Fabrigar, L. R., Wegener, D. T., MacCallum, R. C., & Strahan, E. J. (1999). Evaluating the use of exploratory factor analysis in psychological research. *Psychological Methods, 4*(3), 272-299.

Ganapathy, S., Ranganathan, C., & Sankaranarayanan, B. (2004). Visualization strategies and tools for enhancing customer relationship management. *Communications of the ACM, 47*(11), 93-99.

Gillenson, M. L., Sherrell, D. L., & Chen, L.-D. (1999). Information technology as the enabler of one-to-one marketing. *Communications of the Association for Information Systems, 2*(3), 1-42.

Goodhue, D. L., Wixom, B. H., & Watson, H. J. (2002). Realizing business benefits through CRM: Hitting the right target in the right way. *MIS Quarterly Executive, 1*(2), 79-94.

Grönroos, C. (1990). The marketing strategy continuum: Towards a marketing concept for the 1990s. *Management Decision, 29*(1), 7-13.

Grönroos, C. (1996). Relationship marketing logic. *Asia-Australia Marketing Journal, 4*(1), 7-18.

Gummesson, E. (1990). *The part-time marketer.* Karlstad, Sweden: Center for Service Research.

Gummesson, E. (1994). Making relationship marketing operational. *International Journal of Service Industry Management, 5*(5), 5-20.

Gummesson, E. (2002). *Total relationship marketing.* Oxford: Butterworth Heinemann.

Haeckel, S. H. (1998). About the nature and future of interactive marketing. *Journal of Interactive Marketing, 12*(1), 63-71.

Hakansson, H., & Snehota, I. (1995). The burden of relationships or who's next? In *Proceedings of the IMP 11th International Conference*, Manchester, UK (pp. 522-536).

Jackson, B. B. (1985). *Winning and keeping industrial customers: The dynamics of customer relationships.* Lexington, MA: Heat and Company.

Kaiser, H. F., & Rice, J. (1974). Little Jiffy, Mark IV. *Educational and Psychological Measurement, 34*(1), 111-117.

Konstan, J. A., Miller, B. N., Maltz, D., Herlocker, J. L., Gordon, L. R., & Reidl, J. (1997). Grouplens: Applying collaborative filtering to Usenet News. *Communications of the ACM, 40*(3), 77-87.

Lam, R. H., & Lim, K. H. (2004). Emotions in online shopping: Fulfilling customer's needs through providing emotional features and customizing Website features. *25th International Conference on Information Systems*, Washington, DC (pp. 877-888).

Liu, Y., & Shrum, L. J. (2002). What is interactivity and is it always such a good thing? Implications of definition, person, and situation for the influence of interactivity on advertising effectiveness. *Journal of Advertising, 31*(4), 53-64.

Matthyssens, P., & Van Den Bulte, C. (1994). Getting closer and nicer: Partnerships in the supply chain. *Long Range Planning, 27*(1), 72-83.

Morgan, R. M., & Hunt, S. D. (1994). The commitment-trust theory of relationship marketing. *Journal of Marketing, 58*(3), 20-38.

Mulvenna, M. D., Anand, S. S., & Büchner, A. G. (2000). Personalization on the Net using Web mining. *Communications of the ACM, 43*(8), 122-125.

Munro, N. (1997). The magnetic poles of data collection. *Communications of the ACM, 40*(6), 17-19.

Parvatiyar, A., & Sheth, J. N. (2000). The domain and conceptual foundations of relationship marketing. In J. N. Sheth & A. Parvatiyar (Eds.), *Handbook of relationship marketing* (pp. 3-38). Thousand Oaks, CA: Sage Publications, Inc.

Pavlik, J. V. (1998). *New media technology: Cultural and commercial perspectives* (2nd ed.). Boston: Allyn and Bacon.

Peppers, D., & Rogers, M. (1993). *The one to one future: Building relationships one customer at a time.* New York: Currency Doubleday.

Ravald, A., & Grönroos, C. (1996). The value concept and relationship marketing. *European Journal of Marketing, 30*(2), 19-30.

Romano, N. C. J., & Fjermestad, J. (2002). Electronic commerce customer relationship management: An assessment of research. *International Journal of Electronic Commerce, 6*(2), 61-113.

Romano, N. C. J., & Fjermestad, J. (2003). Electronic commerce customer relationship management: A research agenda. *Information Technology and Management, 4*(2-3), 233-258.

Rowley, J., & Slack, F. (2001). Leveraging customer knowledge—Profiling and personalisation in e-business. *International Journal of Retail & Distribution Management, 29*(8/9), 409-415.

Russell, D. W. (2002). In search of underlying dimensions: The use (and abuse) of factor analysis. *Personality and Social Psychological Bulletin, 28*(12), 1629-1646.

Salam, A. F., Iyer, L., Palvia, P., & Singh, R. (2005). Trust in e-commerce. *Communications of the ACM, 48*(2), 73-77.

Simon, H., & Dolan, R. J. (1998). Price customization. *Marketing Management, 7*(3), 10-17.

Subramani, M., & Walden, E. (2001). The impact of e-commerce announcements on the market value of firms. *Information Systems Research, 12*(2), 135-154.

Tan, X., Yen, D. C., & Fang, X. (2002). Internet integrated customer relationship management: A key success factor for companies in the e-commerce arena. *The Journal of Computer Information Systems, 42*(3), 77-86.

Velicer, W. F., & Jackson, D. N. (1990). Component analysis versus common factor analysis: Some issues in selecting an appropriate procedure. *Multivariate Behavioral Research, 25*(1), 1-28.

Wells, J. D., Fuerst, W. L., & Choobineh, J. (1999). Managing information technology (IT) for one-to-one customer interaction. *Information & Management, 35*(1), 53-62.

Widaman, K. F. (1993). Common factor analysis versus principal component analysis: Differential bias in representing model parameters? *Multivariate Behavioral Research, 28*(3), 263-311.

Williamson, O. E. (1985). *The economic institutions of capitalism.* New York: The Free Press.

Zahay, D., & Griffin, A. (2003). Information antecedents of personalisation and customisation in business-to-business service markets. *Journal of Database Management, 10*(3), 255-271.

Zineldin, M. (2000). Beyond relationship marketing: Technologicalship marketing. *Marketing Intelligence & Planning, 18*(1), 9-23.

Zolkiewski, J. (2004). Relationships are not ubiquitous in marketing. *European Journal of Marketing, 38*(1/2), 24-29.

Chapter IX
Social Implications of Managing Project Stakeholders

Petar Jovanovic
University of Belgrade, Serbia

Marko Mihic
University of Belgrade, Serbia

Dejan Petrovic
University of Belgrade, Serbia

ABSTRACT

This chapter considers the social implications of managing project stakeholders with a special account of e-project management (e-PM), architecture and the importance of project management (PM) portals, and the way they are related to e-projects. The authors argue that PM portals are indispensable in project collaboration and coordination and are closely related to e-projects, since theirs is a key role in both the PM implementation and an adequate incorporation and discussion of all project stakeholders, particularly virtual teams. The authors believe that a detailed analysis of project stakeholders and PM portals presented in this chapter allows for a thorough review of the strengths as well as weaknesses of the e-project approach and is a basis for understanding of social aspects and challenges of modern ICT solutions in e-PM.

INTRODUCTION

The basic features of the modern business environment are openness, complexity and changeability. A high level of instability stemming from these features gives rise to organizational forms that are flexible enough to adapt to a multiproject environment and compact enough to unite the basic management processes. Also, the challenges of change and a large amount of instability alter the traditional approaches in forming strategy and business-venture planning. The change in the organization becomes a rule, not an exemption.

In answer to these challenges, it is necessary that such a management system be defined to bring together an apparent need for change, as reflected in varied numbers and size of projects and programs under execution, and the strategy that incorporates this need. By implementing the concept of project-oriented enterprise as a frame for such a management system, supported by an adequate organization, team work and project culture, it is possible to significantly improve business results, provided that modern PM tools and techniques and information technology (IT) solutions to project collaboration are used.

This chapter highlights the IT tools that support the work of virtual teams and e-projects in general and their features in the process of collaboration among the project stakeholders. Advantages and disadvantages of e-project management are analyzed, as well as sociocultural aspects of team work in virtual teams, whose activities are coordinated by means of portals.

The importance of analyzing project stakeholders and designing complete e-solutions to project collaboration and support is stressed. As part of an integral planning process in the project-oriented enterprise, the analysis of project stakeholders covers the identification of stakeholders and defining their level of interest and influence upon the project. The stakeholder analysis should result in a strategy that will help ensure the favor of key stakeholders and solve controversies in the project-execution phase. Nowadays managing project stakeholders is easier in that the PM methodologies prescribe procedures of project collaboration and advanced IT solutions for project support have been developed—PM portals—whereby the process of collaboration with key stakeholders is simplified and automated.

The chapter also deals with the architecture of the PM portals, with the description of basic functions related to the collaboration between the stakeholders and virtual teams. The advantages of portals in the process of planning and coordinating project stakeholders, as well as their importance in the organization and management of e-projects, which are regarded the basis of e-society are stressed.

LITERATURE AND BACKGROUND

Companies with a large number of geographically distributed programs and projects as well as those whose project teams are separated have a strong need for implementing e-PM. According to Goncalves (2005) and McMahon (2000), the basic features of e-PM are as follows:

- A stronger focus upon adaptation in comparison to optimization
- They are Web-based
- Unreliable functionality
- A large percentage of critical projects
- They are risk driven
- New technologies
- Need for an integration of the speed of change and innovation

Stoehr (2002) argues that the need for implementing e-PM is mirrored in an increasing number of implemented systems of virtual PM, as well as in new approaches in defining traditional PM processes, from initiation and planning, to control and reporting. Such approaches provide numerous benefits related to improving work productivity, coordination and linking the activities of project teams and their members, a more efficient use of resources, reducing operational costs and so forth.

As well as any change in the organization, the implementation of modern e-PM solutions brings numerous challenges (Archibald, 2003). The first group of challenges refers to the capacity and competence of human resources within the organization to accept and implement the designed solutions, especially if these exceed the domain of their expertise (Burke, 2002; Gareis, 2003). A second group is related to fear, tradition or suppressed personal interests that may surface as a result of facing the change (Dinsmore, Englund, & Graham, 2003; Jovanovic, 2004; Miles, 1997). A third group of challenges includes the work of virtual teams and the communication problems that result from dehumanization of work and alienation among the team members (DeMarie, 2000; Kimble, Li & Barlow 2000; Ramachandran, 2005).

One of the biggest problems in e-PM is the maturity of an organization adopting and implementing modern e-PM solutions (Kloppenborg & Opfer, 2002). Since project managers are professionals from various fields of expertise, often outside the IT sector, a clash may occur between the velocity in the development of e-PM support in the organization and the capacity of individuals to adopt and implement it in an adequate way. Therefore the importance of training to raise e-PM capacities in managers gains an increasing importance. The challenge is greater in that the technologies develop very fast, so it is possible that the acquired knowledge may become obsolete at an equally fast rate (Shields, 2001).

According to Dinsmore (1993), Miles (1997) and Wysocki (2004), the implementation of e-PM is frequently faced with resistance from the some of the employees, due to fears, tradition, money or hidden personal interests. Employees most often fear that the change may endanger their place at work or favorable position, their authority and so forth. Also, individuals rarely opt for change, if a large amount of money must be invested into the existing enterprise, which is a basic reason that e-solutions demanding new investments are slowly adopted. Also, some managers are not competent enough to carry out the changes in the e-business sector, therefore they strive to preserve the existing situation and benefits resulting from that position, making them direct opponents to change (Crawford, 2002; Jick & Peiperl, 2003).

Archibald (2003), Goncalves (2005) and Miranda (2003) state that the success of e-PM implementation in an organization depends upon numerous factors, including:

- The scope of the project of change
- Capabilities of the human resources employees working on the implementing the change
- The project term plan
- Budget
- Monitoring and control system
- Resistance to change among the employees

According to Gareis (2003) and Jovanovic, Mihic and Petrovic (2005), the organizational frame of e-PM implementation is the concept of the project-oriented company, which can be defined as a business entity that conducts its activities on the principle of the project organization of work, implementing contemporary achievements of e-PM, that is, using PM or multi-PM. Defining business on the basis of projects allows for increased efficiency and simultaneously decreased cost, for many reasons. One of the basic reasons is that any business or activity is clearly defined following the basic categories (Petrović, 2003):

- Objectives and scope of project
- Project organization
- Project manager and project team
- Key project stakeholders
- Duration of project
- Resources necessary in project execution
- Estimated value of project—budget
- Project execution information and communication systems
- Summing of results and possible corrective activities

A project-oriented company is characterized by changing boundaries and contents (Gareis, 2002, 2003). This changeability, on one hand, is reflected in the permanent change of project numbers and sizes, engagement of constant and temporary resources, coordination in introducing virtual team, and management tasks (Ives, 2005). On the other hand, relations are established with other stakeholders, so that the projects and programs are executed within different social environments to which the company has to adjust (McElroy & Mills, 2000). In order to adequately answer the challenges of a dynamic character of a project-oriented company, it is necessary to define a unique company identity that includes various projects and programs, and whose role is integrative. Such a project portfolio should support the objective and strategy of the company and simultaneously be flexible enough not to endanger the flexible character of the company. (Cooper & Edgett, 2001; Kerzner, 2003; Lyneis, Cooper & Els, 2001; Morris, 1997).

One of the most significant tasks that the project-oriented company's management has to accomplish prior to project or program execution is analysis of key stakeholders and project sponsors.

OVERVIEW OF PROJECT SPONSOR AND STAKEHOLDERS ANALYSIS

Analysis of Project Sponsor

Sponsorship in PM is a specific activity directed towards supplying the necessary technical, personnel, financial and other support to the project/program. (Bolles, 2002). The central position in these activities belongs to the project sponsor or patron, a senior manager of the company in charge of creating a necessary bond between the project execution and the senior management team. In addition, the project sponsor may act on behalf of the project owner, be it for internal or external projects (external project sponsor).

Project sponsorship may take different forms. Usually, the sponsor is not superior to the project manager, however exceptions are possible. Some forms of project sponsorships are as follows (Kerzner, 2003):

- **Individual sponsorship:** This approach includes the individual who will undertake the tasks of project sponsorship.
- **Twofold sponsorship:** Using two sponsors is an approach frequently used, especially when it is necessary to have a person familiar with technical characteristics of project execution.
- **Group (collective) sponsorship:** The group approach is meaningful in some situations and may take the form of a project council or a project board, which is in charge of the sponsorship task.

Characteristic activities of sponsorship in PM may include:

- Maintaining relations with internal and external environments
- Adjusting the project to the strategy, politics and procedures of the company
- Multiproject adjustment of the project at the company level together with the Project Management Office(PMO)
- Supplying the necessary resources for project execution
- Maintaining continual project financing
- Authority and responsibility delegation to the project manager
- Aid in identifying key indicators of success necessary to manage the project successfully
- Approving of or rejecting propositions for changes in the project scope, time, quality and costs

In order to be successful, the project sponsor must have the following qualities (Dinsmore, 2003):

- Interest in the project
- Knowledge and capability of strategic PM
- Ability to influence other managers and important groups
- Basic understanding of the technical aspects of the project
- Closeness with the project manager and the project team

The role of the project sponsor varies as regards the company tradition, the project nature, the sponsor's and the project manager's leadership styles. A powerful project manager with political support may need little support from the project sponsor. On the other hand, a less adjusted project manager with a newly formed team and a nontypical project may badly need a project sponsor's support.

The project sponsor's task is to support the project in all its execution phases (Dinsmore, 2003; Kerzner, 2003; Petrović, 2003):

- **At the beginning of the project:** Ensure that the project strategy, plans and control systems are carried out; provide support for project team composing; check whether the project has been started in an adequate way and whether the team is beginning to form; and ensure political coverage for the project during its execution.
- **As the project advances:** Participate in formal and periodical project checks; be available for support and consulting; track the reports on the project as it advances; and actively participate if the project changes course.
- **As the project nears completion:** Track the transition from the project to the operational implementation phase; stimulate quick project completion; and ensure that the lessons learned are documented.

Analysis of Project Stakeholders

Project stakeholders are the groups or individuals interested in the implementation of the project and can help accomplish the project successfully. Stakeholders have different expectations as to their position and role and the profit or benefit they will gain in the project execution.

It is for this reason that a thorough analysis of all relevant stakeholders is necessary, and it means identification, estimation of influence and a definition of the best ways to meet their interests.

The key project stakeholders are the following:

- **Project sponsor:** A person or group of persons who ensure the financial, personnel and other support for the project. In addition to this, the project sponsor frequently verifies the successful completion of the project.
- **Project team:** A group of persons, working on the execution of the project, who have complementary skills and certain knowledge and experience as regarding the actual project.
- **Management structure:** The managers of the permanent and the temporary organization within the project-oriented company, with special attention paid to those managers who control significant resources, since the PMO and other management structures often come into conflict with them, as a result of their disregarding the strategy and the priorities agreed upon.
- **The individuals and the groups that need not be directly related to the project, but upon whom the project *does exert influence*** to a smaller or a larger extent. This group also includes clients and ultimate users of the project.
- **The individuals and groups that *do influence the project*** to a smaller or a larger extent (politicians and political groups, busi-

ness partners, suppliers, etc). The analysis of this group of stakeholders is of extreme importance since certain groups outside the project/company possess power and position to slow down or even stop the project.

- **Public and other interest groups** (local authorities, NGO, media, etc.) **that influence public opinion**.
- **Other companies and organizations that execute the same or similar projects** or are competitors in some other manner.
- **Institutes, professional associations and other specialized institutions interested in the project execution**, especially in circumstances where the project is to be executed following the procedures or documents prescribed by these stakeholders.

Each stakeholder has his/her own attitude towards the project. These attitudes may often stand in opposition one another and result in conflict. The skill of managing stakeholders is actually in the ability to anticipate possible problems and conflicts, as well as to create alternative strategies in order to gain again the stakeholders' support. Of course, it is easier by far to manage conflicts in the early phases of project execution; therefore, special attention in the project preparation phase should be directed towards the reactions and attitudes of key stakeholders.

Both theory and practice have developed different techniques for project stakeholder analysis, called stakeholder mapping techniques (Milosevic, 2003). Mendelow (1981) developed the environment analysis model based on the stakeholder management concept that includes dynamic environment analysis and the stakeholders' influence upon the organization or the project. According to this author, the basis of stakeholders' power concerning the project lies in the interaction between the stakeholders and the environment. His model is presented by a graph with the basic dimensions of authority and dynamism, where the authority ranges from low to high and the values for dynamism range from static to dynamic. The static environment points to a small probability of change in the stakeholders' authority, while the dynamic environment allows for changes in the ways stakeholders influence the project through changes in the source of power (Jovanovic et al., 2005).

Johnson and Scholes (1999) altered and adapted the previous model and changed the dynamism dimension, renaming it interest level (McElroy & Mills, 2000; Winch & Bonke, 2002). They created an authority/interest matrix that analyzes the answer to the following questions:

- To what extent is each group of stakeholders interested in the expected project decisions and project results?
- Do stakeholder groups plan certain actions and do they possess the authority to carry them out?

By grouping the stakeholders into the authority/interest matrix, the top management and project managers can get a clearer insight into the influence of the stakeholder communication and interaction on the project and its implementation.

On the basis of the authority/interest matrix, Winch and Bonke (2002) developed a "stakeholder map" that analyzes stakeholders' influence in various phases of project implementation. The stakeholder map includes:

- Stakeholders classed as supporters and opponents of the project
- Problems identified by the stakeholders
- Solutions stakeholders proposed to overcome the identified problems

The stakeholder map, combined with executed project decisions, that is, project results executed, serve as basis for creating the tools for assessing the performance and success of the overall procedure of managing stakeholders.

MANAGING PROJECT STAKEHOLDERS THROUGH THE PORTAL

Portal Types and Architecture

There are basic core functions that any portal must provide, such as aggregation, personalization, search, collaboration and security. The exact level of functionality of these core services may vary among different types of portals. Portals can be classed into two large groups: public Internet portals and corporate portals. The corporate portals include private portals and portals open to public.

There is a fundamental and clearly identifiable difference between public Internet portals and publicly accessible corporate portals, based on the business model used to provide an unambiguous and consistent demarcation between the two types.

Since public Internet portals cover such a broad spectrum of general-interest topics and services, they are sometimes referred to as horizontal portals. By this definition, corporate portals become vertical portals, or vortals, since their focus is narrow and confined to their specific business goals.

A corporate portal offers content aggregation, content syndication, search services, collaboration schemes and access to applications, including Web services (Guruge, 2003). Content aggregation, in this context, is the assimilation of information from diverse sources according to the personalization criteria from the target user and the presentation of it in the form of a navigable Web page, replete with title bars, edit buttons and scrolling controls. Content syndication permits diverse data from external sources, in multiple formats, to be dovetailed into a corporate portal's overall framework in a consistent and systematic manner. A powerful and smart search capability is a prerequisite for a good corporate portal.

Collaboration and application accesses are the other two key features of a representative corporate portal. These functions are made possible by the XML platform and Web services. What distinguishes Web services and makes them so popular today is their independence from the hardware and software platform that is used. They can be used and built on any hardware platform, operation system and in any programming language. This is achieved by detaching the interface from the implementation of the Web service, which further allows applications based on them to be loosely linked, component-oriented and present implementations of different technologies.

At a minimum, functionality for a core portal must include (Guruge, 2003):

- Interface to the Web
- User interface management (i.e., presentation services)
- External data access mechanisms
- data management services
- Security, authentication and personalization
- Portal development tools
- Portal administration and management tools

PM Portal Model

PM portals include extranet or intranet corporative portals. They represent developed user applications, completely integrated into the Web environment. Their basic function is the centralization of all project information with an aim to work out and publish quality project documentation, to allow for collaboration and the sharing ideas and information related to the project by project teams and their members' collaboration, and to create easier management and tracking of certain project aspects, such as risk, time, budget, resources and so forth.

The PM portals supply the centralization and coordination of project activities, which is a primary function of the PMO. It is for this reason that in the last few years the use of PM portals has been increasing in numerous companies that carry out various, complex and often geographically distant projects, that is, possess a developed project organization, based on the implementation of the PMO and on the application of temporary organizational structures (projects and programs) (Block & Frame, 2001).

One of the basic ideas is that through PM portals the key stakeholders in the project may have an easy access to the necessary information and be informed in a timely fashion of any relevant changes and news concerning the project. Also, the management of the project-oriented company is in a position to obtain a global picture of the projects or programs under way; at the same time, team members may have an insight into the extent to which the project they are engaged in is executed, that is, into the engagement dynamics and the disposition of responsibilities (Figure 1).

As more PM responsibility is delegated to nonPM personnel, the audience for PM tools is growing. In the light of this, what is still lacking in many projects is an easy means of providing information to various project participants in an easy-to-use, timely manner, while still providing the necessary control for secure access.

The PM portal, integrated with scheduling applications, provides a powerful solution to stakeholders' needs. Through a common interface, team members can submit progress in a timely manner (accessible from anywhere that has Internet access); project managers can rapidly verify progress and update schedules; and all project participants can access the very latest status information in a controlled environment.

According to the Giga Information Group Inc. four key PM portal requirements are (Visitacion, 2003):

- **Project access and information integration:** Gathering and distributing information in a timely manner
- **Project team collaboration:** Providing a means for project stakeholders to communicate and share information
- **Project support tools integration:** Integration of both data and systems within a project
- **Information delivery:** Providing best practice content

In order for a PM portal to be useful it also needs to include several important characteristics:

Figure 1. PM portal model

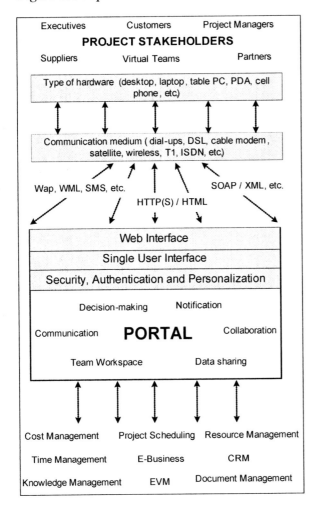

- Ease of use
- Extendibility
- Customizable interface
- Open architecture
- Controlled access

One of the best ways to evaluate a portal solution is to look at the overall benefits of the portal to each department and user group within an organization (Patterson, 2002).

Project Teams
- Enter progress updates through the portal, speeding up the re-planning process
- View real-time reports of work to be performed and live project activities, helping to improve efficiency
- Access project information from disparate sources
- Improve team performance through greater collaboration and communication
- Enable "work anywhere" structures

Project Managers
- Centralize management and control of projects
- Access real-time reports for easier analysis
- Identify potential delays more easily, allowing corrective action to be taken in a timely manner
- Share information and communicate with distributed teams
- Approve team members' progress and update schedule quickly and easily
- Achieve greater project visibility with team and stakeholders
- Build communities around projects and pool expertise

Executives
- Access real-time reports and high-level dashboard indicators

- Monitor project health and status
- reduce project costs and improve time-to-market due to improved efficiency
- Lower cost of ownership and reduce training needs
- Improve knowledge management and project repeatability

Suppliers/Partners/Customers
- Access real-time status reports remotely
- Share information

PM Software Package as Portal

PM software has evolved steadily over the past 20 years with applications growing from stand-alone "person-to-data" systems to today's Web-based "people-to-people" systems.

Portal software is not a new concept. When portals first emerged in the mid-1990s, they were used to consolidate corporate Web sites. Since 1998, they have grown rapidly in user acceptance as a way to improve communications and collaboration across the company, particularly in PM (Seltzer, 1999).

Enterprise PM software packages represent an important component of the PM portal, one that allows for the execution of modern concepts in the multiproject environment, such as program management, virtual PM, managing by projects and so forth. The implementation of these software packages ensures an integrated management of complex projects and collaboration of key project stakeholders. Here will be presented the Microsoft project enterprise model for PM.

The core components of Microsoft's project workgroup collaboration and enterprise PM are as follows (Stover, 2004):

- **Project professional:** This software is the origin of all project data, including tasks, resources, assignments, scheduling dates, costs and tracking information. The Microsoft project database stores all project information managed from the project professional. Through the Microsoft project database, the project professional interfaces with project server.

- **Project server:** This is essentially a server and database custom-designed to convert data to and from the project plan and to an interface with project Web access, using that data. The project server database stores information related to security settings, administrative settings and all other information related to the project Web access. The project server is a separate application containing business logic and functionality to process this data.

- **Project Web access:** This is a Web site with unique capabilities to work specifically with the project server and display targeted project data. It is a view into the project server. This Web site typically lives on the company's intranet and is accessed by project team members via some type of user authentication.

With information on the organization type and the projects under way, it is possible to integrate some additional components into the model:

- Windows SharePoint Services
- Microsoft Outlook
- Active Directory

If the project server is integrated with Windows SharePoint Services, there are three more collaboration features available in the project Web access:

- Document control
- Risk management
- Issues tracking

Documents, risks and issues can be added, tracked, linked with tasks, assigned and eventually closed. These all become an important aspect of managing the project as well as capturing important project archival information for use in planning future projects.

The typical stakeholders included into the enterprise PM model are (Stover, 2004):

- Project manager
- Resource manager
- Team lead
- Team member
- Executive
- Portfolio manager
- Administrator

It is important to note that one stakeholder may have several roles, which depend on the complexity of the organization and the projects, as well as on the architecture of the PM model implemented.

A successful implementation of the standard model of the MS Project group collaboration and the corporate PM means there must be an identification of users, access permissions and defining project responsibilities. In this sense, each of the abovementioned groups is assigned a respective security frame that includes a set of different access permissions.

RELATIONS BETWEEN E-PROJECTS AND PM PORTALS

E-business has become a desired objective of nearly every company and rarely is there a company that does not plan to see part of its future activities within this segment. Today a large number of new business ventures and ideas executed are either directly related to e-business or contain a segment that includes the characteristics and elements of e-business.

The emergence of e-business has triggered the development of entirely new branches that were previously unknown (e-shopping, e-banking, e-insurance, e-health, etc.), as well as the emergence of new organizational units within companies, such as an e-business department, an e-business inovation center and so forth. In this sense, we can say that there is a special project category—e-business project (Stoehr, 2002).

The number of e-projects increases every year, and consequently there is also an increase in the number of companies providing e-business solutions. A successful execution of these projects is often a precondition for a business success of the companies that perceive that it is e-business that their strategic advantage lies in. After the initial delight as a response to Internet development, however, today's views of e-business are more realistic; optimism is moderate and in accord with the reality.

The creation of e-projects has led to a dilemma: in which way are e-projects to be managed?; what are the most appropriate approaches in defining and execution of these projects?; and what knowledge is required in order to carry out e-business projects successfully? Although there is a widespread attitude that these are IT projects, e-business projects differ from classic IT projects by many characteristics (Shields, 2001; Stoehr, 2002).

The basis of e-business projects is Web and the Internet use; they are very dynamic in content; they are executed in a short period of time; and the teams are multidisciplinary, since the project's success is often related to sociological factors, rather than to technology. Contrary to classic IT projects, the project's scope is often ambiguous at the beginning, and the change in scope is one of the main features of these projects. E-business projects also are characterized by different types of objectives than the e-business solution has to achieve (objectives related to IT, marketing, finances, etc.), including a wide range of future e-business solution users (options such as logistics for different languages or adapting to cultural differences are almost compulsory) and application of the latest technological solutions (McMahon, 2000; Shields, 2001).

On the other hand, expectations for e-business projects are often too big and unrealistic, especially from the aspect of project duration and cost. When the e-business solution will be available to the public is a critical factor in the success of many projects. Introducing e-business solutions often requires that the company's work methods be changed. Sometimes companies are not aware of this, but a successful implementation of e-business solutions is a consequence of the change in the previous work methods. Participants in the e-business projects' execution are expected to excel in IT skills, be creative, be competent in fields such as marketing, sales, finances and so forth, and be willing to adapt to changes in the course of the project's execution. (Mihić & Petrović, 2004)

PM portals provide a powerful support for execution of e-business projects. They allow participants to communicate and coordinate any activities required in the execution of e-business projects. PM portals also allow individuals not directly included in the e-PM, but who are indispensable in the successful execution of the project, to be adequately included in the operation. PM portals provide timely and protected access to information to all the participants in the e-business project. The possibility of information integration, on one hand, and the adaptation and personalization of the approach to the data, on the other hand, are key advantages to PM portals in e-PM.

The execution of e-business projects by means of PM-portal support allows for an intensive collaboration and communication among all the participants in the project. The structure of the group included in e-business projects is often very heterogeneous (expert pools, for example) and geographically spread out, and they need to collaborate virtually in real time (DeMarie,

2000; McMahon, 2000). Similarly, PM portals make it possible for insight into all the activities and projects carried out in accord with the company's e-business strategy, as well as the relations between individual projects and their influence upon the achievement of the company's objectives in real time.

All of this leads to the conclusion that e-projects are not only a type of IT project but much more than an IT project. The successful execution of e-projects, therefore, requires an adequate use of PM knowledge. Managing e-projects can be characterized by the implementation of classic PM knowledge and skills, as well as the application of specific knowledge of e-projects. The PM portal should play a key role in the implementation of an adequate PM and an adequate linking of all the participants in these projects' execution.

SOCIAL AND CULTURAL ASPECTS OF TEAMWORK THROUGH PORTALS

The trends contributing to an ever stronger demand for forming virtual teams are as follows (Goncalves, 2005, Stoehr, 2002):

- Globalization
- Strategic alliances
- Telecommunications
- Downsizing
- Trend of outsourcing

The abovementioned are strongly supported in analyses by Visitacion (2003) and the Cutter Consortium (2005) in which the following is given:

- Fifty percent of new software projects are Web based.
- Twenty percent of them are critical.
- Thirty-one percent of an organization's IT budget is spent on Web projects.

- Ninty-five percent of these projects are to be accomplished "within a year."

The sociocultural aspect of team work is a very significant component, since the team members generally execute the planned activities independently. The basic factors of a successful team as regards the sociocultural aspects are as follows:

- Nonexistence of a direct authority
- Limited social interaction
- Team members organizationally competent
- Time management as the most important skill
- Self-motivation of team members
- Concentration upon the task, regardless of the physical distance from the team members

In recruiting the virtual team, human resources must consider the character traits of candidates. These men and women should have independent personalities; be creative in view of designing e-conditions of work (PM portals, e-conferences, Web forums, PM software packages, etc.); be goal setters; be oriented to solving problems independently; and able to work under pressure (Mihić & Petrović, 2004).

According to Goncalves' research (2005), the basic tasks accomplished by virtual teams as a percentage of their participation in the project manager's working hours are as follows:

- Business relations and communication with clients (35%)
- Defining, planning and organization of the project (25%)
- Measuring progress and quality control (15%)
- Coordination and communication within the team (10%)
- Technical problems solving (10%)

- Managing virtual working environment (5%)

The data show that the project manager pays considerably more attention to communication with clients in comparison to communication with team members and other stakeholders. This may lead to problems in communication, alienation among the team members, loss of team spirit and the synergy effect, which is one of the most important cohesive factors, regardless of the type of the team.

The basic advantages of virtual teams that coordinate their work via portals are the flexibility of access; the possibility of a choice of the extent to which the stakeholders will be included in the work of the team; the creation of so-called knowledge tanks; and the establishment of contacts that go beyond the limits of time and space. The disadvantages are generally reflected in the language and culture barriers. Problems related to words, accents or ways of expressing oneself are successfully solved by use of electronic translators. These have proved to be a more efficient and less expensive means of communication, when compared to language courses and training interpreters. The understanding of messages' context is a much greater problem than knowledge of foreign languages. The dialogue between different cultural groups allows for mutual understanding, thereby coming to a consensus about a common frame of work that is flexible enough to give credit to each member of the team (Kimble, Feng, & Barlow, 2000).

CONCLUSION AND FUTURE TRENDS

In this chapter we analyzed the project stakeholders and the possibilities of enhancing the efficiency of their coordination and communication via PM portals as e-solutions to integration and information sharing. PM portals provide all project par-

ticipants with a secure, Web-based environment that they can use to collaborate, access project information and stay up-to-date on the project's status. Project portals can dramatically improve communication within project teams and raise project visibility to stakeholders.

PM packages make an integral component of PM portals. Their main role is to estimate project parameters and monitor and report on the execution of the project. In addition, their implementation allows for the integration and sharing of project information (project portfolio, risks, quality, documentation, etc.) in a Web environment, which provides independent solutions to managing project stakeholders.

A special challenge in IT implementation is represented by the human factor, that is, the work of virtual teams, integration of the employees into the new environment as well as their potential for adopting the change. Therefore, regardless of the quality of the IT solution implemented, the final success in achieving an efficient e-PM system will depend upon the sociocultural aspects of the organization and the teams engaged in the direct preparation and execution of organizational projects.

In discussing the implementation of IT solutions in project collaboration and support, attention should be paid to the future trends that, on one hand, include an ever-expanding implementation of the PMO concept as means to integrate e-PM into the organization on the operational and strategic levels, while, on the other hand, they mean a dynamic growth in ICT technologies in the years to come. The companies whose employees efficiently adapt to the dynamic development of modern technologies are certainly in an advanced position, therefore an increasing importance is expected to be assigned to education and trainings in the fields of PM portal and PM software solutions, as well as to the human aspects of organizational change initiated by the e-PM implementation.

REFERENCES

Archibald, D. R. (2003). *Managing high-technology programs and projects.* New York: John Wiley & Sons.

Block, T. R., & Frame J. D. (2001). Today's project office: Gauging attitudes. *PM Network, 15*(08), 50-53.

Bolles, D. (2002). *Building project management centers of excellence.* New York: AMACOM

Burke, W. (2002). *Organization change: Theory and practice.* London: Sage Publications.

Cooper, R. G., & Edgett, S. J. (2001). *Portfolio management for new products.* Ancaster, Canada: Product Development Institute.

Crawford, J. K., (2002). *The strategic project office: A guide to improving organizational performance.* New York: Marcel Dekker.

Cutter Consortium. (2005). Retrieved from http://www.cutter.com

DeMarie, S. M. (2000). *Using virtual teams to manage complex projects: A case study of the radioactive waste management project.* Department of Management, College of Business, Iowa State University.

Dinsmore, C. P. (1993). *The AMA handbook of project management.* New York: AMACOM.

Dinsmore, C. P, Englund, R. L, & Graham, J. R. (2003). *Creating the project office: A manager's guide to leading organizational change.* San Francisco: Jossey-Bass.

Gareis, R., (2002). *PM Baseline, version 1.0.* Wien, Austria: PMA.

Gareis, R. (2003). *Competencies in the project-oriented organization.* Paper presented at the IPMA World Congress, Moscow, Russia.

Goncalves, M. (2005). *Managing virtual projects.* New York: McGraw-Hill.

Guruge, A. (2003). *Corporate portals.* Digital Press, Elsevier Science.

Ives, M. (2005). Identifying the contextual elements of project management within organizations and their impact on project success. *Project Management Journal, 36*(1), 37-50.

Jick, T., & Peiperl, M. (2003). Managing change—Cases and concepts. New York: McGraw-Hill.

Johnson, G., & Scholes, K. (1999). *Exploring corporate strategy.* London: Prentice Hall.

Jovanovic, P. (2004). *Project management, faculty of organizational sciences.* Belgrade.

Jovanovic, P., Mihic, M., & Petrovic, D. (2005). *Relation between project power and project management maturity model.* Paper presented at the IPMA World Congress, New Delhi, India

Kerzner, H. (2003). *Project management* (8th ed.). NJ: John Wiley & Sons.

Kimble, C., Li, F., & Barlow, A. (2000). *Effective virtual teams through communities of practice.* Strathclyde Business School.

Kloppenborg, T., & Opfer, W. (2002). The current state of project management research: Trends, interpretations and predictions. *Project Management Journal, 33*(2), 5-18.

Lyneis, J. M., Cooper, K. G., & Els, S. A. (2001). Strategic management of complex projects: A case study using system dynamics. *System Dynamics Review, 17*(3), 237-260.

McElroy, B., & Mills, C. (2000). Managing stakeholders. editors In R. Turner & S. Simister, *Gover handbook of project management* (pp. 757-775). Gower Publishing Limited.

McMahon, P. E. (2000). *Virtual project management: Software solutions for today and the future.* New York: CRC Press.

Mendelow, A. (1981). Environmental scanning: The impact of stakeholder concept. *Paper presented at the II International Conference on Information Systems*, Cambridge, UK.

Mihić, M., & Petrović, D. (2004). Project-oriented managers—Results of the new approach to managers education. *Paper presented at the International Scientific Days*, Nitra, Slovak Republic.

Miles, R. H. (1997). *Leading corporate transformation*. San Francisco: Jossey-Bass Publishers.

Milosevic, D. (2003). *Project management toolbox*. NJ: John Wiley & Sons.

Miranda, E. (2003). Running the successful hi-tech project office. Boston: Artech House.

Morris, W. G. P. (1997). *The management of projects*. London: Thomas Telford.

Patterson, D. (2002). Using project management portals to integrate and share project information [white paper]. WST Corporation.

Petrović, D. (2003). *The concept of multiproject management in company*. Belgrade, Serbia: FON.

Ramachandran, S. (2005). *Effect of cultural protocols on media choice in global virtual teams*. San Antonio: Department of Information Systems, The University of Texas.

Seltzer, L. (1999). The virtual office. *PC Magazine, 18*(18), 150-164.

Shields, M. G. (2001). *E-business and ERP: Rapid implementation and project planning*. NY: John Wiley & Sons.

Stoehr, T. (2002). *Managing e-business projects*. Berlin: Springer.

Stover, T. (2004). *Microsoft office project 2003 inside out*. Redmond: Microsoft Press.

Visitacion, M. (2003). *Project management best practices: Key processes and common sense*. Giga Information Group Inc.

Winch, G., & Bonke, S. (2002). Project stakeholder mapping: Analyzing the interests of project stakeholders. In *The frontiers of project management research* (PMI chapter 23).

Wysocki, K. R. (2004). *Project management process improvement*. Boston: Artech House.

Chapter X
B2C Failures:
Toward an Innovation Theory Framework

Anil M. Pandya
Northeastern Illinois University, USA

Nikhilesh Dholakia
University of Rhode Island, USA

ABSTRACT

Using the product and services innovation failures literature, this chapter develops a framework to help understand why so many Internet-based business-to-consumer (B2C) "dot-com" companies failed to fulfill their initial promise. Viewed collectively, B2C dot.com crashes constitute an initial wave of failure of an entirely new class of technology-driven services. Such services sought to inform, promote, sell and deliver B2C items in radically unfamiliar ways. Besides ignoring basic precepts of sound business practice, unsuccessful B2C firms failed to realize they were marketing innovative services. We place B2C dot-com ventures on a continuum of need-solution context of innovations, in conjunction with the notion that seller/buyer perceptions about the scope of innovations are not necessarily concordant. Matched perceptions between sellers and buyers lead to success. Sellers as well as buyers, however, can misjudge the nature and scope of innovations. Using case evidence, the chapter illustrates the explanatory power of the framework and contributes to e-commerce issues by clarifying why, despite resource availability, many early B2C firms failed due to misjudged perceptions of sellers and/or buyers.

INTRODUCTION

The social impact of the so-called "dot-com crash" was enormous. Vast amounts of market capitaliza-tion was wiped out; thousands of highly skilled workers were left jobless; and consumers and media were turned into scathing skeptics about the promises of information technology (IT).

Perhaps most insidiously, the pillars of modern faith in the power of scientific and technological innovation were corroded—beyond repair in some cases.

This chapter proposes a framework to help understand why so many Internet-based B2C companies failed to fulfill their initial promise. B2C dot-com crashes represent special types of innovation failures. Our analysis shows that the class of innovation called "B2C e-commerce," in its initial incarnation, was flawed.

With increasing cost pressures, there is increasing reliance on consumers' interactions with technology to create services instead of receiving services from live employees (Zeithaml, Bitner, & Gremler, 2006). Most B2C dot-com firms were geared to be such technology-based service provision firms (Pandya & Dholakia, 2005).

Marketing literature calls this new class of service technologies self-service technologies (SSTs) (Bitner, 2001). Across a wide range of industries and applications, it has been found that consumers have strong feelings about SSTs: consumers love SSTs when they work and hate them intensely when they fail (Meuter, Ostram, Roundtree, & Bitner, 2000).

Chances of service failure are high in new services, especially in SSTs service delivery models of B2C firms (Pandya & Dholakia, 2005). What irked customers the most were SST failures in terms of downed Web sites, shipping delays or failures; Web sites that were difficult to navigate and maneuver, having to use a plethora of usernames and passwords; and inadequate "recovery" efforts by B2C providers when failures occurred (Bitner, 2001; Meuter et al., 2000). For B2C firms to succeed, the service delivery elements had to be smoother and simpler than the interpersonal services that these SSTs substituted—in many cases, it was the opposite (Pandya & Dholakia, 2005). Our framework shows how difficult this task can be as it entails creating perceptual concordance between suppliers and buyers.

In B2C settings, consumers balance the cost of time and effort, against services received, and make judgments about service quality (Berry, Seiders, & Grewal, 2002) and its continued use. In such an environment, service quality depends on: (1) the perceptions about the service quality and (2) the gap between the perception of the service and the experience of the delivered service (Brady & Cronin, 2001). Services are high in experience and credence qualities, and consumer evaluations of the actual experience relative to the perception of the service is critical to the purchase and repurchase decision (Zeithaml & Bitner, 2003; Zeithaml et al., 2006), which are central to the profitable operation of e-commerce firms. According to a high-technology product innovation research stream, two factors shape perceived vs. expected performance in innovative high-tech decisions: (1) the need-solution context of innovations (Leonard-Barton, Wilson, & Doyle, 1995) and (2) the congruence of perceptions between technology innovators and technology consumers (Rangan & Bartus, 1995).

In this chapter, we propose that in the initial wave of B2C service innovations, buyers and sellers marched down divergent paths. Technology innovators and sellers saw B2C technologies as being capable of radically exceeding buyers' expectations, while buyers saw B2C innovations as relatively inconvenient ways of performing familiar shopping tasks. Many B2C firms in the first wave focused more attention on marketing and front-end technology and less on timely delivery and customer satisfaction. The results were persistently high customer acquisition costs without sufficient revenues (Agarwal, Arjona, & Lemmens, 2001; Barsh, Blair, & Grosso, 2001). Research confirms that most B2C firms failed to adhere to these conventional management principles (Agarwal et al., 2001; Barsh et al., 2001; Varianini & Vaturi, 2000). Thus, we ask: Why did so many firms with resources and talents fail to use time-honored management principles? What was it about this new technology and service delivery method that these managers misread? We argue that the firms failed to realize they were dealing with a new innovative services management situation, which needed a new orientation (Achrol & Kotler, 1999). And as we argue later in the chapter, the innovative technology required B2C firms to alter their view of business-customer relations. We develop a framework to show how an innovation context can lead to problems of concordance of perceptions between buyers and sellers. Managers have to figure out how to navigate this maze of perceptions to be successful.

The chapter is organized as follows. The next section examines the scope of the B2C failure problem and reflects on some early diagnoses of it. The section that follows presents the proposed innovation theory-based framework and provides illustrative evidence. The concluding section draws together the main arguments and makes recommendations for managers and researchers.

SCOPE OF THE B2C PROBLEM

B2C e-commerce failure was a system-wide failure. It was not the case where a few managers in a few start-up firms made poor judgment calls. The finding that managers of these firms failed to follow well-known management truths (costs cannot consistently exceed revenues; pricing correctly is critical; acquisition costs must decline; or customer loyalty and customer services are important for long-term success [Agarwal al., 2001; Barsh et al., 2000; Baker, Lin, Marn, & Zawada, 2001; Marn, 2000; Varianini & Vaturi, 2000]) is important and necessary but not in itself sufficient. Incompetence is not a satisfactory answer when a large number of firms fail. This section first describes the enormity of the B2C failure, followed by a brief review of the empirical findings from a careful look at the B2C failures. This discussion sets the stage for

our contribution and develops our framework to address the question of why these managers in all these firms failed.

The Size of the Crash

The B2C market crash was massive and economically destabilizing. It wiped out billions of dollars of market capitalization and led to huge loss of employment. Between 1995 and 2000, a total of 492 Internet-related companies raised $36.3 billion in capital in the public markets. By 2000, just 11% of these companies were trading at prices greater than their offer price. A third of them were trading below 80% of the offer price. In 1999, 230 initial public offerings (IPOs) raised $18.2 billion. In 2000, 130 IPOs were offered and raised $12.8 billion, but 133 IPOs, representing $10.4 billion, were withdrawn from the market. The market capitalization of the Internet sector in 1999 was $881 billion. This plunged to $208 billion by December 2000 (Anderson, 2001). Layoffs in the industry in the year 2000 were 4,805 in September, 5,677 in October and, by December, the total layoffs stood at 22,267. Unemployment reached 700,000 for the year 2001 (Corcoran, 2002; Rock, 2000). Table 1 shows profiles of some of the B2C firms that failed during the 1999-2000 period.

Preliminary Diagnosis

In most B2C debacles, there was persistent discrepancy between high customer acquisition costs and low revenues. In early 1999, B2C companies spent more than $1,100 to acquire a typical customer, who spent only $400. In late 1999, the average cost of customer acquisition reduced to $800, but customer spending remained at or below $400. The average monthly losses per B2C site were $1 million and $1.1 million, respectively, in the first and second half of 1999, despite the reduction in customer acquisition costs (Agarwal et al., 2001).

As supplemental revenue sources, B2C Web sites relied on subscription fees and advertising. But by the end of 1999, advertising revenue per visitor had declined from about $1 to 50 cents, and the rates charged to advertisers had declined between 3% and 12%. Among the content providers, fewer than 10% were garnering subscription revenues in late 1999 (Agarwal et al., 2001).

In the false hope that the Internet was a price-elastic market, many B2C businesses maintained low margins. However, in reality, instead of clicking across multiple sites, 80 to 90% of buyers of books and CDs visited only one site, even though prices of books and CDs across Web sites varied by as much as 25 to 30%. Online shopping habits varied by product category. The percent of buyers who bought from their first purchase Web site were 89% for books, 84% for toys, 81% for music, 76% for electronics, 65% for computers and 55% for travel (Jupiter Media Metrix as reported in Baker et al., 2001). Only 8% of Internet shoppers were found to be bargain hunters (Forsyth, Lavoie, & Mcguire, 2000). Hence it appears that in this segment of the B2C market, instead of deep discounting, astute firms could have charged higher prices without sacrificing revenues and profits (Marn, 2000). Baker et al. (2001) argued that e-commerce companies should maintain their prices within the consumer's pricing-indifference band, which varied between 0.2% for personal loans to 17% for branded health and beauty products.

Table 1. Examples of B2C failures in 1999-2000

B2C firm	Internet business	Lifespan	Status	Failure date
Redrocket.com	Nickelodeon's toy sales site	January 1995-May 5, 2000	Acquired by Viacom in 1999	May 2000
BBQ.Com	Grilled meats and sauces	June 15, 1999-May 15, 2000	Standing as Barbequemall.com	May 2000
DEN	Digital Entertainment Network	1996-May 17, 2000	Investment $50 million; $75 million IPO shelved	May 2000
Toysmart.com	Smart "good" (not destructive or faddish) toys. Encouraged parents to "click on your child's potential."	January 22, 1999-May 19, 2000.	Controlling interest by Disney in August 2000 with $50 million investment.	Disney stopped support
Pixelon	Investment scam	1996-August 2000.	Bilked $30 million from investors. Promoter lived in his car. Spent half the capital on launch.	Turned himself over to the police
Pop.com	Received $50 million from Paul Allen of Microsoft.	The 80-employee content site never launched	The site—backed by Steven Spielberg, Jeffrey Katzenberg, David Giffen, Ron Howard and Brian Grazer—burned $18 million.	Closed 14 days prior to the launch
Pseudo.com	Streaming media	1994-September 18, 20000	Received $18 million in 1999 and $14 million in spring of 2000	With 10 channels chasing 10 different genres and with streaming rich-media content across broadband, Pseudo could not establish its core audience
Ingredients.com	The company developed and manufactured personal-care products for Web distribution.	1998-October 2000	Received $4.5 million in funding	Many beauty sites; competition from major brands and lack of originality or funding saw to its demise

Only a small but solid group of companies managed to achieve visitor conversion rates of 12%, customer churn rates below 20% and repeat purchase rates of around 60% (Agarwal et al., 2001). Online prices for hot products like video games and luxury cars were found to be 17 to 45% higher than off-line prices. Some business-savvy companies increased their revenue and profits by understanding supply–and-demand conditions. One electronic supplier increased profits by 25% (Baker et al., 2001). The majority of the B2C failures, however, were caused by "fatal attraction": luring visitors to the site but failing to convert them into customers (Agarwal et al., 2001). Successful firms generated nearly three times the gross income from repeat customers as from onetime buyers. This difference in performance was the result of superior skills in acquiring (keeping the customer acquisition cost low), converting (keeping the purchase process simple) and retaining customers (making operational execution satisfactorily reliable, i.e., sites download quickly, on-time delivery and ease of return or exchange of purchases). Additionally, the successful companies followed the tried-and-true principles from the brick-and-mortar world: (1) focus on core product or service propositions that fit the needs of well-defined customer segments; (2) control extensions of product lines and business models, and focus on the core products; and (3) avoid "bleeding-edge technologies" (i.e., leading but unproven technologies) and focus on basic product presentation features, customer service tools and logistics.

In short, to be successful, a firm must find its natural customers efficiently, offer them what they want and deliver it reliably (Agarwal et al., 2001).

B2C Internet businesses were hemorrhaging money because they failed to follow basic marketing principles. When electronic commerce was young, it seemed that marketing expertise could be cast aside. A speedy grab for a large share of the market with the aim of getting as many visitors as possible to the site became the immediate objective. It was assumed, falsely by most B2C firms, that at some stage these visitors would translate into profitable repeat customers (Varianini & Vaturi, 2000).

Collectively, these findings confirm that most B2C firms failed to adhere to conventional management principles of efficiency and consumer focus. This raises important questions: Why did so many firms with so much talent and easy access to capital (some profiled in Table 1) fail to use time-tested management principles? Why did they fail to realize that managing a B2C e-commerce required acumen similar to that required in the conventional brick-and-mortar world? What was it about this new technology and service delivery method that most B2C managers misread? Why could these companies not convert visitors into profitable and loyal customers? The following section addresses these questions.

Toward Innovation Theory-Based Diagnosis

The Internet implies a revolutionary shift in marketing approach. From being agents of the seller, B2C firms have to become agents of the buyer (Achrol & Kotler, 1999). The Internet allows B2C firms to get close to their customers in ways not possible before. For the first time, these firms can represent buyers to the producers of goods, rather than the other way around. They can figure out what their customers want and communicate that demand to the producers. B2C firms failed to appreciate this change and did not quite grasp that their business represented a radical service innovation, not a new technology business. Additionally, they were offering known products to customers in a new, more convenient and faster way than what was possible before. This new service concept emerged from the new technology but that is not the whole story. Old retail knowledge about assessing demand, buying, creating an assortment, managing inventory, developing displays, managing supplier relationships and improving delivery technology has to be seamlessly integrated to create a satisfied customer. This subtle, but strategic, shift in perspective could have refocused B2C managerial efforts from being preoccupied with the new technology and market share dominance to providing consistently high-quality customer service and convenience, geared towards fostering buyer loyalty and customer retention. While acknowledging that many B2C firms strayed from simple and conventional—but nonetheless vital and relevant—management principles, we present a theory-based framework to capture some of the additional underlying complexity of B2C failures and to identify ingredients for B2C success.

INNOVATION THEORY-BASED FRAMEWORK AND EVIDENCE

The classical theory of innovation diffusion suggests that, to be widely adopted, innovations must be compatible with existing habits, provide incentives to change, and pose low physical, social, economic and psychological risks to adopters. Overlaying this set of barriers is the inherent difficulty of maintaining consistent service quality, which becomes important at the back end of a B2C operation. At the front end, not all customers are equally savvy about technology, so their involvement can lead to frustration when it comes to navigating Web sites. Thus B2C managers face serious problems involving customer perceptions and behavior change when purchasing goods on the Internet. The service quality model well known in the services marketing literature identifies four gaps: (1) not knowing what customers expect; (2) not knowing the right service design and standards; (3) not delivering to standards; and (4) not matching performance to standards (Zeithaml & Bitner, 2003; Zeithaml et al., 2006). While these approaches are insightful, they do not fully address the problems that B2C technology innovations pose to sellers as well as buyers. We

argue that, in part, B2C firms failed because they failed to perceive correctly the nature and scope of their innovation. This eventually led to the problems of matching consumer expectations as the context of innovation changed. This is particularly important in the context of high-technology innovations, where the question of the precedence of technology voice or customer voice remains a contested issue. We extend the current discussion on innovations, combine high-technology product development literature and present a new framework to show an additional dimension of difficulty regarding perceptual problems created by the nature and scope of the innovation itself. Our model explores the problem of concordance and discordance between buyers and sellers about the innovation in different innovative contexts. Our model adds texture and substance to the theory of diffusion and service quality model in the context of technology innovation.

Viewing the Initial B2C Wave as Innovation

As a global concept, B2C represents a major innovation in the way marketing is done. It offers goods and services to consumers through the Internet. It reduces search costs. It is convenient, quick, easily accessible and less expensive. In this sense, it is a "new service innovation" for consumers as well as the world. When firms offer traditional products, such as books, CDs, groceries and toys, via the Internet, they are not merely marketing known products to known customers. Instead they are offering fast, highly competitive, interactive and technologically facilitated means of information access and transaction. Using such means, consumers are able to shop from home or the office, make comparisons and receive door-to-door service at a price they consider reasonable. The failure of B2C firms thus can be construed as a failure of an entirely new class of Internet-mediated service, not just a failure of the particular firms involved (Pandya & Dholakia, 2005).

Conceptually, therefore, the B2C debacle needs to be seen as a failure of a new service product. Putting this observation into the overall context of innovation research, however, it is evident that this experience is not unique. Failure rates of new products generally continue to be as high as 95% (Brown & Eisenhardt, 1995). When viewed as a major innovation in marketing methods, B2C systems, if not more, are equally susceptible to such punishing rates of failure.

Newness of Innovative Solutions and Needs Addressed by Innovations

In the 1980s, Hewlett-Packard (HP) found that successful innovators had a deep understanding of user needs. HP also found that the primary cause of difficulties in the marketplace was a failure to understand user needs, and the clarity reached in understanding user needs was the key determinant of new product success (Leonard-Barton et al., 1995). But the process of figuring out needs in varied market contexts is difficult. The difficulties are compounded when markets are new.

New products entering existing markets address known needs. In such cases, satisfaction gaps with existing products can be identified with relative ease and incorporated in the new product. But in new markets, customer needs are uncertain, and the needs and products coevolve, giving rise to four need-solution contexts (as elaborated on in Table 2). These are respectively an improved solution for a known need, a new solution for a known need, a new solution for an anticipated need and an evolving solution for an uncertain need (Leonard-Barton et al., 1995).

Concordant and Discordant Perceptions of Innovations

What should drive new product development: technology or the customers? Views of innovators and customers regarding the nature of product "breakthroughs" may not be concordant. Such mismatches in innovator-customer perceptions could lead to failure of innovations (Rangan & Bartus, 1995). Breakthroughs usually employ new technology, create new markets and represent conceptual change. Conversely, increments represent a continuation of existing products or practices. Furthermore, suppliers and customers find it easy to understand increments (Rangan & Bartus, 1995), while breakthroughs, requiring technology and applications development, are driven by technologists (and may be less readily understood by customers). Hence, increments tend to evolve from the demands of customers and the customer's voice (rather than the technologist's voice), which guide incremental innovations. Additionally performance at a price, rather than performance per se, usually becomes a design criterion for incremental innovations. Hence, when one side (the seller) thinks a particular innovation is a breakthrough, while the other (the buyer) thinks it is an increment, we have the potential for discordance. Clearly, failures are more likely in such discordant settings, and successes are more likely where the two sides agree about the nature of the innovation, be it a breakthrough or an increment.

In the initial B2C wave, there were many possibilities for discordance:

- Large firms treated B2C extensions lightly, as mere increments, but their customers did not.
- B2C startups were enamored of the technology and thought they had breakthroughs on hand. Conversely customers felt they were buying regular products (clothes, detergents, books, CDs, toys). The only difference was that these were being presented through a different (and probably a better, faster, more convenient) channel.

Our understanding of the B2C e-commerce success vs. failure phenomenon increases substantially when we integrate concordance in buyer/seller perceptions with the need solution context (Table 2). If innovations are to succeed, not only must the perceptions of sellers and buyers of innovations match, but innovators also must recognize the inherent uncertainty in finding solutions for customer needs in situations where contexts change.

Integrative Innovation Theory Framework

Table 2 is, thus, constructed using four dimensions: (1) customer need (known to uncertain); (2) nature of solution (improved to evolving); (3) the scope of innovation (incremental to breakthrough); and (4) buyer-seller agreement (concordance to discordance). These four dimensions on which the framework is constructed give rise to 16 cells. Table 2 shows only 12 cells because the right-hand column (where buyer/sellers disagree about newness) shows only four cells instead of eight cells. To save space, unlike the left column, we have not bifurcated, the rightmost column into breakthrough and increment columns. Also, each of the eight cells in this right column has a "discordant" entry. Thus looking at Table 2, as a whole, we see that in the buyer/seller agreement column, there are only two concordant situations, one under breakthrough and the other under increment. The remaining six cells are false perceptions, overly optimistic assessments or overly pessimistic assessments. These cases are unlikely to lead to success. In the buyer/seller disagreement column on the right, all eight cells (only four of which are shown) show discordance with high chance of failure.

The three right-hand columns of Table 2 characterize the level of concordance or discordance of the buyer and the seller about the perceived newness of the innovation. The left-hand column reflects a kind of technology continuum, ranging from the relative comfort of low-tech/known-need to the extreme of high-tech/high uncertainty.

Concordant innovations occur when needs are known, and both sellers and buyers agree the solution is incremental (and, therefore, understandable and quickly adopted) and chances of success are high. But when one party thinks it is a breakthrough, while the other thinks it is an incremental solution, we have discordant expectations with greater chances of failure. In rare cases, there may be the possibility of a "false dawn," when an incremental innovation is misperceived as a breakthrough by both sides, and there is concordance—where failure occurs after a bubble of enthusiasm.

When needs are unknown, both parties must think it is a breakthrough, otherwise perceptions will be discordant, and success will be unlikely. There is also the rare possibility of "unrecognized promise," when sellers and buyers both see only incremental benefits in a truly innovative solution, which may remain underpromoted and underappreciated. As Table 2 shows, for each solution/need pair, there are concordant and discordant conditions. However, it is proposed here that the concordant condition is more likely to lead to success, while the discordant condition will most likely lead to failure.

It should be noted that the framework presented here will behave differently in different market conditions faced by buyers and sellers. Competitive conditions will make the problem of new services and goods marketing certainly more complicated. We are, however, addressing a central issue in high-technology products and services development literature, which argues that—for the success of innovations—concordance between buyers and sellers is essential. How that concordance is to be created depends on the need/solution context of the innovation. It should be further noted that the framework in Table 2 also suggests that if all cells were equally likely, concordance is possible in only two out of 16 possibilities, or about 12% of the time. Discordance is likely 88% of the time. It is not surprising, therefore, to find that most

Table 2. Concordant and discordant states of innovations/markets (Source: Authors' integration of ideas from Leonard-Barton et al., 1995; Rangan & Bartus, 1995)

Technology continuum	Buyer/seller concur that the innovation is:		Buyer/Seller disagree about newness
Need-Solution Context	BREAKTHROUGH	INCREMENTAL	MISMATCH
Improved solution/ known need	*FALSE DAWN*	CONCORDANT INNOVATION	*DISCORDANT INNOVATION*
New solution/ known need	*MINOR BREAKTHROUGH*	*UNDERESTIMATED INNOVATION*	*DISCORDANT INNOVATION*
New solution/ anticipated need	CONCORDANT INNOVATION	*UNRECOGNIZED PROMISE*	*DISCORDANT INNOVATION*
Evolving solution/ uncertain need	*PERILOUS OPTIMISM*	*CAUTIOUS OPTIMISM*	*DISCORDANT INNOVATION*

innovations fail. When we see the first wave of B2C e-commerce in this light as a service innovation, we can explain the high failure incidence of this wave. Understanding such failure will help managers to conceive and plan the development of their innovations better. In the next section, we examine published evidence to validate the various dimensions of this model.

Evidence of B2C Innovation Discordance

There is evidence of considerable discordance in B2C settings. In early 2000,

Josh Harris, founder of the streaming-media company Pseudo.com, declared with certitude on the CBS television show *60 Minutes* that he was there to put companies like CBS out of business (Useem, 2000). At the time, the Internet was seen as a "disruptive" or "breakthrough" technology that would favor new entrants and send old-line brick-and-mortar companies scurrying for cover. Pseudo.com, of course, no longer exists, but streaming media are being used extensively on the Internet, along with other media. In hindsight, the discordance inherent in such views is obvious.

Many established merchants perceived B2C as a breakthrough innovation and deliberately created "pure play" (i.e., purely Internet-based commerce) divisions, insulated from the parent. Examples include Borders.com and Grainger.com. Subsequent learning has often changed these perceptions. For example, after the first flush of enthusiasm, WW Grainger, a Chicago-based warehousing company, later reabsorbed Grainger.com. According to Grainger's president, it became obvious that the Internet unit needed greater interdependence with the originating company (Useem, 2000).

Michael Dell was far more insightful. He created an independent online division within the firm and appointed Scott Eckert, the CEO of the Internet company. Eckert used a highly creative strategy to get the whole organization to adopt the fledgling unit once it became a success, to integrate the division into their existing business groups and to make it a part of the larger firm. enabling them to access the small business and household consumer segment (Harvard Business School Publishing, 1998). Dell clearly saw B2C as a new growth opportunity for his firm but only as an extension of existing Dell-Direct business and not a breakthrough.

In direct contrast to Dell, many B2C startups mostly assumed they were breakthroughs and spent enormous capital on acquiring new customers and upgrading technologies. Some estimate that customer acquisition costs of online firms were four times as high as those of off-line companies (Useem, 2000). Agarwal et al. (2001) also found that companies spent three to four times the amount a customer spent at the Web site to acquire a new customer. The presumption here was that customers, once acquired, will soon learn the wonders of the breakthrough technology and eventually will spend enough money at the Web site to justify the acquisition costs. Customers were probably looking for price and good delivery experience. Discordance in perception set the stage for gaps in expectations to arise, leading to dissatisfaction with the firms.

Boo.com is the prototypical breakthrough-enamored B2C startup. It got entangled in creating Web site with the best possible aesthetic, but it failed to incorporate the basic desire of customers to view and compare fashion products quickly in order to make the buying decision. Launched with a blaze of publicity, it burned through $135 million even before it went public (Isaacs, 2001). Insiders say Boo.com failed because it spent too much money on marketing (Isaacs, 2001). While Boo.com Web designers fretted about aesthetics, customers were actually looking for good deals and fast delivery service. Discordance carried the day.

Petstore.com, Pets.com, Toysmart.com and other similar ventures also failed to take off. They offered nothing new by way of products or services to the customers. These Web sites had neither inexpensive products nor inexpensive and reliable delivery systems. They targeted ultrathin product niches for which demand had never been proven (Isaacs, 2001), and they also did not augment their offers with high quality and timely service. Toysmart.com did not have a chance in a crowded space occupied by Toys-R-Us and other e-tailers (Isaacs, 2001). These

B2C e-commerce companies addressed a known need, but their offer did not match either customer expectations of better and cheaper service or the offers of already existing new and traditional suppliers. E-Toys failed first to forecast demand, and then overreacted and overstocked products that quickly became obsolete. It could not fulfill customer expectations, despite the fact that its top management team consisted of experienced Disney executives. Here again we see examples of innovative companies and their customers, where perceptual discordance eventually led to service quality failure.

Misperceptions about Breakthroughs and Network Externalities

The "breakthrough" notion, prompted by the idea that the Internet was a disruptive technology, also spawned the "instant company" approach (Useem, 2000), resting on illusory first-mover advantages and nonexistent "network-externality" effects (i.e., the positive impact on all members of an ever-expanding network). These ideas led companies to build major brands supported by marketing and advertising expenditures. Only some networks, however, are capable of positive network externalities (Arthur, 1996). Networks where members are not interdependent do not exhibit positive externalities. B2C seller-buyer networks are usually star-shaped, where each buyer is connected to a single seller. An increasing membership base, therefore, does not necessarily confer network externality benefits.

In the first B2C wave, this was the case. B2C players did not have specialized partners—transporters, parcel couriers, third-party logistics providers, fulfillment houses, payment systems and producers of main and peripheral products. Lacking such services, "the eyeballs the Web sites managed to attract did not turnout to be loyal" (Useem, 2000, p. 84). For example, CDNow, a music e-tailer, had name recognition of 83%, but only 17% loyalty. Under such conditions, brand promotion did not turn into first mover or network advantage.

A notable trend is that these hard-learned lessons have made subsequent and surviving B2C players attentive to how networks function. The survivors created partnerships to provide interdependent services and have learned to differentiate their products on the Internet. Such positive externalities are more evident in m-commerce networks, where consumers can access increasing number of services from suppliers of games, music, and news and sports bulletins.

Misperceptions About First-Mover Advantages

Because the Internet offers instant market access, it can also instantly wipe out the first-mover advantage of B2C pioneers. In general, me-too competitors can enter just as rapidly as the first movers did. Only firms capable of creating sustainable advantages can hope to build customer loyalty. Perceptions that B2C offerings in a sector are interchangeable commodities, quite logically, generate commodity-like response from customers. In such contexts, savvy second movers sometimes win the competitive game.

Breakthrough on the Customer Relationship Side

While B2C methods may not be the disruptive "breakthroughs" that the initial wave of B2C players believed them to be, they are certainly different because they bring the sellers and the buyers together in new ways. B2C methods disrupt old ways of doing business and change the customer-company relationships. Given this, in B2C settings, the customer's voice must take precedence over technology's voice. B2C settings create new demands on managers to listen and respond to the "voice of the customer." This is not easy. A Deloitte Consulting study of 850 top firms (Reed, 2000) found that only 13% of the companies paid attention to creating customer loyalty networks (integration of marketing and servicing activities through technology) and supply-chain collaborations (streamlining of finance and human resources and the creation of e-chain connectivity, involving collaboration and customization of manufacturing and supply processes amongst supply chain partners).

In practice, the first-wave of failed B2C firms appears to have seen themselves as providers of goods by technically new alternative means. Late entrants and survivors were substantially more customer centric. They focused on basic product presentation, customer service, on-time and efficient delivery, no hassle returns and so on. In other words, they designed their services and aligned them with the needs of the customers, thus creating concordance.

IMPLICATIONS FOR MANAGERS AND FOR FURTHER RESEARCH

B2C retail methods offer low startup costs, ease of entry and greater geographic exposure, but these advantages do not make B2C business models simple. For example, Amazon.com, the leading B2C survivor, has increased the assortment of goods offered. Amazon is continually augmenting the "B2C innovation" by adding features, such as a full-text search of books, recommendation engines, reviews and ratings, time-based Gold Box specials, referral bonuses, payment system discounts, political campaign coverage and contribution channels, and so forth. Amazon came to realize that:

1. The first wave of B2C innovation was an increment.
2. It is essential to keep pushing this innovation so that the "Amazon.com shopping experience" moves towards the two highlighted concordant cells of Table 2.

By 2004, Amazon had still not met conventional rubrics of retail profitability, but it was inching towards that goal.

The foregoing discussion has several implications for B2C managers. Compared to brick-and-mortar counterparts, the B2C operation must be viewed and studied as an innovation. In most cases, such an innovation would turn out to be more incremental than breakthrough in nature, at least from the customer perspective. Therefore, it becomes necessary to figure out the segments of customers to whom the B2C option will deliver substantial (and more than merely incremental) advantages. Amazon found this segment amongst book buyers. The B2C advantages, however, cannot be static. Such advantages need to be constantly augmented and communicated to the customers. Rather than lapsing into technoeuphoria, the baseline position of B2C managers should be this: it is going to be exceedingly difficult to create and meet high customer expectations.

E-Toys thought it would present serious competition to brick-and-mortar toy sellers, like Toys-R-Us, by removing the hassle of shopping, especially during frenzied holiday periods. In its TV ads, E-Toys created expectations of a failure-proof service. In practice, however, E-Toys ran out of key inventories, stocked the wrong inventories and failed to process orders correctly. The result was that customers experienced serious delays, particularly during the busy holiday gift-giving season. If E-Toys had positioned its innovation incrementally, say as an online birthday toy gift registry, perhaps it could have engendered and successfully met the lower expectation levels, and thus remained in business.

SUMMARY AND CONCLUSION

In summary, we have used historical examples in an eclectic cross-sectional fashion across the B2C retail sector to illustrate our proposed innovation theory-based framework for B2C success and failure. We started by questioning the findings of recent empirical studies as to why so many firms, with so much talent and easy access to capital, failed to use time-tested management principles. Why did they fail to realize that managing a B2C e-commerce required acumen similar to that required in the conventional brick-and-mortar world? What was it about this new technology and service delivery method that most B2C managers misread? Why could these companies not convert visitors into profitable and loyal customers? We have argued that it is not incompetence that led to the collapse of many of these ventures, but a misperception of their basic business, on the one hand, and a mistaken positioning of their innovative services for their customers. These errors we believe led to discordance in perceptions between buyers and sellers, and misallocation of resources within the firm, more so at the front end for customer acquisition and technology, than on customer retention and delivery.

These problems eventually resulted in serious lapses in service quality, and customer desertion and abandonment of the B2C delivery methods of many of the dot-com pioneers. Our framework captures the problem of creating concordance between buyers and sellers in the context of high-tech innovations, and it shows by implication that managers have to be aware of the nature and scope of the innovations and then ensure that they are in concordance with their customer base. The framework underlines the necessity of correctly choosing between the voice of the customer and the voice of technology. For known needs and improved solutions, attention to customer voice tends to lead to concordance. But as needs become uncertain and solutions are evolving, customers know less about the needs and will depend on the "magic of technology" to address their problems. But if managers assume falsely that they have breakthrough innovations, and chances of such assumptions are high in high-tech settings, they will alienate their clients and will not succeed. The framework, thus, can be of great use to managers involved in developing and marketing innovative products and services, especially in the e-commerce context. Managers carefully can assess the need-solution context in which they are operating and then strive for concordance and avoid false optimism or undue pessimism.

While such an approach has value, it also has obvious limitations. First, there are reasons other than innovation failure that potentially help to explain the dot-com B2C crash phenomenon. These alternative approaches warrant further in-depth study to understand the colossal economic collapse of the dot-com era. Second, even within the innovation theory framework that we offer, there is need for further systematic in-depth studies that go deep into specific B2C cases. More systematic comparisons of B2C failures also are needed.

In conclusion, we believe that historic case based studies of e-commerce methods—such as in this chapter—offer insights into how technology shapes, and is shaped by, social factors. As the advanced and emerging nations move headlong into a future that is heavily invested in IT, it is imperative to take a balanced stand in terms of understanding the false promises and pitfalls of such technologies—in addition to the usual reveling in and singing the praises of the glorious potential of such technologies.

REFERENCES

Achrol, R. S., & Kotler, P. (1999). Marketing in the network economy. *Journal of Marketing, 63*(special issue), 146-163.

Agarwal, V., Arjona, L. D., & Lemmens, R. (2001). E-performance: The path to rational exuberance. *The McKinsey Quarterly,* (1), 31-43.

Anderson, J. (2001). Carnage.com. *Institutional Investor, 35*(1), 90.

Arthur, W. B. (1996, July-August). Increasing returns and the new world of business. *Harvard Business Review, 74* (4), 100-109.

Baker, W. L., Lin, E., Marn, M. V., & Zawada, C. C. (2001). Getting prices right on the Web. *The McKinsey Quarterly,* (2), 54-63.

Barsh, J., Blair C., & Grosso, C. (2000). How e-tailing can rise from the ashes. *The McKinsey Quarterly,* (3), 98-108.

Berry, L. L., Seiders, K., & Grewal, D. (2002). Understanding service convenience. *Journal of Marketing, 66,* 1-17.

Bitner, M. J. (2001, Spring). Self service technologies: What do customers expect? *Marketing Management, 10*(1), 10-11.

Brady, M. K., & Cronin, J. J., Jr. (2001). Some new thoughts on conceptualizing perceived service quality: A hierarchical approach. *Journal of Marketing Research, 65*(3), 34-50.

Brown, S. L., & Eisenhardt, K. M. (1995). Product development: Past research, present findings, and future directions. *Academy of Management Review, 20*(3), 343-383.

Corcoran, E. (2002). Digital diaspora. *Forbes, 169,* 74-80.

Forsyth, J. E., Lavoie, J., & Mcguire, T. (2000). Segmenting the e-market. *The McKinsey Quarterly,* (4), 23-25.

Harvard Business School Publishing. (1998). *Dell online.* Boston: Harvard Business School Publishing.

Isaacs, N. (2001). Crash & burn. *Upside, 13*(3), 186-192.

Leonard-Barton, D., Wilson, E., & Doyle, J. (1995). Commercializing technology: Understanding user needs. In K. Rangan, B. P. Shapiro, & R. T.

Moriarty, Jr. (Eds.), *Business marketing strategy: Cases, concepts, and applications* (pp. 281-305). Chicago: Irwin.

Marn, M. (2000). Virtual pricing. *The McKinsey Quarterly,* (4), 128-130.

Meuter, M. L., Ostram, A. L., Roundtree, R. I., & Bitner, M. J. (2000). Self service technologies: Understanding customer satisfaction with technology-based service encounters. *Journal of Marketing, 64,* 50-64.

Pandya, A., & Dholakia, N. (2005), Conceptualizing B2C businesses as a new category of services. *Journal of Electronic Commerce in Organizations, 3*(1), 1-12.

Rangan, K., & Bartus, K. (1995). New product commercialization: Common mistakes. In K. Rangan, B. P. Shapiro & R.T. Moriarty, Jr. (Eds.), *Business marketing strategy: Cases, concepts, and applications* (pp. 63-75). Chicago: Irwin.

Reed, J. (2000). For success, building a customer-centric strategy is key. *Electronic News, 46* (42), 54-59.

Rock, J. (2000). The hostile market hurts more than just dot-coms. *Weekly Corporate Growth Report, 11068*(1118), 11057.

Useem, J. (2000). Dot-coms: What have we learned? *Fortune, 142*(10), 82-104.

Varianini, V., & Vaturi, D. (2000). Marketing lessons from e-failures. *The McKinsey Quarterly,* (4), 85-97.

Zeithaml, V.A. & Bitner, M.J. (2003). *Services marketing: Integrating customer focus across the firm.* Boston: McGraw-Hill-Irwin.

Zeithaml, V. A., & Bitner, M. J., & Gremler, D. D. (2006). *Services marketing: Integrating customer focus across the firm* (Rev. ed.). Boston: McGraw-Hill-Irwin.

Chapter XI
An Empirical Investigation of the Role of Trust and Power in Shaping the Use of Electronic Markets

Raluca Bunduchi
University of Aberdeen Business School, UK

ABSTRACT

This chapter discusses the role that social relational characteristics, such as trust and power, play in shaping the use of a particular type of e-business application—electronic markets (EM)—to support exchange relationships with suppliers that exhibit predominantly transactional characteristics. The analysis is based on a case study of an EM in the electricity sector. The study finds that the EM is used to take advantage of a superior power position, in order to achieve cost reductions, breeding mistrust and eroding the suppliers' bargaining power. The findings support the argument that social relational characteristics, such as trust and power, are significant factors in shaping the use of EM in transactional-oriented relationships.

INTRODUCTION

The rapid commercial adoption of the Internet in the mid-1990s has been one of the most dramatic changes for organizations in the recent history. Since the invention of the Mozaic browser in 1993, businesses have encountered a range of opportunities to use the emerging Internet to support communication, commercial transactions, business processes, service delivery, learning and collaboration. The Internet enables the creation of new forms of interactions between organizations and new kinds of social relationships (Evans & Wurster, 1999) leading to profound social changes in the way organizations operate (Castells, 2000). This chapter addresses the social implications of the Internet on the way organizations manage their interorganizational relationships.

The use of Internet to support the buying and selling of goods and services, to service customers and to collaborate with business partners, to enable learning and knowledge sharing both within and outside the organizational boundaries, as well as to conduct electronic transactions within an organization has been coined with the term "e-business" (Turban, King, Viehland, & Lee, 2006). The impact that the adoption of e-business has on the nature of interorganizational relationships has been studied extensively in existing literature from an economic perspective. The first studies in this area have adopted a transaction costs economics (TCE) stance (Clemons, Reddi, & Row, 1993; Malone, Yates, & Benjamin, 1987), and, by and large, the following research has followed the TCE tradition emphasizing the impact that e-business has on the transaction costs and risks (Bakos, 1998; Orman, 2002). The social implications of e-business, in terms of changes in the social nature of interorganizational relationships, have become only lately part of the e-business research agenda.

However, even before the advent of the Internet, information systems (IS) research identified social relational attributes issues, such as power and especially trust, as crucial in shaping the use of IS between organizations (Hart & Saunders, 1998; Kumar & van Dissel, 1996; Meier, 1995). In an e-business context, the majority of studies that address the social relational implications of e-business use focus on trust rather than power.[1] In the context of Internet based EM, which is a particular type of e-business application, existing studies on trust and power tend to focus on collaborative exchanges, characterized by high levels of trust and resource dependency (Christiaanse, van Diepen, & Damsgaard, 2004; Markus &

Christiaanse, 2003). The implications that EM has on relational trust and power in transactional-oriented exchanges remain largely unaddressed by current research.

The objective of this chapter is to identify the role that trust and power play in shaping the use of EM to support exchange relationships with suppliers that exhibit predominantly transactional characteristics.[2] This objective is achieved through an in-depth study of the use of EM in a multiutility company (Utilia). The study contributes towards understanding the role that e-business technologies play in shaping the social nature of interorganizational relationships.

BACKGROUND

Definitions

This chapter focuses on the use of a particular type of Internet-enabled application—EM—to support interorganizational relationships with suppliers.

Organizational research generally differentiates between two types of buyer-supplier relationships: transactional, or arms-length relationships, and collaborative, or obligational relationships. The former are characterized by low interdependence, short-term commitment, prearranged terms and conditions in a written contract, narrow communication channels, low trust and low asset specificity. In contrast, the latter are characterized by strong interdependencies, high levels of trust and commitment, long-term span, high transaction costs, terms and conditions loosely specified and high asset specificity (Morgan & Hunt, 1994; Sako, 1992). Transactional relationships, therefore, can be characterized as economic exchanges, concerned with the economic exchange of goods and/or services between parties. Collaborative relationships involve economic as well as social exchanges, such as interdependencies, friendships, closeness and trust (Easton, 1997) and are referred to in the literature as relational exchanges to differentiate them from the purely transactional exchanges (Lambe, Wittmann, & Spekman, 2001).

This study follows Bakos (1998) in defining EM as an online marketplace where buyers and sellers meet to exchange goods, services, money or information. According to Bakos' interpretation, EM fullfil three functions: (1) to match buyers and sellers, (2) to facilitate the exchange of information, goods, services and payments associated with market transactions, and (3) to provide an institutional infrastructure, such as a legal and regulatory framework, that enables the efficient functioning of the market. In this way, the difference between a traditional market and an EM is that the later leverages Internet technology to perform these functions with increased effectiveness and reduced transaction costs, resulting in more efficient (in the sense of lower transaction costs) markets. This definition emphasizes the transactional nature of interorganizational relationships that are mediated by the EM by focusing on the sale transaction and the price, rather than on the collaborative aspects of the exchange, such as joint inventory management or fullfilment (Christiaanse et al., 2004). This interpretation of EM serves the purpose of this chapter, which is to analyze the social implications of e-business in relationships characterized predominantly by transactional exchanges, rather than collaborative behavior.

This study addresses the implications that the use of EM has on two social attributes of interorganizational relationships: power and trust.

According to Pfeffer (1997), "Power means being able to get things one wants, against opposition—not predicting what is going to happen anyway, and then advocating that outcome" (p. 54). It is based on resource interdependencies between organizations (Salancik & Pfeffer, 1974). Such dependencies appear in connection with scarce and needed resources (Pfeffer, 1997) and dictate the balance of power between business

parties (Fill, 1995). For example, the higher the dependency of one partner on the other, the lower his power in the relationship.

Following Nooteboom (1996) and Smith Ring and Van de Ven (1992), this research focuses on the analysis of goodwill trust defined as confidence in the other party's intentions to perform according to agreements. Goodwill trust emphasizes faith in the goodwill of others, which is developed through repeated interpersonal interactions, and it is based on the assumption that personal relationships are a necessary condition of trust (Smith Ring & Van de Ven, 1992). Trust can be defined at two levels: the personal level, that is, *trust in another individual*, and at the organizational level, that is, *trust between organizations* (Luhmann, 1979; Zaheer, McEvily, & Perrone, 1998), as individuals in an organization may "share an orientation toward another organisation" (Zaheer et al., 1998, p. 143). The organizational and personal dimensions are interrelated, as interpersonal relationships between individuals that enact interorganizational relationships serve to shape and modify interorganizational relationships, and are at their turn conditioned by legal systems and organizational role responsibilities (Smith Ring & Van de Ven, 1992).

Trust, Power, and E-Business

In general, existing studies concerning trust and Internet-based EM converge on the belief that the use of such technologies can enhance the level of trust between the parties, however, such an outcome depends of the type of EM functionalities used (Bunduchi, 2005). Transaction driven functionalities, such as auctions and catalogs, tend to reinforce transactional outcomes and hamper trust, while collaborative functionalities, such as cooperative purchasing tools and shared databases, support trust building in collaborative relationships (Bunduchi, 2005; Markus & Christiaanse, 2003). Direct monitoring of the exchange, the use of feedback mechanisms and the adoption of cooperative norms, such as flexibility, solidarity and information sharing (Pavlou, 2002), the provision of constantly available information, and the opportunity to order products and services directly (Bauer, Grether, & Leach, 2002) also were found to support trust between buyers and sellers in Web-based business-to-business (B2B) exchanges. Based on the findings of EDI research, Ratnasingam, Gefen and Pavlou (2005) suggest that structural assurances embedded in Internet-based EM, such as common information technology (IT) standards, security norms, IT connectivity and uniform product descriptions, are likely to facilitate trust building between the participant firms. A follow-up study of the use of Internet-based e-business technologies in Cisco found that structural assurances in the form of the security of technical solutions over time leads to the development of interpersonal, goodwill trust (Ratnasingam, 2005).

By and large, the research concerning the outcome that e-business technologies has on trust has focused mostly on risk-based trust, rather than goodwill trust, especially in a B2C context (Chen & Dhillon, 2003; McKnight, Choudhury, & Kacmar, 2002). The justification has been that familiarity and repeated interactions, which are significant sources of goodwill trust, do not apply to electronic transactions, hence the emphasis has to be placed on risk-based trust, which is impersonal and relies on reputation information and economic reasoning (Ba & Pavlou, 2002). While this might be true for consumer EM, empirical studies of EM in B2B settings suggest that despite the potential of using online EM to bring together anonymous buyers and sellers, often such technologies are still used with known partners. For example, in the automotive industry, although the original goal of Covisint was to provide a single point of entry for the entire industry, it ended up being used only by a limited number of well-known tier-one suppliers (Ratnasingam & Pavlou, 2005), with the founding car companies maintaining strict control over the

participants based on predefined contracts (Gerst & Bunduchi, 2005).

The argument that EM tend to be used with known parties is further supported by empirical studies that found that the extent of e-business use in B2B settings (Soliman & Janz, 2004; Vlosky, Fontenot, & Blalock, 2000) is positively correlated with the level of trust, which implies a priori knowledge of the exchange partner. Consequently, the use of EM in B2B settings is influenced not only by the presence (or lack) of risk based trust, but also of trust based on familiarity and personal interactions, as the parties know each other prior to engaging in the B2B relationship.

In the absence of trust, e-business systems are found to lead to ill feelings and resentment within the user community and to tensions and conflicts and ultimately to the withdrawal of some of the users from the system (Allen, Colligan, Finnie, & Kern, 2000; Gerst & Bunduchi, 2005). Even before the advent of the Internet, trust between existing parties was seen as critical to the success of an interorganizational system (IOS) or electronic market (Hart & Saunders, 1998; Meier, 1995). The importance of trust was seen as directly related to the balance of power between the firms engaged in electronic transactions. As Meier argued in 1995, "trust is a key ingredient in establishing and maintaining a successful IOS because of the mutual dependence of system participants and the ensuing coordination requirements" (p. 145).

The use of EDI systems creates dependency between the parties involved in the exchange, due to the costs involved in switching to a different system (based on a different standard) for the users (Meier, 1995). Some users may also loose bargaining power as often the benefits of using the system are not symmetrically distributed among participants. Nakayama's study (2000) of EDI e-commerce between grocery suppliers and wholesale distributors found that suppliers obtain more accurate and timely information on product sales and their partners' operational status and gain higher market flexibility because the system makes it easer for them to change prices, product specifications and promotional plans. Consequently, as EDI systems are likely to create dependency between the users and the system provider, users would be deterred to adopt it. This explains why coercive power often has been used by the more powerful firms to influence their trading partners to adopt EDI (Hart & Saunders, 1998; Webster, 1995). However, coercive power is found to lead to underperformance (Ratnasingam, 2000), while trust is seen as a mechanism to alleviate the users' perceived loss of power (Meier, 1995).

Existing trust between the parties (Hart & Saunders, 1998) and the provision of price incentives to support such trust (Nakayama, 2000), rather than the use of coercive power, were found to positively influence the use of EDI. Studies of Internet-based systems supported Meier's arguments, finding that lack of trust acted as the prime motivation for the more powerful firms to exercise control by manipulating the data standards embedded in the system. Control over standards meant that the more powerful firms were altering the rules of the trade that were embodied in these standards. The use of coercive power was found to degrade the relationship, to breed more mistrust and, finally, to trigger serious threats to the future of the e-business system (Allen et al., 2000). Lack of trust and the erosion of the power also explained the failure of Internet-based EM in the automotive industry (Gerst & Bunduchi, 2005).

However, other authors have suggested that the use of the Internet will make power and dependency less relevant in interorganizational exchanges. Clemons et al. (1993) and Turban et al. (2006) argue that the Internet will reduce the dependency between EM participants, due to the Internet's open standards and low costs. Supporting this argument is an empirical study by Vlosky et al. (2000) that finds no correlation between the balance of power between the firms and the extent of their use of Internet e-business systems.

Consequently, existing research suggests that social relational characteristics, such as trust and power, have a significant impact on the way organizations use e-business systems in collaborative relationships. Trust is nurtured by collaborative functionalities of e-business systems. Mutual dependency can be created by the high costs, proprietary data standards and unfair distribution of benefits associated with the system use; and the use of coercive power breeds mistrust, leading to the demise of collaborative relationships and consequently affecting the performance and extent of e-business use. But what are the outcomes of e-business on trust when the relationships are not collaborative? What is the role that power plays when e-business is implemented in relationships that exhibit mainly transactional features? The case study below attempts to provide some answers to these questions.

RESEARCH METHOD

This research is based on what Stake (1995) calls an instrumental case study. The adoption of a single instrumental case study research design allows us to understand the dynamics present within a single settings. The objective of this research is to explore the role that trust and power play in shaping the use of EM within a particular context—the relationships that Utilia develops with its suppliers—and not to identify general patterns that apply across a multitude of contexts. The case study design does not and cannot represent a "sample" of the total population, and generalization is possible only at the level of the theoretical propositions, not at the level of the populations as it is the case with quantitative studies (Yin, 1994). The aim of the investigator here is to understand a particular issue (Stake, 1995)—the implication of EM use on social relational attributes— not to enumerate instances in which the findings hold true (Yin, 1994).

Semistructured interviews were used for data collection, complemented with internal documentation and other sources of secondary data (published reports, company communications). Nine interviews were conducted in total with representatives of Utilia's procurement office and the EM management, as well as IT offices and internal users. The semistructured nature of the interview built flexibility into the interviewing process, enabling the researcher to pursue new avenues of inquiry as they appeared to be relevant during the interview. To ensure the validity of the interview, the transcripts were sent to respondents within a day of the interview (Payne, 2000). Interview data also were checked, where possible, with the data gathered through documentation, for example, the data regarding the impact of regulation on supplier relationships were checked against the data provided by other interviewees.

Categorical aggregation (Stake, 1995) was used to reduce the data. Coding was approached deductively (Miles & Huberman, 1994), starting with a provisional list of codes created prior to the fieldwork and based on the literature review. The initial list included two categories: (1) concepts regarding EM applications, such as extent of use and type of exchange, and (2) concepts concerning the social relational characteristics, that is, trust and power. As suggested by Miles and Huberman (1994), based on these codes, descriptive and explanatory data displays were generated to explore the relation between EM use and trust and power. The displays served to reduce the data and to capture the relationships among concepts, in order to draw and verify conclusions. The analysis of data displays followed the techniques outlined by Miles and Huberman (1994), making comparisons, noting relationships among variables, and developing patterns and themes. Finally, case narratives (Stake, 1995) were used to explore and understand the relationships among the concepts under study.

CASE STUDY

The case study discusses the use of an EM application to mediate the exchange with suppliers in a multiutility company based in the European Union (EU) called Utilia, an integrated multiutility company, including gas and electricity businesses. The company is involved in all four activities in the energy supply chain: generation, transmission, distribution and supply. The tight regulation in the electricity market, especially the requirement to comply with EU legislation regarding procurement activities, has a strong impact on the way Utilia manages its supplier relationships. Both EU and national regulations are intended to ensure open competition and discourage anticompetitive behavior. According to EU regulations,[3] for all procurement contracts worth more than £3,000, utility companies must publicly announce the request for suppliers (invitation to tenders) in the Official Journal of European Community (OJEC). Subsequently, the negotiation of the contract and the criteria used for selecting the supplier must be transparent in order to give equal opportunities to all potential suppliers. In addition, contracts cannot exceed two years in length. While such a transparent and competitive approach encourages competition, it hampers the ability of the company to nurture collaboration with suppliers during the search and selection stages of the transaction. Moreover, since all relationships are limited to two years, collaborative behavior is discouraged even during the concluding stage of the transaction, as suppliers have little incentives to make any sort of specific investments in the relationship.

At the time of the study, Utilia was using an EM application to support its procurement requirements. The EM, called Utilia.com, was jointly funded by Utilia and three other utility companies.

Supplier Relationships in Utilia

Supplier relationships are categorized in Utilia into two groups, partnership approach (PA) and competitive tendering (CT). The criteria that separate the two categories include the financial value of the contract and the criticality (for Utilia) of the items purchased: PA is adopted with suppliers whose contracts represent a high financial value and/or with suppliers who deliver products/services that are of vital importance for Utilia, while the opposite is true for CT relationships.

The way Utilia treats and manages the interaction in supplier relationships can be described according to the three transactional stages: search (gathering information about suppliers), selection (assessing suppliers and negotiations) and concluding (delivery of items/service, control and monitoring the exchange).

Search and Selection Stages

The treatment of all suppliers, either PA or CT, is similar during the first two stages of the transaction.

Any new supplier must have the same opportunities as any supplier we have been friend with [sic]. Even if there are people that we've worked before with, [sic] even if it's a supplier that we've trusted, and built a relationship with, we need to follow the European legislation and treat everyone equal. (General Manager)

The respondents emphasized that all supplier relationships are managed in an equal and competitive manner. Personal relations play no role during search and negotiation, which must be based on transparent and nondiscriminatorye criteria. All suppliers are subjected to impersonal and standardized treatment. The rationale for such competitive treatment is the requirement to abide by EU regulations.[4]

Concluding Stage

The treatment of suppliers is differentiated only during the concluding stage. In CT relationships, there is little information sharing after the contract is awarded. Such limited interaction means that neither personal nor organizational trust have the time to develop.

Standardized treatment of CT suppliers reduces Utilia's switching costs. Since no customization is involved in the contract and the product is not a critical item for Utilia, the organization can easily change suppliers. Consequently, dependency on CT suppliers is limited.

In contrast, PA relationships involve extensive information sharing and regular face-to-face (FtF) meetings. These informational exchanges facilitate social exchanges, enabling personal trust building that is seen as critical to ensuring a satisfactory outcome in PA relationships.

We wanted to ... work more closely together. In the end, it all boiled down to trust. We have different ways of working from our contractors, and these problems don't disappear if we just decide to have a partnership. (Supply Chain Manager)

Consequently, it seems that all supplier relationships are treated equally during search and negotiation to satisfy EU regulations. The development of trust, which becomes critical during the conclusion stage with PA suppliers, is forbidden during the first two stages. A closer look at the interviewees' comments suggests, however, a slightly different picture. The general manager, for example, while emphasizing the equal treatment during the search, made the following comment:

We need to follow the procedures set by EU. If we spot a supplier that we are interested in, we might wake him up [sic] a bit if he doesn't reply to our tender invitation [sic]. (General Manager)

Moreover, the supply-chain manager mentioned that when trust was broken with a particular PA supplier, then no future exchanges were made with that supplier. In contrast, with two other PA suppliers with whom trust developed during the duration of their initial contract with Utilia, future contracts were awarded.

These examples suggest that personal and organizational trust influence the search and selection stages, even in what appears to be a transactional type of relationship (i.e., standardized treatment during search and selection, competitive bidding, short-term contract). Trusted suppliers with whom previous exchanges have taken place are almost inevitably included in the selection process by Utilia. Furthermore, trust developed during previous exchanges can influence the negotiation stage and lead to the continuation of the relationship. It thus became clear that the treatment of PA suppliers during search and selection is affected by the existence of trust developed in previous transactions, which contravenes to the espouse theory, that is, equal and competitive treatment of all suppliers. Nevertheless, the ability to support such organizational trust during the concluding stage is restricted by the limited duration of the contract; suppliers have limited incentives to make adaptations (which create dependencies) and/or to invest in trust-building efforts that support collaboration, since they have to compete again for the contract in two years.

The products/services delivered by PA suppliers involve a high degree of customization, as well as effort and adaptations on the part of Utilia, such as meetings to monitor performance, cross-sharing information and collaborative design. These adaptations create dependency between the parties. Again, due to the limited duration of the contract, the effort that Utilia invests in a particular relationship is limited.

In conclusion, Utilia develops "pure" transactional relationships with its competitive tendering suppliers, since dependency and trust are absent. In contrast, although primarily transactional, the relationships with partnership suppliers exhibit some trust and dependency, reflecting the existence of some forms of collaborative behavior.

The Use of EM—The Role of Trust and Power

Utilia uses EM to support its exchanges with suppliers only during the first two transactional stages—search and negotiation. The EM application includes two different technologies: e-publishing and electronic auctions (e-auctions), which have been used by both CT and PA suppliers for two years at the time of the study.

During the search for suppliers, the EM is used to support the electronic publication of the invitations to tender. These invitations are electronically sent and then published in the OJEC. During the selection of suppliers, e-auctions replace FtF negotiations to choose a particular supplier and award the contract.

The e-auctions used in Utilia are reverse auctions, where the buyers place the items under request for bids. Potential suppliers bid for the contract, reducing the price gradually. The "price" can include single or multiple variables.[5] Several rounds of bidding take place, and the winner is the supplier with the lower bid. The use of e-auctions by Utilia was described by one of the interviewees as follows:

We sit on one side, and the suppliers are on the other side, [the e-auction] is something as a vehicle. For example, when we like to tender some offers, the suppliers are on the other side and while they are bidding, they can see their own price and the lowest price, and then they drop their price if they want to be still in the bid. It runs for 20 minutes, and the price gets constantly lower. ... We are thinking at the moment to put through an action for fuel. In this case it is all about the price ... For example, for transformers you are comparing other features as well, some transformers lose more electricity than others, so all these types of cost[s] need to be taken into account. With vehicles, we have considered things such as the residual value and the operating cost. The suppliers saw the whole life cost, i.e. the operating costs minus the residual value, so in the end we got the cheapest life cost. (General Manager)

The e-publishing tool allows Utilia to store electronically all tender documents, to simultaneously (and electronically) manage the distribution and communication with all potential bidding supplies, and to handle electronically the evaluation of responses from suppliers. These functionalities reduce interaction costs during the search. Neither trust nor dependency are mentioned as relevant at this stage of EM use.

Purchasing cost reductions are the prime motivator for using e-auctions during selection. For example, the evaluation of the success or failure of an e-auction was in terms of the level of purchasing cost reductions were obtained.

There was another e-auction ... and everybody who participated, even those that were resistant at the beginning, said that it was a great success, as the discount level that they've got was incredible. (Supply-Chain Manager)

These cost reductions are made possible as e-auctions dramatically increase the transparency of the negotiation process between Utilia and its potential suppliers. E-auctions bring together (simultaneously) all bidding suppliers who are able to see each other's prices (in contrast with individual FtF negotiations where suppliers are less aware of the prices offered by competitors). As described by one of the interviewees:

In traditional auctions, when [suppliers] are bidding, they wouldn't know how far they need to drop their prices. In electronic auctions, if the lowest price is 11 and they bid 12, then they would stop dropping their price. Electronic auctions have a huge transparency, which stop them, in this case, to drop margins. We are advantaged [sic]as well because before we would have said to them that you need to drop the price as the other suppliers have lower prices, but now, because the auction is transparent, they can see by themselves which is the lowest price and they drop theirs. So the transparency works both ways: they drop their prices and thus gain the business, and we gain a lower price than we would have otherwise obtained. Traditionally, we would have had FtF negotiation, and then the supplier had no idea what prices he was competing with. He didn't know what the next supplier would offer. (General Manager)

In e-auctions suppliers are more aware of the demand and number of their competitors. More awareness means that in the situation in which there is high demand and a large number of competitors, suppliers are more inclined to drop their prices in order to gain the business. These two conditions were emphasized as requirements that have to be met for the e-auction to be successful (i.e., achieve reduced purchasing cost).

E-auction works only in specific circumstance[s], when there is sufficient competition and enough hunger for your business. (Supply-Chain Manager)

If [the electronic auction] is big enough, can be boiled down to a commodity, and there is a market here, then we will use an auction. All conditions are important, but the most important one is to have enough participants, so for the auction to have a dynamic of its own. (General Manager)

High demand and large number of suppliers mean that e-auctions are used only when the supplier's bargaining power is low, that is, when Utilia has an advantageous power position vis-à-vis its suppliers. Consequently, Utilia uses e-auctions only when it is in a stronger power position than its suppliers. Under these conditions, the transparency inherent in e-auctions leads to higher purchasing cost reductions for Utilia. In other words, e-auctions allow Utilia to make a better use of its advantageous power position, thereby leading to higher purchasing cost reductions.

In contrast with the e-publishing tool, which was used with both CT and PA suppliers, e-auctions are used only with PA suppliers. The rationale for the selective use of e-auctions is that they involve high set-up costs for Utilia. As the supply-chain manager mentioned:

The costs for running an auction are as high as for adding a middleman in the process, and I need yet [sic] to see how much value they can add to the process. Some of the costs for tender exercises were around 20,000£. (Supply-Chain Manager)

Such set up costs can be recouped only if the costs savings achieved as a result of using an e-auction are high. The amount of purchasing costs savings achieved depends on the value of the contract. As described before, in contrast with CT suppliers, PA relationships have a high financial value, which potentially can generate large savings. For this reason, e-auctions are used in Utilia only with PA suppliers.

By replacing FtF negotiation, e-auctions not only diminish the costs involved in dealing with suppliers, but also reduce the relevance of trust during the selection stage for suppliers involved in previous relational exchanges. According to the theory in use concerning the differential treatment of suppliers, the trust between SP and its suppliers with whom it has been involved in former relational exchanges plays an important role during the selection stage. At the same time, e-auctions impede the ability of new exchange parties to make social exchanges that lay the foundation for the development of personal trust. Furthermore, e-auctions allow Utilia to take advantage of its favourable power position during the selection stage, which also hampers the

development of organizational trust later on in the relationship. Although trust and collaboration were not mentioned as required during the search and selection stages, the interviewees argued that they are essential during the concluding stage with partnership suppliers. Therefore, e-auctions can lead to negative social outcomes, since their use obstructs the development of trust during the initial stages of the transaction.

DISCUSSION AND CONCLUSION

The Utilia case study suggests that the use of Internet based EM can have potentially harmful consequences on the nature of relationships with suppliers.

First, as suggested by a number of quantitative studies of EDI and Internet-based e-business systems (Hart & Saunders, 1998; Soliman & Janz, 2004; Vlosky et al., 2000), EM are used in Utilia in relationships characterized by higher trust. However, in Utilia's case, there is no direct relationship between the existence of trust and the extent of EM use. The reason why EM is used only with more trusted "partnership" suppliers is that such relationships involve high-value contracts, and, hence, the potential cost reductions resulting from the use of e-auctions are high enough to offset the costs associated with setting up the e-auction. Hence the correlation between trust and the extent of EM use can be explained indirectly through the balance between the potential costs reductions and the investments in running the EM.

While the existence of trust does not directly influence the use of EM, the balance of power plays a significant role in the decision whether to use e-auctions to support the selection of suppliers. Utilia purposefully uses the transparency inherent in e-auctions to take advantage of a superior power position vis-à-vis its suppliers, in order to achieve its cost reduction objectives. These findings seem to support the branch of IS research that argues that power influences the adoption of e-business systems (Gerst & Bunduchi, 2005; Ratnasingam, 2000). In Utilia's case, a stronger power position leads the customer to enforce the use of EM with its suppliers.

Second, in Utilia the use of EM adds to the existing environmental forces (e.g., regulations) that inhibit trust development with suppliers during the selection stage. This increases the pressures on the buyer to find additional ways of supporting trusting behavior during the concluding stage of the transaction, where such behavior is beneficial. Additionally, far from reducing the dependency between exchange parties through the use of open standards as advocated by some researchers (Clemons et al., 1993, Turban et al., 2006), the case study showed that Internet-based EM applications can be used to reinforce the advantageous power position of powerful buyers, in a similar way that pre-Internet technologies used IOS (Webster, 1995), regardless of the negative effect such a use has on the ability to support trust in the relationship later on.

The study has a major limitation that is inherent in its designed. The single instrumental case study design enabled the researcher to gather an in-depth understanding in the role that social relational characteristics play in shaping the use of EM in transactional interorganizational relationships. However, to obtain such a detailed picture, a generic overview of the role that power and trust play in B2B EM was sacrificed. Further research should involve multiple case study research that is design to include other industries where EM are used, such as the chemical and the automotive industry, to enable the findings to be generalized. Such a qualitative approach could be aided by the use of surveys of EM users to confirm the results through triangulation. Future research also should address the different dimensions of trust that were not included in this study, such as risk-based trust. The integration of power and trust to explain the use of e-business technologies in both transactional and collaborative relationships is also an avenue that should be explored further,

as most existing studies focus on only one or the other of these concepts.[6]

Despite this limitation, the study makes an important contribution to the e-business research in that it finds that EM breeds mistrust and increases the dependency of suppliers, which negatively affects interorganizational relationships that exhibit predominantly transactional characteristics. This finding suggests the adoption of e-business has significant social implications, not only in relationships characterized by strong collaborative behavior, but also in exchanges that are closer to the transactional model.

REFERENCES

Allen, D. K., Colligan, D., Finnie, A., & Kern, T. (2000). Trust, power and interorganisational information systems: The case of the electronic trading community TransLease. *Information Systems Journal, 10*(1), 21-40.

Ba, S., & Pavlou, P. A. (2002). Evidence of the effect of trust building technology in electronic markets: price premium and buyer behaviour. *MIS Quarterly, 26*(3), 243-268.

Bakos, Y. (1998). The emerging role of electronic marketplaces on the Internet. *Communications of the ACM, 41*(8), 35-42

Bauer, H. H., Grether, M., & Leach, M. (2002). Building customer relations over the Internet. *Industrial Marketing Management, 31*(2), 155-163.

Bunduchi, R., (2005). Business relationships in Internet based electronic markets: The role of goodwill trust and transaction costs. *Information Systems Journal, 15*(4), 321-341.

Castells, M. (2000). The information age: Economy, society, and culture. *The rise of the network economy* (Vol. 1). Oxford: Blackwell Publishers.

Chen, S. C., & Dhillon, G. S. (2003). Interpreting dimensions of consumer trust in e-commerce. *Information Technology and Management, 4*(3-4), 303-318.

Christiaanse, E., van Diepen, T., & Damsgaard, J. (2004). Proprietary versus Internet technologies and the adoption and impact of electronic marketplaces. *Journal of Strategic Information Systems, 13*(2), 151-165.

Clemons, E. K., Reddi, S. P., & Row, M. C. (1993). The impact of information technology on the organization of economic activity: The move to the middle hypothesis. *Journal of Management Information Systems, 10*(1), 9-35.

Easton, G. (1997). Industrial networks: A review. In D. Ford (Ed.), *Understanding business markets* (pp. 102-128). London: The Dryden Press.

Evans, P., & Wurster, T. S. (2000). *Blown to bits.* Boston: Harvard Business School.

Fill, C. (1995). *Marketing communications. Context, content and strategies.* London: Prentice Hall.

Gerst, M., & Bunduchi, R. (2005). Shaping IT standardisation in the automotive industry—the role of power in driving portal standardisation. *Electronic Markets, 15*(4), 335-343.

Hart, P. J., & Saunders, C. S. (1998). Emerging electronic partnerships: Antecedents and dimensions of EDI use from the supplier's perspective. *Journal of Management Information Systems, 14*(4), 87-111.

Kumar, K., & van Dissel, H. (1996). Sustainable collaboration: Managing conflict and cooperation in interorganisational systems. *MIS Quarterly, 20*(3), 279-300.

Lambe, C. J., Wittmann, C. M., & Spekman, R. E. (2001). Social exchange theory and research on business-to-business relational exchange. *Journal of Business to Business Marketing, 8*(3), 1-36.

Luhmann, N. (1979). *Trust and power.* UK: John Wiley & Sons.

Malone, T. W., Yates, J., & Benjamin, R. I. (1987). Electronic markets and electronic hierarchies. *Communications of the ACM, 30*(6), 484-497.

Markus, M. L., & Christiaanse, E. (2003). Adoption and impact of collaboration electronic marketplaces. *Information Systems and E-Business Management, 1*(2), 139-155.

McKnight, D. H., Choudhury, V., & Kacmar, C. (2002). Developing and validating trust measures for e-commerce: an integrative typology. *Information Systems Research, 13*(3), 334-359.

Meier, J. (1995). The importance of relationship management in establishing successful interoganisational systems. *Journal of Strategic Information Systems, 4*(2), 135-148.

Miles, M. B., & Huberman, A. M. (1994). *Qualitative data analysis: An expanded sourcebook.* Thousand Oaks, CA: Sage Publications.

Morgan, R. M., & Hunt, S. D. (1994). The commitment-trust theory of relationships marketing. *Journal of Marketing, 58*(2), 20-38.

Nakayama, M. (2000). E-commerce and firm bargaining power shift in grocery marketing channels: A case of wholesalers' structured document exchanges. *Journal of Information Technology, 15*(3), 195-210.

Nooteboom, B. (1996). Trust, opportunism and governance: A process and control model. *Organization Studies, 17*(6), 985-1010.

Orman, L. V. (2002). Electronic markets, hierarchies, hubs, and intermediaries. *Information Systems Frontiers, 4*(2), 213-228.

Pavlou, P. A. (2002). Institution-based trust in interorganizational exchange relationships: The role of online B2B marketplaces on trust formation. *Journal of Strategic Information Systems, 11*(3-4), 215-243.

Payne, S. (2000). Interview in qualitative research. In A. Memon & R. Bull (Eds.), *Handbook of the psychology of interviewing* (pp. 89-102). Chichester, UK: John Wiley & Sons.

Pfeffer, J. (1997). *New directions for organisation theory*. NY: Oxford University Press.

Ratnasingam, P. (2000). The influence of power on trading partner trust in electronic commerce. *Internet Research*, I(1), 56-62.

Ratnasingam, P. (2005) Trust in inter-organizational exchanges: A case study in business to business electronic commerce. *Decision Support Systems, 39*(3), 525-544.

Ratnasingam, P., Gefen, D., & Pavlou, P. A. (2005). The role of facilitatinh conditions and institutional trust in electronic marketplaces. *Journal of Electronic Commerce in Organisations, 3*(3), 69-82.

Sako, M. (1992). *Prices, quality and trust: Inter-firm relations in Britain and Japan*. Cambridge: Cambridge University Press.

Salancik, G. R., & Pfeffer, J. (1974). Organisational decision making as a political process: The case of a university budget. *Administrative Science Quarterly, 19*(2), 135-151.

Smith Ring, P., & Van de Ven, A. H. (1992). Structuring cooperative relationships between organisations. *Strategic Management Journal, 13*(7), 483-498.

Soliman, K. S., & Janz, B. D. (2004). An exploratory study to identify the critical factors affecting the decision to establish Internet-based interorganizational information systems. *Information & Management, 41*(6), 696-706.

Stake, R. E. (1995). *The art of case study research*. Thousand Oaks, CA: Sage Publications.

Turban, E., King, D., Viehland, D., & Lee, J. (2006). *Electronic commerce. A managerial perspective*. NJ: Prentice Hall International.

Vlosky, R. P., Fontenot, R., & Blalock, L. (2000). Extranets: Impacts on business practices and relationships. *Journal of Business & Industrial Marketing, 15*(6), 438-457.

Webster, J. (1995). Networks of collaboration or conflict? Electronic data interchange and power in the supply chain. *Journal of Strategic Information Systems, 4*(1), 31-42.

Yin, R. (1994). Case study research: Design and methods. Second edition. Beverly Hills, CA: Sage Publishing.

Zaheer, A., McEvily, B., & Perrone, V. (1998). Does trust matter? Exploring the effects of interorganizational and interpersonal trust on performance. *Organization Science, 9*(2), 141-159.

ENDNOTES

[1]   See Gerst and Bunduchi (2005) and Ratnasingam (2000) for some exceptions.

[2]   Transactional relationship trust and power are not considered significant (Lambe, Wittmann, & Spekman, 2001; Morgan & Hunt, 1994; Sako, 1992).

[3]   That is the Suppliers Directive 93/36/EC and the Utilities Directive 93/38/EC.

[4]   It is interesting to note that although such regulations exist within the national legislation as well, the interviewees focus only on the EU legislation. Such an emphasis on EU, rather than national legislation, can be explained by the fact that where EU law is applicable, it prevails over national law. EU legislation is enforced more severely, and the sanctions are harsher than in the case of the national legislation. The threat of substantial fines for a breach of the EU regulations increases Utilia's incentives to assure compliance with EU legislation. Additionally, the emphasis on the EU also could be the result of the extension of Utilia's strategic

interest, which does not focus exclusively on the domestic market but looks to compete in an extended EU energy market.

[5] Just the price of the item, or the total lifecycle cost of the product, that includes several cost variables.

[6] For an exception, see the study by Allen et al. (2000) of an IOS between the UK's motor vehicle leasing and contract hire companies and their repair agents.

Chapter XII
Social Aspects of Open Source Software:
Motivation, Organization, and Economics

Spyridoula Lakka
University of Athens, Greece

Nikolas E. Lionis
University of Athens, Greece

Dimitris Varoutas
University of Athens, Greece

ABSTRACT

Open source software/free software (OSS/FS), also abbreviated as FLOSS/FOSS (free/libre and open source software), has risen to great prominence. Existing literature from diverse disciplines or through interdisciplinary studies have tried to explain the growth and success of the phenomenon. This chapter describes and discusses OSS/FS under the scope of three major aspects: motivations that lead to OSS/FS, the organization of OSS/FS communities and the economic theory as a means of explaining the manifold phenomenon. Furthermore, the chapter analyzes the social implications that lie underneath the OSS/FS diffusion, together with the social processes that take place in OSS/FS communities in an effort to enhance our understanding of the diverse mechanisms that disseminate OSS/FS rapidly.

INTRODUCTION

"Free software" is a matter of liberty, not price. Free software is a matter of the user's freedom to run, copy, distribute, study, change and improve the software. In order to be able to make changes and to publish improved versions, one must have access to the source code of the program. Therefore, accessibility to source code is a necessary condition for free software. The freedom to improve a program and release it to the public, so that the whole community benefits, complies with the philosophy that introduced free software: the prosperity and freedom of the public in general.

The idea of open software is not new for institutes and universities, yet its rapid growth and significance to mainstream information technology (IT) business was not accomplished before the Internet became widespread and the emergence of electronic commerce (e-commerce). The spread of the Internet made possible the collaboration of communities and the ability to handle massive decentralized projects, while a significant portion of e-commerce runs on OSS/FS.

OSS developers from around the world collaborate, self-organize and rarely meet face-to-face. Questions about their motivations, about the organization of their communities, and the ethics and social implications of the phenomenon inevitably arise. This chapter, by presenting and analyzing recent developments and discussions of the existing literature, aims to contribute to the understanding of the economic and social aspects related to the open source phenomenon.

BACKGROUND

In 1985, Richard Stallman (1992) created the Free Software Foundation (FSF) (2006) and designed the GNU General Public License (GPL) (GNU General Public License, 1991), OSS/FS's first formal licensing contract.

The FSF's definition of free software stresses the abandonment of property rights, which it terms "copylefting." Copyleft uses copyright law, but flips it over to serve the opposite of its usual purpose; instead of a means of privatizing software, it becomes a contractual means of keeping software open.

The Open Source Initiative (OSI)[1] was founded by Eric Raymond. While the FSF and the OSI work to help each other, they are not the same

thing. The FSF uses a specific license and provides software under that license. The OSI seeks support for all open-source licenses, including ones from the FSF. The infrastructure and philosophy of the two movements has sometimes led them to divergence, yet the two groups are working toward the same goal, which remains a conciliating factor. The terms OSS/FS and FOSS as used in this document will refer to both movements.

ORGANIZATION OF OSS COMMUNITIES

The OSS/FS organizational structure follows a bottom-up approach that relies on generally accepted protocols of communication and a shared notion of validity. The strength of these elements is enhanced by the peculiar characteristics of the software good and the structure of the OSS/FS license.

Licenses are the basic element in the structure of FOSS projects and there are almost as many open licenses as OSS/FS projects. Most of these projects are released under GPL copyleft license, whose design allows attuning the incentive of the FOSS developers, serving the goals of the FOSS community better than other legal frameworks. The GNU GPL was the first and is still the most popular open license enacted, but there are also other widely used licenses that are known to be compatible with the GNU GPL, such as the GNU library or Lesser General Public License (LGPL), original MIT/X (The MIT License, 2006) and BSD (The BSD License, 2006).

Copylefting is a means of copyrighting a program, but at the same time a programmer actually signs the GPL. With this arrangement, the program is simultaneously freely usable, but protected from becoming someone's private intellectual property. It is also a way of linking the programmer and his contribution together permanently, while the contribution is publicly observable. This creates an environment where programmers have an incentive to signal their abilities via the copyleft community.

Another characteristic of open licenses is in the two kinds of agents it links together: the agent who originally attaches an open license to an asset, establishing it as an OSS/FS project, and the agents who have subsequently obtained the copylefted product. As using the product constitutes implicit acceptance of the contractual terms of the open license attached to it, an agent becomes an adopter by procuring the copylefted product. Together, program-creators and adopters constitute a community (Von Hippel, 2001).

The abandonment of property rights, however, has become a major controversy from an ethical and sociopolitical point of view. Some researchers are skeptical (Lerner & Tirole, 2005; Marty, Kevin, Don, & Keith, 2002; Mundie, 2001), while governments remain inactive to the establishment of a general legal framework. What if adopters attempt to generate revenue by improving or distributing the copylefted product? The answer lies in the nature of copyleft, which by its definition diminishes such a possibility. Lerner and Tirole (2005) also talk about the problem that might occur if the project leader decides to transition from one license to another more "flexible" one, and they find that again such a procedure actually would be impractical under the open source definition.

Under this skepticism, FSF (Stallman, 1992) argues that free knowledge requires free software and a free file format, and, subsequently, it is essential to free the code as a contribution to the social welfare. The FSF philosophy has an increasing number of advocates, who in turn become members of the community.

Managing the OSS/FS Community

It is apparent that OSS/FS communities are organized and maintained under common goals and beliefs that span traditional boundaries of ownership. OSS/FS projects, however, pose a great management difficulty, in that the peer groups exist in a virtual community with a large diversity of members, who may never see each other face-to-face. However, many OSS/FS projects are successful, even if they appear to eschew the traditional project coordination mechanisms, such as formal planning, system-level design, schedules and defined development processes. Many researchers (Crowston, Annabi, Howison, & Masango, 2004; Elliott & Scacchi, 2003) believe that FOSS is a growing component of software engineering as a human and team practice, and it is a good practice for those who seek to improve the effectiveness of their projects, by learning from the social and sociotechnical practices of FOSS development teams.

First of all Internet technology has made it possible to resolve communication problems and handle massive decentralized projects. Elliott and Scacchi (2003) in a sociotechnical study identify the social processes that facilitate the successful development of OSS/FS. The OSS/FS project groups are characterized as occupational communities (Trice & Beyer, 1993; Van Maanen & Barley, 1984) with beliefs, values and norms that influence their software development practices, including tool choices and conflict resolution. In fact, the OSS/FS developers share similar goals, work practices, interests and value systems, and they are bound by socially constructed rules and ethics that promote formation of shared ideologies and cultural forms. The study further showed that strong organizational cultural beliefs in a virtual community, ties a group together so that conflict is more easily mitigated and finally resolved. It also pointed out that conflicts within a group can also be faced with the use of computer-mediated communication, such as mailing lists and related artifacts in the form of Internet-relay chat.

Bonaccorsi and Rossi (2003) identify two factors that shape the lifecycle of a successful OSS/FS project: a widely accepted leadership that sets the project guidelines and drives the decision process, and an effective coordination mechanism among the developers based on shared communication protocols.

Raymond's (1999a) bazaar metaphor is a famous model of the OSS/FS process. Developers are likened as merchants in a bazaar, who autonomously decide how and when to contribute to project development. While popular, the bazaar metaphor has been broadly criticized. It disregards important aspects of the OSS/FS process, such as the importance of project leader control and the existence of hierarchical organization.

For instance, in the Debian Project (Debian, 2006), the project leaders were elected by the developers, but had total authority over those who worked on their projects. Mozilla (Mozzila.Org, 2006) is an example of open-source management structure that demonstrates control. A small group of Netscape employees oversee the Mozilla community and play the role of benevolent dictators who arbitrate what happens in a module.

Most successful FOSS projects, display a clear hierarchical or onion-like organization (Crowston et al., 2004), with a small core group of developers at the center, surrounded by codevelopers, active users and finally the passive users. Although it is obvious that the core is at the highest level of the hierarchy and is responsible for oversight[2] of the design and evolution of the project, the roles within the hierarchy are not strictly assigned. As the project grows, the authority of the project leaders (core group) arises naturally from a bottom-up investiture, as a result of the contributions to the commonly agreed goal.

A widely known successful project with an onion-like hierarchy is Linux. The most important feature of Linux is its small and compact kernel. The system can be extended by independent modules, which are configured and inserted inside the Linux kernel, obtaining a monolithic kernel. In this way, programmers can add modules without interfering with other parts of the program (Barfield Diego, Tanabe-Hines, Shaffner, & Yelden, 2003).

OSS/FS projects may not always be successful. There is a danger of information overload and burnout and the possibility of conflicts that cause a loss of interest in a project or forking, that appear in many projects (Bezroukov, 1999). In these cases, the leadership plays an important role by selecting the best fitting solution. The support of the members of the community is also crucial for the project to be viable. A mitigating fact is that agents choose freely to focus on problems that they think best fit their own interests and capabilities. Under these conditions, a developer could achieve the best of his/her performance. In general, the coordination mechanisms of OSS/FS communities are successful, despite the obstacles of diversity, size and distance.

Motivation of OSS/FS Contributors

It is true that the OSS/FS movement has challenged traditional reasoning by suggesting that individuals behave altruistically and contribute to a public good, despite the opportunity to free-ride. As explained above, one of the reasons that developers join the OSS/FS community is because of their beliefs. Lerner and Tirole (2002) also made a thorough analysis of the programmer's incentives to OSS/FS. They argue that a developer's participation in an OSS/FS project aspires to net benefits from the work, with net the benefit based on both immediate and delayed rewards.

Immediate rewards include monetary compensation, as well as the opportunity to fix a bug or customize a program for their own benefit. Delayed rewards stem from the *signaling incentive* (Lerner & Tirole, 2002). This includes the *career concern incentive,* which refers to future job offers, shares in commercial open source-based companies or future access to venture capital, and the *ego gratification incentive,* which expresses the desire for peer recognition. Though different in some regards, both have been shown to be stronger when the work is visible to people the programmer wants to impress (colleagues, venture capitalists, the IT market, etc.). Signaling incentive prevails, where the spotlight on the programmer's contribution counts most.

Generally, with OSS/FS, a programmer is his/her own boss and can take full responsibility for the success or failure of a task. In typical commercial projects, programmers have to work with (or around) their supervisor, thus the individual contribution is harder to measure.

The proprietary nature of the code generates income, making it possible for firms to reward programmers immediately with salaries. Unlike the commercial projects, however, OSS/FS projects have the advantages of *alumni effect* and that of customizing projects *for personal use* (Lerner & Tirole, 2002). The first advantage refers to open-source products, as knowledge acquired from their school time and, therefore, is more familiar. Secondly, programmers like to be free to use the modified programs in many ways, that is, for improving their work.

Finally, in OSS/FS, people have greater flexibility when moving from one project to another, building knowledge and "tools" as they go. By contrast in commercial firms, people are restricted by proprietary code specific to that firm. So in a sense, they have to start all over again when they switch jobs.

A number of surveys have been conducted to measure developers' motivations. The Boston Consulting Group (BCG) (2003) survey identifies the top motivations for participating in OSS/FS and divides developers into four major groups: those for learning and stimulation: for skill improvement and fun by 29%; hobbyists: need the code for a nonwork reason by 27%; professionals: for work needs and professional status by 33.8%; and community believers: believe source code should be open by 19%. The FLOSS Survey (Ghosh, Glott, Krieger, & Robles, 2002) finds similar results with 79% saying they joined to *learn and develop new skills* and 50% saying they joined to *share their knowledge and skills*.

The BCG survey (2003) took things one step further and compared the different motivations cited by paid versus volunteer contributors. The comparison showed that those who are paid to contribute to OSS are motivated by the desire to do their job more effectively. This shows that financial rewards are not a primary driver of OSS/FS communities.

Motivations for IT Enterprises

However, unpaid volunteers are not the only possible source of labor for OSS/FS. IT enterprises may have incentives to "accommodate" labor for the development of open source, and, in several cases, it has been done in some extent. The main incentive remains revenue, yet business may benefit by indirect sale values. For instance, funding an OSS/FS project could stimulate the demand for other products or services of the firm. Spolsky (2002) argues that investing in open source would prove a good business strategy for enterprises. This argument is based on the idea that every product in the marketplace has substitutes and complements. A substitute is another product one might buy if the first product is too costly, while a complement is a product that one usually buys together with another product. Since the demand for a product increases, when the prices of its complements decrease, companies try to commoditize their products' complements. For many companies supporting OSS/FS products, turning a complementary product into a commodity, results in profit growth. In this situation a company will want to have extensive knowledge about the OSS/FS movement and may even want to encourage and subsidize OSS/FS contributions. Both reasons will lead company to allocate some programmers to an OSS/FS project.

In addition, many commercial companies released some existing proprietary code in order to further develop it as an open source project. This kind of participation by commercial firms in OSS/FS is again motivated by profits that may be created in the firm's complementary activities. The release of proprietary code under an open-source license makes sense if the profit increase in the proprietary complementary segment offsets any profit from the primary segment. It also applies to the situation when the product is lagging behind leaders' products and is making little profit. In this case, if the open-source project succeeds and the program is utilized more widely, the firm may gain the leadership of the market and increase its profitability through the complementary segment.

Finally, some firms encourage their programmers to participate and contribute in open source projects to learn about the strengths and weaknesses of this development approach. The scope of this strategy may be to improve their proprietary closed-source products, in order to achieve a better competitive position in the software market.

All this together with the e-commerce and networking growth mean that the distribution of free products in software markets is likely to increase. New business models are being created. They are enterprises that uphold the FOSS principles and at the same time aim to make direct or indirect profit.

ECONOMICS OF OSS/FS

Diffusion of OSS/FS

The open-source phenomenon and the turnover of standards (proprietary software) have attracted the interest of the economists, in order to explain and forecast the diffusion of open source among users and among companies.

According to economic theory, information goods, such as software technology, are different in their nature from traditional economic goods. The two fundamental characteristics that distinguish information goods are the *increasing returns* they exhibit in their production (e.g., the development of a new software would cost far more than

the reproduction of a copy) and the *consumption externalities* that drive their demand (the utility derived from the software depends on the number of people using the same or compatible software). As David (1985) and Arthur (1989) showed, the immediate and important consequence of these special demand and supply characteristics of information goods is that their diffusion process is subject to lock-in and path dependence.

The lock-in effect occurs when a large network of old users makes the adoption of a new information good less desirable, while path dependence occurs when insignificant events may give an initial advantage in adoption to one of the competing information goods. This good may then improve more than the others, so it may appeal to a wider proportion of potential adopters. Thus, it may eventually corner the market of potential adopters, with the other information goods becoming locked out.

In this respect, given the presence of network externalities, the lock-in mechanism seems an inevitable outcome in the software diffusion process. That is, if a piece of software manages to gain a significant market share, a cycle is set in motion such that consumers will have even more incentive to use it; there will be an increase in the supply of complementary products (applications, maintenance); and that particular piece of software will start to dominate the market and become the standard. Interestingly, the development of open source contradicts this prediction in that it is eroding, for instance, the market share of Microsoft's dominant standard. The question that arises is what determines the diffusion pattern of OSS/FS technology.

Dalle and Jullien (2000) refer to local interactions to explain the dissemination of the Linux system in place of Windows NT. In their view, what is important in the choice of an operating system is not so much the total number of other individuals who use it, but the number of those who do so within the group with whom the individual interacts. In other words, local consumption externalities are very important in the diffusion phenomenon of open source. Indeed, many leading members of the open-source movement emphasize the central role of advocacy (Pavlicek, 1999). Advocacy is a form of one-to-one or one-to-few marketing, whereby the users of open-source programs are invited to convince other members of their group to do likewise and to abandon the commercial sector. Moreover, advocacy is important for diffusion because it has an exponential growth. Its aim is not only to transform an individual into a new disciple of the open-source movement, but also to make the new member a potential advocate. The role of an open-source advocate is, thus, very similar to that of Witt's (1997) diffusion agents. These agents not only disseminate information about the new technology, but also try to convince a group of potential users to do so simultaneously, so as to contrast those diseconomies that in the presence of network externalities, penalize those who first choose a new technology.

Another approach adopts the theory of collective action to explain the diffusion of OSS/FS. The theory of collective action applies to the provision of a public good. Interestingly, the OSS/FS projects have all the features of a public good. As a digital product, it can be easily and cheaply copied for each individual. Thus, the usage by an individual does not limit another to use it. OSS/FS also has the impossibility of exclusion property by its definition. This approach points out that OSS/FS is developed through collective action by numerous individuals and, thus, suggests that software produced outside commercial channels is just an instance of the general issue of *collective action* (von Hippel & von Krogh, 2003).

Hardin (1982) underlines the significance of the heterogeneity of resources and interests within the group of individuals who may participate in the collective action. A small set of strongly motivated and resourceful subjects (small group) is often capable of overcoming the initial phases of the supply process of the collective good, setting in motion a virtuous circle that possibly enables the phenomenon to be self-sustaining. The small group of individuals that are necessary to initiate the supply process is called *critical mass*. The basic idea is that it is sufficient to have an initial group capable of producing the collective good (e.g., hackers), in order to discourage opportunistic behavior in the rest of the group. Marwell, Oliver and Prahal (1993) argue that the role of strongly interested subjects is not to provide the good entirely themselves, but to create the necessary conditions for production to become easier. This is the role played by those who originate an OSS/FS project, deciding which problem to work on and implementing the central nucleus of the code, which will subsequently be modified, perfected and enriched by other contributions.

Analyzing the diffusion of technologies with network externalities, Hurberman and Loch (1999) conclude that the heterogeneity of the group is positively related with the minimum achievement time of critical mass. In particular, their simulations demonstrate that if there is a small group of individuals with double the tendency for innovation in relation to the group average, the critical mass is reached almost immediately. This result underlines the role of hackers and their culture in the diffusion of open source movement. Their existence is important not only to explain how the phenomenon arises and finds an economic application, but also to explain how it spreads.

More recently Bonaccorsi, Rossi, and Giannangeli (2003) simulate a diffusion model of OSS/FS in which the new software is adopted if its intrinsic value is high, if other members of the population adopt it and if there are direct coordination benefits from exchanging pieces of code. The results of their exercise confirm that the diffusion of a network technology in presence of a well-established standard is difficult and takes a long time. The diffusion of OSS/FS depends on the initial distribution of the potential users' beliefs and on the activation of network externalities. Thus, they conclude that commercial software and OSS/FS are likely to coexist even in the limit.

To sum up, the recent diffusion of OSS/FS seems to satisfy the hypotheses of the existence of critical masses, which permit an alternation of standards, as opposed to the long-term dominance of a given software technology predicted by path dependence and lock-in. Heterogeneity among users, local interactions and advocacy play a central role in the whole diffusion process, since they facilitate the achievement of the necessary critical mass. This latter point also explains the observed differences of OSS/FS adoption between the server and the client markets and supports the general claim that OSS/FS and closed-source software are likely to coexist in the future.

Interaction of Open- and Closed-Source Software

Bessen (2002) underlines that OSS/FS can be customized by its user and presents a model where complexity affects the provision of software. He concludes that when heterogeneous-user needs make software complex, proprietary software does not meet the needs of all users, even when contract programming and custom applications are considered. Standardized products address relatively simple applications, especially popular applications in large markets. Customized software addresses more specialized needs, especially for high value consumers. OSS/FS, provided in addition to proprietary software, allows additional users to develop software that meets their own particular needs. In this respect, OSS/FS is not an alternative to the proprietary software market but it is an innovation that complements the provision of standardized software. Standardized software succeeds by delivering a common denominator product to diverse consumers but cannot satisfy all specialized needs.

In contrast, open source incorporates specialized features from diverse consumer/producers.

The question that arises is how the OSS/FS movement affects the market for proprietary software. Khalak (2000) simulates the effects of the introduction of an OSS/FS product onto a proprietary market. When only proprietary products are available in the market, there is a tendency for monopolies to emerge. However, the stability of the monopoly position is not guaranteed, when a new firm could displace the market leader by offering a code at a low price. In the case where the users' adoption decision was based on market share, the OSS/FS was able to completely dominate the market. The worst scenario for open-source products was when advertising constitutes the sole criterion for purchasing software. Khalak's model suggests that even if open source is of equivalent quality and is free of charge, it must still gain a critical mass of the market share from those dissatisfied with the product of the market leader, to gain enough inertia to capture the entire market. The software adoption decision depends on the market share, that is, network externalities and advertising.

Another approach of the interaction between a closed source monopolist and an open-source community is provided by Mustonen (2003). In his model, there is an open-source program that is a substitute for a program provided by a profit maximizing monopolist. It is assumed that consumers' valuations of either program are proportional to the amount of development effort that went into the program. Consumers face an implementation cost, which is equal for both programs, on top of the price they pay to buy a program. A large population of programmers can choose to work for the monopolist at a wage that the monopolist sets or can choose to belong to the open source community and receive complementary income. In order to increase development effort, the monopolist must hire more programmers, which requires offering a higher wage, while the amount of open-source development is determined by the occupational choices of the programmers. Due to open source activity, the monopolist faces constraints in the programmer labor market and competition from a substitute copyleft program in the consumer market. Whether the open-source program will be available in the market or not depends on the consumer' implementation costs for programs. In particular, if this cost is sufficiently low, some consumers will choose the open-source program and the monopolist will take into account when choosing its price and will not be a monopolist.

A number of studies explore not only the competitive forces among open and closed code products but also their impact on the welfare of the society. In particular, Casadesus-Masanell and Ghemawat (2003) depict competition between an open-source operating system available at no cost and a proprietary commercial product. The crucial feature of their model is the network externalities on the demand side. In this setting, the presence of an OSS/FS operating system leads the commercial firm to set lower prices, which in turn means that the overall use of operating systems is higher. However, the value of the commercial one for users is lower because, for instance, the presence of a competing product may lead third-party developers to develop fewer complementary products for the commercial operating system. This model also suggests that in some cases, the proprietary operating system may be able to drive the market share of the open source alternative to zero, an action that may occur even if it is not socially desirable.

The implicit assumption of the above competitive models is that open source and proprietary software are perfect substitutes, although Bessen (2002) noted the OSS/FS is not an alternative but a complementary to the proprietary software market.

In Gaudeul's (2004) model, OSS/FS has both costs and benefits relative to proprietary software. OSS/FS suffers from some lack of coordination in the sense that the same code may be written twice or not at all. Further, it is assumed that the developers of OSS/FS may not bother developing interfaces that appeal to unsophisticated users. By contrast, the profit-maximizing proprietary software firm is keener to develop such an interface, but, on the other hand, it must pay its developers and, despite good project coordination, may choose to develop a limited set of features. The proprietary software is sold to users at a positive price that excludes some possible users. In equilibrium, the OSS/FS, if it survives, is used either by low-demand or low-income consumers, who cannot afford to buy the proprietary software, or by sophisticated users who like the potentially larger set of features and do not care about the missing or insufficient user interface. The presence of OSS/FS raises welfare, if it does not discourage the development of proprietary software with a good interface.

Importantly, the open-source phenomenon has spawned a number of firms that are trying to make profits from business activity based on copylefted programs. According to Lakhani and Von Hippel (2003), the motivations for undertaking some necessary tasks (e.g., giving online help about the Web server Apache) are similar to the ones governing high-level activities, such as developing and debugging the software. The emergence of new hybrid business models seems to solve this kind of problem. The new model has been spurred by the entry of companies and software houses producing free software, giving it away to customers free of charge and shifting the value from licensing agreements to additional services, such as packaging, consultancy, maintenance, updating and training.

Bonaccorsi, Rossi, and Giannangeli (2003) study the business models of the firms that enter the software industry by producing under the open-source license scheme. They find significant heterogeneity among them as many agents supply both proprietary and OSS/FS. Raymond (1999b) identifies seven different business models: The firms that use OSS/FS to maintain a market position for a related proprietary software product; the firms that sell hardware with open-source driver software; the firms that distribute OSS/FS and sell service and support contracts; the firms that sell accessories for OSS/FS, such as documentation; the firms that sell closed source software with a license that makes it OSS/FS after a specified time period; the firms that sell other developers a brand that certifies their OSS/FS technologies are compatible with all others who use the brand; and finally the frims that develop an open-source product that receives proprietary content that the firm sells.

FUTURE TRENDS

The OSS/FS phenomenon evokes several research, policy and social issues and attracts the interest of people working in various disciplines. This chapter is an attempt to enhance the understanding of the economic and social aspects related to this phenomenon.

Although there has already been plenty of discussion and interdisciplinary study of open-source software development, OSS/FS is still growing. Plenty of issues remain open. One major issue is government intervention and policy towards it. Can open software allow for sufficient standardization? What about national and international intellectual property laws—how are they affected?

Future research in the economics of OSS/FS also could be focused on business models that software firms adopt in response to the OSS/FS diffusion and the pricing schemes appropriate to compete with the proprietary software.

A comparative empirical study in the management of OSS/FS communities could give very interesting results from a sociotechnical point of view, offering valuable information in disciplines like software engineering and social studies. The results of this study also could be applied in the design of an electronic-business (e-business) or e-commerce organizational structure. It would also be very interesting to find the necessary elements

from an OSS/FS process and how they would be best used by an e-business model.

Finally, the above study could be expanded to include the case of digital or electronic-government. Digital government encourages the adoption of modern IT business practices that exploit the Internet and e-commerce capabilities to improve the government operations and public services. How can open source and to what extent support these procedures?

CONCLUSION

The OSS/FS phenomenon has an impact on many aspects of society, including the economy, employment and education. The economy is affected by the change in the structure of the software market and the strategies commercial firms (i.e., the business community, the computing industry and the entertainment industry) use to compete. Also new kinds of business models are introduced. Consequently, employment is affected by the emergence of new conditions in labor.

The collaborative nature of open source has a strong cultural affinity to higher education and its mission to advance and share knowledge for the greater public good. Educational communities also can benefit from the use of OSS/FS, either as a teaching tool or as teaching subject and methodology. The underlying code is (by definition) open for student inspection and can become invaluable in the classroom.

Richard Stallman (1992) declares that free software is not only for a close group of people but is made to serve the public. This implies that the whole society can benefit not only from the ideals of knowledge sharing and free thinking but also from the services OSS/FS offer, such as portability and independency of price limitation in choice .

OSS/FS communities, though massive and with a sense of a prevailing anarchy, can be governed in the most efficient manner. Teams rely on a variety of social control mechanisms; the social bonds and the common beliefs prove to be an important factor in the coordination process. The underlying democratic elements increase the performance of the developers and, consequently, the quality of the product, but the developers are not only attracted by their democratic governance. A number of strong enough motives, besides direct or indirect funds, have been identified and presented.

In addition, there are a surprising number of reasons for a private enterprise to support OSS/FSS. New business models are created and invest in free software development for direct or indirect profit. Commercial firms, though seemingly competitors to OSS/FS turn out to have various kinds of rewards. Also, widespread networking and the growth of e-commerce facilitate the rapid dissemination of digital products at almost no cost, creating the best conditions in market for the introduction of free products. Under these circumstances, the massive diffusion of OSS/FS has been an inevitable procedure.

ACKNOWLEDGMENT

This work is partially supported by the Greek Ministry of Education and Religious Affairs under a Pythagoras Grant.

REFERENCES

Arthur, W. B. (1989). Competing technologies, increasing returns, and lock-in by historical events. *Economic Journal, 99,* 116-131.

Barfield, M., Diego, M., Tanabe-Hines, S., Shaffner, M., & Yelden, G. (2003). *Managing innovation on the Internet: Analysis of open-source networks.* Pacific Lutheran University.

Bessen, J. (2002). Open source software: Free provision of complex public goods.

Bezroukov, N. (1999). A second look at the cathedral and the bazaar. *First Monday* (4), 12.

Bonaccorsi, A., & Rossi, C. (2003). Why open source can succeed. *Research Policy, 32*(7), 1243-1258.

Bonaccorsi, A., Rossi, C., & Giannangeli, S. (2003). *Adaptive entry strategies under dominant standards: Hybrid business models in the open source software industry.* Sant' Anna School of Advanced Studies.

Boston Consulting Group. (2003). *Boston Consulting Group/OSDN hacker survey.* Boston: Boston Consulting Group.

Casadesus-Masanell, R., & Ghemawat, P. (2003). *Dynamic mixed duopoly: A model motivated by Linux vs. Windows.* Graduate School of Business Administration, Harvard University.

Crowston, K., Annabi, H., Howison, J., & Masango, C. (2004). Effective work practices for software engineering: Free/libre open source software development. In *Proceedings of the 2004 ACM Workshop on Interdisciplinary Software Engineering Research.* Newport Beach, CA: ACM Press.

Dalle, J., & Jullien, N. (2000). NT vs. Linux or some explanations into economics of free software. In Ballot & Weisbuth (Eds.), *Applications of simulation to social sciences* (pp. 399-416). Paris: Hermis.

David, P. A. (1985). Clio and the economics qwerty. *American Economic Review, 75,* 332-337.

Debian. (1997-2006). Retrieved April 15, 2006, from http://www.debian.org

Elliott, M. S., & Scacchi, W. (2003). Free software developers as an occupational community: Resolving conflicts and fostering collaboration. In *Proceedings of the 2003 International ACM SIGGROUP Conference on Supporting Group Work* (pp. 22-29). Sanibel Island, FL: ACM Press.

Gaudeul, A. (2004). *Competition between open source and proprietary software: The LaTex case study.* Universities of Toulouse and Southampton.

Ghosh, R. A., Glott, R., Krieger, B., & Robles, G. (2002). *Free/libre and open source software: Survey and study FLOSS.* The Netherlands: International Institute of Infonomics, University of Maastricht.

GNU General Public License. (1991). Retrieved November 15, 2005, from http://www.gnu.org/licenses/gpl.html

Hardin, R. (1982). *Collective action.* Baltimore: John Hopkins University Press.

Hurberman, B., & Loch, C. (1999). A punctuated equilibrium model of technology diffusion. *Management Science, 45,* 160-177.

Khalak, A. (2000). *Economic model for impact of open source software* [working paper]. MIT.

Lakhani, K., & Von Hippel, E. (2003). How open source works: "Free" user-to-user assistance. *Research Policy, 32,* 923-943.

Lerner, J., & Tirole, J. (2002). The simple economics of the open source. *Journal of Industrial Economics, 50*(2), 197-234.

Lerner, J., & Tirole, J. (2005). The scope of open source licensing. *Journal of Law, Economics, and Organization, 21*(1), 20-56.

Marty, J. W., Kevin, B., Don, G., & Keith, M. (2002). Open source software: Intellectual challenges to the status quo. In *Proceedings of the 33ʳᵈ SIGCSE Technical Symposium on Computer Science Education* (pp. 317-318). Cincinnati, KY: ACM Press, 317-318.

Marwell, G., Oliver, P., & Prahal, R. (1993). *The critical mass in collective action. A micro-social theory.* Cambridge: Cambridge University Press.

Mozilla.Org. (1998-2006). Retrieved April 15, 2006, from http://www.mozilla.org/about/

Mundie, C. (2001). *The commercial software model.* Retrieved December 10, 2005, from http://www.microsoft.com/presspass/exec/craig/05-03sharedsource.mspx

Mustonen, M. (2003). Copyleft—the economics of linux and other open source software. *Information Economics and Policy, 15,* 99-121.

Pavlicek, R. (1999). *Keys to effective Linux advocacy within your organisation.* Retrieved from http://users.erols.com/plavlicek/oreilly/alsfullpaper-1999.txt

Raymond, E. S. (1999a). *The cathedral and the bazaar: Musings on Linux and open source by an accidental revolutionary.* Cambridge: O'Reilly Associates.

Raymond, E. S. (1999b). *The magic cauldron.* Cambridge: O'Reilly Associates.

Spolsky, J. (2002). Strategy letter v: The economics of open source. In J. Spolsky (Ed.), *Joel on software*: Apress, 1-3.

Stallman, R. (1992). *Why software should be free.* Retrieved April 15, 2006, from http://www.gnu.org/philosophy/shouldbefree.html

The BSD License. (2006). Retrieved April 15, 2006, from http://www.opensource.org/licenses/bsd-license.php

The Free Software Foundation. (2006). Retrieved April 15, 2006, from http://www.fsf.org

The MIT License. (2006). Retrieved April 15, 2006, from http://www.opensource.org/licenses/mit-license.php

Trice, H. M., & Beyer, J. M. (1993). *The cultures of work organizations.* Englewood Cliffs, NJ: Prentice Hall.

Van Maanen, J. V., & Barley, S. R. (1984). Occupational communities: Culture and control in organizations. *Research in Organizational Behavior, 6,* 287-365.

Von Hippel, E. (2001). Innovation by user communities: Learning from open-source software. *MIT Sloan Management Review, 42,* 82-86.

Von Hippel, E., & Von Krogh, G. (2003). Open source software and the "private-collective" innovation model. *Organization Science, 14*(2), 212-213.

Witt, U. (1997). Lock-in vs. Critical masses. Industrial changes under network externalities. *International Journal of Industrial Organisation, 15,* 753-772.

ENDNOTES

[1]   The official open-source definition as given at www.opensource.org describes open-source software as the software whose distribution terms should comply with the following criteria:

- **Free redistribution:** The license shall not restrict any party from selling or giving away the software as a component of an aggregate software.
- **Source code:** The program must include source code and must allow distribution in source code as well as compiled form. Deliberately obfuscated source code is not allowed. Intermediate forms such as the output of a preprocessor or translator are not allowed.
- **Derived works:** The license must allow modifications and derived works, and must allow them to be distributed under the same terms as the license of the original software.

- **Integrity of the author's source code:** The license may restrict source code from being distributed in modified form, only if the license allows the distribution of "patch files" with the source code for the purpose of modifying the program at build time. The license must explicitly permit distribution of software built from modified source code. The license may require derived works to carry a different name or version number from the original software.
- **No discrimination against persons or groups:** The license must not discriminate against any person or group of persons.
- **No discrimination against fields of endeavor:** The license must not restrict anyone from making use of the program in a specific field of endeavor. For example, it may not restrict the program from being used in a business, or from being used for genetic research.
- **Distribution of license:** The rights attached to the program must apply to all to whom the program is redistributed without the need for execution of an additional license by those parties.
- **License must not be specific to a product:** The rights attached to the program must not depend on the program being part of a particular software distribution.
- **License must not restrict other software:** The license must not place restrictions on other software that is distributed along with the licensed software. For example, the license must not insist that all other programs distributed on the same medium must be open-source software.

- **License must be technology neutral:** No provision of the license may be predicated on any individual technology or style of interface.

2   In order to keep track of the insertions and/or modifications of open source modules, many projects use the concurrent versioning system (CVS) log. CVS is an important software tool, which stores source code, along with programmers' comments.

Chapter XIII
Challenging Digital Inequalities:
Barriers and Prospects

Norman Bonney
The Robert Gordon University, UK

Olufemi Komolafe
The Robert Gordon University, UK

Elizabeth Tait
The Robert Gordon University, UK

ABSTRACT

There are substantial inequalities in access to and use of the Internet. These inequalities build on enduring social and economic inequalities that have themselves been rooted in previous rounds of the development of electronic technologies and have largely resisted public policies designed to remedy them. Rapid developments in the use of the Internet have great potential for commercialization and democratization, but digital inequality means that this potential is not always exploited to the advantage of the poorer sectors of the community. Recent public policies have attempted to remedy digital disadvantage, but there is little evidence that they are fundamentally transforming them. Constant innovation enables the more advantaged sectors to advance their position, while many are still excluded from compensatory attempts at catch up. An increasing body of experience suggests ideas for new approaches, but the magnitude of the challenge of eroding digital inequality should not be underestimated.

INTRODUCTION

The increasing availability and use of advanced information and communications technologies (ICT) have transformed many aspects of social life, business, education, government and democracy, and enthusiasts of the new technologies perceive even more profound productive, liberating and democratizing transformations in the future. At the same time, there has been increasing concern that large sectors of national and global populations have been excluded from the benefits of these innovations and that they may be used to further entrench the position of the advantaged and the powerful. This paper explores the mixed blessings of the ICT revolution particularly as it relates to ideas of electronic commerce (e-commerce), electronic government (e-government) and electronic democracy (e-democracy); places the analysis in a longer historical frame that helps to assess both the positive and the negative features of recent significant developments in ICT; and explores aspects of the emerging patterns of digital inequality and the challenges for policies designed to tackle them.

DIGITAL INEQUALITY

The concept of *digital inequality* is perhaps a better way of conceptualizing the issues that surround the concept of digital exclusion or the digital divide, since it is differences in degree of exposure to and use of digital technologies, rather than complete exclusion, that best summarizes the reality of the phenomenon and the ideas that motivate study in these fields. Digital inequality relates to phenomena with a much wider span than the Internet, but it is access to and use of this medium that is the subject of this chapter. Although the focus is also upon the United Kingdom, the issues that it deals with relate to other states and also, of course, have a global dimension as well.

In this chapter, it is argued that inequalities in access to and use of the Internet are additional manifestations of patterns of social, political and economic inequality that have been continually experienced by the poorer and more disadvantaged sectors of society. Poverty and inequality are relative phenomena that have been persistent features (although with varying characteristics and degrees of incidence over time) in modern

societies. Constant processes of technological innovation inevitably mean that some sectors of society are better placed to take advantage of the new methods of production or service delivery and, thus, forge ahead in benefiting from them. While other sectors eventually benefit from the trickling down of these innovations and their elaborations at a later stage, when the first-time beneficiaries or replacement innovators are moving on to benefit from yet further rounds of innovation.

Digital inequality, like social and economic inequality, is reproduced through the generations. People are born to financially resource rich or poor households or somewhere in between, and households differ in the degree to which they are able to benefit from technological and social innovation. There are also major differences in cultural resources and repertoires in these different households. The ability to benefit from formal systems of education and acquire valued educational qualifications differs greatly between them. The expansion of educational systems in the last 100 years, including the development of higher education, has only modified, in a minor way, the association between levels of education and social privilege or disadvantage. Successive governments over the last half-century have specifically attempted to remedy the educational disadvantage of poorer households, but the broad structure of social and educational disadvantage has remained the same even after a further eight years of New Labour initiatives in the field (Kelly, 2005).

Reich (1993) has distinguished between social strata in the degree to which they are able to manipulate symbol systems, arguing that advanced abilities in this respect are the key to ensuring that workers are able to take advantage of opportunities in a modern knowledge-based economy. In the present day, these differences are manifest in the use of digital technologies and the Internet. Different social class abilities to utilize and benefit from them are, thus, the most recent manifestation of much more enduring and persistent sets of major social-class differences in levels of cognitive and occupational skills and educational attainment. Just as generations of attempts to produce equality of educational opportunity have not removed the problem of educational inequality because as general educational standards are raised, some groups continue to forge ahead to higher levels to keep their absolute and relative advantage; so there is a constant challenge of catch up as specific initiatives to remedy the digital handicap operate in an environment where new innovations are enabling the more advantaged to maintain or advance their position ahead of the field.

150 YEARS OF ELECTRONIC COMMUNICATION

There is a danger in discussions of the impact of the Internet and digital technologies to exaggerate their novelty and significance. The introduction of the telegraph and the global extensions of cable telegraphy in the 19th century have been seen by some as revolutionary in their impact in their times as the Internet in more recent decades (Fuller, 1851; Standage 1999). Such innovations were as integral to the global capitalist revolution of the 19th century, with its outbursts of productivity and the creation of global labor, capital markets and networks, as the Internet is to today's remarkable changes. Indeed there are those that argue that the years leading up to 1914 witnessed greater relative degrees of globalization than in the present day (House of Lords, 2003). If these and subsequent electronic innovations were as integral to the development of global capitalism and its associated international and internal state inequalities, why then should one expect any lesser degree of inequality from the more recent developments in electronic communication?

If we examine the diffusion of major household electronic communication technological innovations in the course of the 20th century subsequent to telegraphy, such as the landline telephone, the radio, black and white and then color television, personal computers, mobile telephones and so forth, we observe a geographical spread and social trickling down of these innovations as they emerge in key metropolitan urban centers of technological development. They are initially taken up by richer households that can afford the new devices at relatively high initial prices, then gradually percolate down the class social structure and eventually become more generally adopted as they become more efficient and cheaper. In the early days of mass personal computing in the 1990s, the neophyte domestic and office users experienced many hiccups. They needed the assistance of technical advisors or more expert friends in order to make use of the, by contemporary standards, less sophisticated hard- and software that was then available. These experiences were very similar to those experiences of people who can remember the spread of black and white television in the 1950s, when friends and neighbours advised on how to adjust the controls on the TV set in order to receive a good picture.

In time, the continuous improvement of successive rounds of development in these technologies makes them much more user friendly and more widespread and valuable in their use. Also, these reflections emphasize the importance of assistance from family, friends and work colleagues in making best use of these new devices. The human culture surrounding them ensures better use and needs to be considered as a factor supporting the spread and use of innovations. Think, for instance, about the talk that surrounds the use of mobile phones by young people as they demonstrate new features to friends and use them to communicate. There are perhaps here some clues to help in propagating knowledge and interest about digital communications amongst groups with less familiarity and skills in the use of new technologies.

INEQUALITIES IN ACCESS TO AND USE OF THE INTERNET IN THE UK

What, then, is the evidence about the dissemination of one of most recent electronic forms of communication to be made available to mass publics—the adoption and use of the Internet and its place in the pattern of social inequality in the United Kingdom?

According to National Statistics Online (2005) in May 2005:

Over half (55%) of households in Great Britain (13.1 million) could access the Internet from home in May 2005. Almost two thirds (60%) of adults in Great Britain had used the Internet in the three months prior to interview in May 2005, of which 58 per cent had bought or ordered goods, tickets or services. A higher proportion of men (63%) than women (52%) had used it for purchases. People aged 25-44 were most likely to buy on-line (61%) while people aged 55-64 were the least likely to buy on-line (48%).

Of those adults who had used the Internet for personal or private use, in the 12 months prior to interview, the most common purchases were travel, accommodation or holidays (52%), videos or DVDs (41%), music or CDs (40%) and tickets for events (35%).

Just under one third (32%) of adults had never used the Internet in May 2005. Of those who had not used the Internet, 43% stated that they did not want to use, or had no need for, or no interest, in the Internet; 38% had no Internet connection; and 33% felt they lacked knowledge or the confidence to use it. These adults were also asked which of four statements best described what they thought about using the Internet. Over half (55%) of non-users chose the statement I have not really considered using the Internet before and I am not likely to in the future'. This core group of non-Internet users represented 17% of all adults

in Great Britain.

In summary about one-third of the UK population still does not use the Internet (with about half of those indicating that they are not likely to use it in the future). Another third of the population takes advantage of the Internet for the purchase of goods and services and the final third has other uses for it.

Data from the 2002 *British Social Attitudes Survey* (Economic and Social Data Services (ESDS), 2005), gives some information on how access to and use of the Internet was structured socially. In that year, 45% of households had access to the Internet, but this access varied from 12% in households with an annual income below £6,000 to 80% in households with incomes of more than £44,000. There was also a marked variation in use of the Internet by highest educational qualification; 86% of those with a university degree having used it compared to 30% of those with the lowest school-leaving qualifications and only 10% of those with no qualifications at all—a group which constituted a quarter of the whole adult population sampled (ESDS, 2005). In social class terms, 71% of professionals and managers used the Internet, but among working class occupations, the figure was 27% (Bromley, 2004). According to the recent Office of the Deputy Prime Minister (ODPM) report (2005), in 2004 85% of professional and managerial households had home computers with Internet access compared, at the other end of the social scale, to 35% of those people who were unemployed or relied on social benefits.

To a marked degree, then, access to and use of the Internet is highly socially structured with groups that are more socially and economically advantaged also having greater exposure to this rapidly developing and important social and technological innovation. In terms of gender differences, men are slightly more likely to use the Internet than women (53% compared to 48%, in 2003).

A 2000 study of usage of the Internet in the EU indicated that the primary uses of the Internet (among, of course, that minority of the population that used the Internet) were e-mail with friends, family and work colleagues (69%); 47% used it for online education and training, 38% for product information, 38% for sport and recreational information, 28% gaming, 23% for job searches and 15% for government Web sites. Similar findings are evident in the United States (Barney, 2004, citing Norris). The *British Social Attitudes Survey of 2002* indicated that the major uses of the Internet were e-mail for 33% of the whole sample interviewed (i.e., including nonusers in the base figure); 19% for shopping, travel and weather information; and 13% for the news and education and training (ESDS, 2005).

There are clear age differences in use of the Internet with younger people becoming much more familiar with its resources and opportunities, than older people. In 2003, it was estimated that 74% of 18 to 24 year olds used the Internet, compared to only 15% of those over 65 (Bromley, 2004). In 2002, two in three 11 to 18 year olds used the Internet for school work; 70% used computers for games; and 90% for school work (National Statistics Online, 2005). We should note that these figures still indicate that about one in four 18 to 24 year olds did not use the Internet —another indication of the education and skills deficit among some of the more recent graduates of the educational system.

The use of the Internet is, thus, becoming more and more common in British society, but there are substantial sectors of the population—about one in three—that have never used it. These nonusers are heavily concentrated among the poorer, older and less educated sectors of the population, with the pattern of digital inequality closely mirroring the pattern of social and economic inequality. Users in turn can be differentiated into heavy users, who use it extensively for work, leisure, friendship, kinship, education, commerce and recreation, and a more casual set of users with less intensive patterns of involvement in the Internet.

E-BUSINESS AND DIGITAL INEQUALITY

The significance of this social patterning of inequality in access to the Internet is all the more important when one considers the rapid developments in the services available and how they impact on peoples' lifestyles and economic opportunities.

It has long been argued that "the poor pay more" (Caplovitz, 1967), and there is no reason why innovations in Internet-based services should necessarily countervail this tendency. Rapid developments in the services now available on the Internet mean that people without access to it, or the skills to utilize it, are probably missing out on all types of new and improved services and opportunities. Some relevant examples follow. First are travel services, which is, as we have seen one of the major uses of the Internet. These examples also demonstrate that while official government policy statements emphasize the productivity and cost-lowering gains from e-commerce in relation to, say, the growth of budget airlines, it does not explicitly state that these gains may not be available to some categories of the population. Overall the report estimates that use of the Internet saves the average user £268 per annum with benefits, of course, that accrue to the better-off sectors of the population that can afford and utilize the equipment (ODPM, 2005).

In relation to transport services, poorer people are much more likely to rely on intercity bus services for their longer distance travel, but they may not be able to take advantage of new cheaper intercity bus services that reduce costs by improving load factors and lowering administrative costs through Internet-based seat booking. This disadvantage can be mitigated in that some providers allow bookings by telephone. But credit or debit card numbers may be required to make these bookings, and many poorer people lack these means of credit. Ten percent of Scottish households, for instance, do not have a bank or building society account (Scottish Executive, 2005). Some new budget hotels and low-cost airline flights can, however, only be booked over the Internet—potentially excluding large sectors of the population from benefiting from these new services because of the lack of the appropriate technology, skills, financial status or lifestyle to have appropriate financial credit.

Travel agents, who have in the past been able to deliver holidays in the sun and elsewhere on an attractive price basis to shoppers in the High Street, often from modest income households, are finding bookings decreasing as bookings by individuals over the Internet become more common. New businesses that offer such services electronically over the Internet are expanding rapidly, while conventional travel agencies find their business diminishing. People, who rely on travel agents for foreign travel and holiday bookings, may find themselves with a decreased array of opportunities. Travel agencies are seeking to meet this challenge by providing new more exotic and challenging destinations, where individual travellers might prefer to have the security of agency assistance. However these opportunities are at the more expensive end of the market. Perhaps there is a role for low-cost agents to be electronic assistants to poorer and less Internet adept customers as they have historically, in many cases, been for the less well-off general public.

Another area where the less advantaged might be further deprived by their lesser ability to access and utilize the Internet could involve networks of interpersonal relations. As we have seen, e-mail is becoming an increasingly common form of communication among people for business reasons but also for personal, friendship and kinship relations. The success of sites such as Friends Reunited is an indication of how the Internet can enrich peoples' personal networks and keep them in touch with a wider circle of friends. Given that social isolation is a known concomitant of social and economic deprivation (Hills & Stewart 2005), the inability to access and utilize these new channels of interpersonal social communication may further enhance the social exclusion of the less advantaged sectors of contemporary society.

E-DEMOCRACY AND E-GOVERNMENT

There has been no shortage of vision with respect to the implications of new information and communications technologies for democracy and the business of government. Some see a potential transformation in the effectiveness of democracy in the ability of citizens to interact with their government representatives through the new electronic means of communication (Berra, 2003; Chadwick 2003; Ward, Gibson, & Lusoli, 2003). E-mail (like the telephone before it) potentially enables closer contact between citizens and elected representatives. Interactive Web sites can enable more responsive and speedier communications between them. Both tools also allow citizens to communicate and organize more effectively amongst themselves. Other analysts (Mehta & Darier 1998; Shelley, Thrane, Shulman, Lang, Beisser, Larson, & Mutiti, 2004; Wilson 2003) are more skeptical about the liberating and democratizing potential of the new technologies, placing greater emphasis on the exclusionary and socially distributed nature of access to the Internet and the differences in information literacy among the population that mean that some groups are less able to take advantage of these new opportunities.

E-democracy concerns the roles of citizens and residents, collective organizations, political parties and elected representatives in utilizing ICTs to support or enhance their involvement in influencing the decisions of governments. E-government is about using ICTs to facilitate the business of government, the administration of services, the propagation of information and the delivery of entitlements to citizens and residents. As the above discussion suggests, e-democracy has proven more problematic than e-government. Many of the operations of government are business-like, and the business of government can be more readily organized on a systematic or electronic basis, than can the more messy politics of democracy. (Not that large scale government computing projects have not had their share of major organizational problems.) Governments have exemplary Web sites and organize more of their activities and services on an electronic basis. Three quarters of UK government services are now available electronically. Four million taxpayers accessed self-assessment online in 2004. There are 8,600 job centers with touch-screen employment search facilities (and plans for extensive staff lay offs), and 21 million benefit payments are being made electronically into bank or building society accounts.

The use of ICT for the business of government raises all sorts of issues that concern its relationship with its citizens in a democratic society. Is universal electronic service delivery a valid objective, when large sectors of society are not able to utilize the technology effectively? Should it be a condition of school graduation or the granting of citizenship that individuals are competent with ICT so that they can effectively deal with electronic government? How can the old, the ill, the disabled and the illiterate be enabled to benefit from available services? As a society we are still in the early stages of appreciating the scale of the challenges involved and developing appropriate responses.

TACKLING DIGITAL INEQUALITY

How, then, do we meet the challenges of digital inequality? Is it possible to devise strategies that

might help the disadvantaged to catch up or, at least, lessen the distance from the groups benefiting most from newer and more established opportunities?

Given that social and economic inequality are so deeply rooted and that patterns of digital inequality are enmeshed in differential patterns of social advantage and privilege that have proved so difficult to eradicate, there are grounds for skepticism about any major initiative to eliminate or substantially modify the known patterns of digital inequality. If decades of major initiatives to produce equal educational opportunity have proved so unsuccessful, why should specific initiatives in this direction have any greater chance of success? In this context, we might note the contrast between the recognition of the persistence of continuing gross social class inequalities in educational opportunity as expressed in the comments of the Secretary of State for Education and Skills, despite decades of attempts to remove social differences in educational opportunity, (Kelly 2005), and the more upbeat and visionary expectations of the new UK Digital Strategy (ODPM, 2005) to reduce the digital divide, which envisages turning in 2008 to mop up the residual problems that will remain.

There also, perhaps, requires some discussion about whether governmental intervention is an effective way of dealing with social inequalities in access to and use of the Internet. After all, the major forces promoting the use and dissemination of the Internet seem to be in the market, the work place and the home. Home and work are by far the most important places whereby individuals access the Internet. Libraries and community centers come way behind with the respective percentages being 75 at home, 20 at work and 11 in libraries and community facilities. For people aged 18-24, the respective percentages are 68, 46 and 17 (Bromley, 2004). As Internet access becomes cheaper, the home computer with an Internet connection will probably become as common a domestic electrical device as the television and CD player. There is certainly a need to think through whether the most effective way to challenge digital exclusion might be through domestic-based services, assisting with the provision of relevant hardware and training in homes or stimulating interest and in-home use through clubs frequented by potential or actual users, as opposed to focusing on community facilities.

The strongest argument for governmental policy initiatives seems to lay with the fact that the government is determined to offer all its services electronically and it will require and expect that citizens benefit from and receive their services though these media. While three quarters of government services are now available electronically, it is a salutary reminder of the challenge ahead in meeting government ambitions that there are only 5 million users, out of a population of 59 million, registered with the Government Gateway for 50 electronic services from 20 government departments (ODPM, 2005).

Given then that there is a case for governmental policy initiatives to modify and where possible eliminate digital inequality, if only to ensure that all citizens are able to take advantage of the electronic delivery of services (and to participate in emerging forms of democracy, markets and social participation as well), then there needs to be consideration of the forms that these initiatives should take and how they should be delivered.

Issues of timing will have great importance in this respect. Perhaps the most effective way to ensure the widest reach of such policy initiatives in the longer term is through the primary and secondary school system through which nearly all UK adults graduate. Such a strategy will reach nearly all of the population, but it will, of course, take decades to percolate through the whole population. There is increasing emphasis in school-based education on information and communication technology literacy. We have seen how younger people are much more equipped with the necessary skills and more familiar with

the uses and benefits of the Internet and digital technologies. As more and more cohorts of young people graduate through the school system and go to higher education, greater and greater proportions of the successive generations are going to be able to take advantage of the resources of the digital age. But we should be aware that there are still major problems with adult literacy. We cannot be certain that the education system will succeed in ensuring that all school graduates are properly equipped to take advantage of the possibilities of the new era and are sufficiently adaptable to take advantage of subsequent innovations that come along. On the basis of past performance of the education system and society at large, the existence of an educational underclass, lacking the necessary basic skills for the exploitation of the opportunities of the digital age, cannot be ruled out for the future. Even more certain, however, is the likelihood of there being continuing digital inequalities in terms of great variations in the relevant knowledge, skills and abilities of people graduating from the various levels of the education system, from those leaving at age 16 or earlier—including some lacking basic literacy skills—to those leaving after age 26 with advanced post-graduate training.

A second major set of institutions that could be the basis of policy initiatives to confront digital inequality among those who have already passed through the system of primary and secondary education are those involved in adult basic and community education. They would seem to be very well placed to take a lead in strategy in this field, since they usually have premises and staff that are well suited for the purposes.

A third base for initiatives to reach those in need of access to the Internet and assistance with the development of skills to utilize it effectively is the national library system, which is gradually adapting its services to meet the needs of the present day. The wide provision of library premises and staff suggest that they would be a good base for the delivery of digital and Internet access and training, and they are to some extent undertaking such roles.

COMMUNITY-BASED INITIATIVES

Voluntary and community sector organizations continue to be seen by the present government as key partners in the delivery of social and ICT services, especially in areas of social deprivation. They have been involved centrally in initiatives to tackle digital inequality. The Scottish Executive Public Internet Access Initiative launched in 2002 (Scottish Executive, 2004) provided up to five personal computers (PCs) with Internet access available in shops, pubs, post offices, hairdressers and community centres and in organizations devoted to disadvantaged social groups, such as single parents, ethnic minorities and New Deal clients. By 2003, 1,300 PCs had been provided in venues with an average of 2.2 PCs per site. The wide dispersal of these machines meant, however, that they were often not accessible or usable and often lacked technical support. The researchers state that:

The majority of machines we came across were either switched off or powered down. Many users had problems logging on and getting started. This is likely to be off-putting to anyone wanting to get quick access to the Internet.

In many cases, staff members were unable to provide assistance to learners and users. Business sites (shops, Internet cafes), which accounted for the majority of the provision (61%), were more readily visible and accessible than public provision (libraries); these in turn were more visible and accessible than nominal community provision. Estimated use levels were at about 3% of the population of Scotland. It was also estimated that between 170, 000 and 220,000 people used the machines annually, including tourists and non-residents. The program has added to resources, particularly in disadvantaged areas, and has been of use to the unemployed, but the report argues that it does not appear to be a good way of attracting new users or older potential users.

The Scottish digital inclusion strategy does not appear to have been as effective as the English program, based upon UK online centers. The Scottish initiative dispersed PCs in small batches in numerous locations, which were not necessarily accessible and did not necessarily have adequate technical and learning support for learners. The online centers, which are currently established in 88 neighborhood renewal areas and 2,000 deprived council wards, were more concentrated in learning centers, where there was technical and learning support (ODPM, 2005). The 2005 UK digital strategy (ODPM, 2005) proposes a competition to build the best local authority-based ICT public service centers that would enable citizens to access e-government services, would offer ICT training and would be specially targeted, initially, to the most disadvantaged localities, but also available more generally. This seems to be a good concept, since it would allow the provision of well-resourced centers staffed with technical assistants and trainers, as well as the relevant hard- and software. There is an initial challenge here in deciding on the location of such centers. Should they be based in areas of social deprivation or more centrally in the city, where they would be available to a wider range of citizens? Even then it might prove difficult to find one location that is adequately centered for all areas of deprivation. Is there not a case for investigating a proposal for mobile facilities that could serve neighborhoods on a regular basis, in the way that mobile library services operate? And, although initiatives might focus on areas of social deprivation, does this approach effectively reach the large numbers of the socially deprived people living in neighborhoods that are not officially classified as deprived?

CONCLUSION

There is now a considerable volume of experience and a wide network of institutions that attempt to overcome inequalities in access to and use of the Internet, but rapid, continuing technological and commercial developments mean that there is a constant challenge to assist the less fortunately placed to participate in and benefit from the new digital economy and society. There is little evidence to suggest that the combined effect of these institutions and policies do anything fundamentally to reverse the patterns of educational, social and digital inequality that are so entwined with one another and have developed out of long historical processes. At each social level, there is a process of "skimming," whereby the most qualified, eligible or prepared actually benefit from innovations or come forward to receive training and support in ICT innovations. There is no "Heineken" policy solution that reaches the parts that others do not reach. The aspiration in the recent digital strategy for the United Kingdom (ODPM, 2005), which states that by 2008 the government can attend to whatever residue there is of the digital divide, is excessively optimistic. New digital inequalities are being created and reinforced at the same time as official policies seek to remedy older ones. The digital divide will remain as a continuing and dynamic issue that constantly needs attention.

Given the scale and the continuity of the current challenges, there is a need for some new ideas to tackle digital inequality. While the formal systems of learning outlined above are clearly basic to the task, they need supplementation by initiatives that might begin by recognizing the importance of informal learning—stimulating interest in learning by those in need by forming clubs and providing advice and assistance through informal channels, such as friends and others who are in regular contact with them, that is, developing and extending an informal culture that extends beyond the formal sites of learning into the lives of those in need of support. There is still a big gap between the education, community and voluntary sector institutions that seek to deliver support and the actual lives of many of the more deprived sectors of the population. Age Concern England, which is greatly concerned with digital exclusion for the older citizen, has in place a number of initiatives to bridge this gap. Numerous other initiatives have similar aims but confront major challenges in reaching throughout the community. New approaches are needed to bridge the gap between aspiration and achievement. Perhaps they can build on the superior knowledge, motivation and abilities of younger people who are much more familiar with the new technologies and their potential. Can school pupils and young people be encouraged to assist peers and older relatives, neighbours and community contacts to acquire the necessary skills and interests? But as the contrasts between English and Scottish initiatives demonstrate, there is also a clear need for physical bases and more formal technical and learning support to make the most of such initiatives.

It is clear that we are only at the earliest stages of realizing the profound implications of the widespread application of innovations in ICT, for the way in which business, the political system and society is organized and for assessing their impact on the different social groups. There is ample evidence of the liberating and productive aspects and potential of the new technologies, but there are also continuing and worrying implications for social control and social inequality that may need monitoring and mitigation. Genuine and significant policy innovations have been made to attempt to redress the newly emerging patterns of inequality that build upon inherited and entrenched patterns of economic and social inequality. Overcoming them is no easy task, and there is much to be learned from examining the experiences of existing initiatives and seeking new approaches that can overcome their deficiencies. Business itself probably has a considerable incentive to be a partner in this process by extending electronic literacy into all sectors of society, not only to cultivate the skills and competencies of its own work forces, but also to help develop new markets and products that will help it prosper.

REFERENCES

Barney, D. (2004) *The network society.* Oxford: Polity.

Berra, M. (2003). Information communications technology and local development. *Telematics and Informatics, 20,* 215-234.

Bromley, C. (2004). Can Britain close the digital divide? In *British social attitudes: The 21ˢᵗ report.* London: Sage and National Centre for Social Research.

Caplovitz, D. (1967). *The poor pay more.* London: Collier Macmillan.

Chadwick, A. (2003) Bringing e-democracy back in. *Social Science Computer Review, 21* (4),443-445.

Economic and Social Data Services (ESDS). (2005). *British social attitudes survey 2002.* Retrieved July 2005, from www.data-archive. ac.uk/esds

Fuller J. (1851). *The Telegraphic computer: A most wonderful and extraordinary instrument by which business of every possible variety are instantly performed.* New York: Jon Fuller.

House of Lords Select Committee on Economic Affairs. (2003). *Globalisation* [first report]. London: House of Lords. Retrieved June 26, 2004, from http://www.publications.parliament.uk/pa/ld200203/ldselect/deconaf/5/507.htm

Hills, J., & Stewart, K. (2005) *A more equal society?* Bristol: Policy.

Kelly, R. (2005) *Equity and excellence: Education and social mobility* [speech]. Retrieved July 26, 2006, from www.ippr.org.uk

Mehta, M. D., & Darier, E. (1998) Virtual control and discipling on the Internet: Electronic governability in the new wired world. *The Information Society, 14,* 107-116.

National Statistics Online. (2005, September). Retrieved from http://www.statistics.gov.uk/

Office of the Deputy Prime Minister (ODPM). (2005). *Connecting the UK: Digital strategy.* London: ODPM.

Reich, R. (1993). *The work of nations.* London: Simon and Shuster.

Scottish Executive. (2004) *Evaluation of the public Internet access initiative* [first draft]. Retrieved from http://www.scotland.gov.uk/library5/finance/epiapi-00.asp

Scottish Executive. (2005). *Scottish household survey 2003/4.* Edinburgh.

Shelley, M. C., Thrane, L., Shulman, S., Lang, E., Beisser, S., Larson, T., & Mutiti, J. (2004). Digital citizenship: Parameters of the digital divide. *Social Science Computer Review, 22*(2), 256-269.

Standage, T. (1999). *The Victorian Internet.* London: Weidenfield and Nicholson.

Ward, S., Gibson, R., & Lusoli, W. (2003), Online participation and mobilisation in Britain, hype, hope and reality. *Parliamentary Affairs, 56*(4), 652-668.

Wilson, A. D. (2003) Shrinking the digital divide: The moderating role of technology environments. *Technology in Society, 25,* 83-97.

Chapter XIV
A Social Shaping Perspective of the Digital Divide:
Implications for E-Business

Audley Genus
University of Newcastle upon Tyne, UK

Mohd Ali Mohamad Nor
University of Newcastle upon Tyne, UK

ABSTRACT

The digital divide is a phenomenon associated with disparities among groups and societies in the adoption and diffusion of electronic information and communications technology (ICTs) and electronic-business (e-business) practice. The chapter argues that, in rhetoric, at least, the innovation, adoption and diffusion of ICTs bear the hallmark of technological determinism (i.e., that of a technical imperative) in which social, economic and political factors are underplayed. By way of contrast, the chapter considers the merits of a social-shaping approach to the analysis of innovation in ICTs to assess the prospects for ameliorating the digital divide between developed and developing countries and for stimulating economic development in the latter through the promotion of e-business. The chapter suggests how future research on the social shaping of ICTs, e-business and the digital divide between developed and developing nations can meet the challenges discussed herein.

INTRODUCTION

In the wake of initiatives, such as those promoted by then Senator Al Gore during the 1992 U.S. presidential campaign and the Bangemann report (Europe and the Global Information Society), a series of national-level policies have been produced, aiming to a greater or lesser extent to create information-based societies, including some occurring in developing countries. In Europe, these include the French Information Autoroutes, the Danish Information Society 2000 and the

United Kingdom's Information Society initiative. In Asia, one may identify Singapore's Intelligent Island strategy, Malaysia's Vision 2020, Japan's high performance information infrastructure plan, China's NII 2020 policy and Vietnam's IT 2000, amongst others (Ducatel, Webster, & Herrmann, 2000, pp. 1-17). Yet there remains a marked disparity between developed and developing countries in their take up and ability to use the ICTs central to the creation of information societies, the growth of e-business and electronic commerce (e-commerce), and thence economic development.

This chapter explores the extent, nature and factors affecting bridging of this digital divide, drawing on and reviewing the literature related to "technological determinism" and the "social shaping of technology," whilst identifying implications for e-business and economic development in developing nations. Vestiges of the former, which tends to be treated as theoretically passé, remain pervasive, whilst social shaping approaches have yet to provide any effective analysis of the digital divide as it applies to developing compared with developed countries. The chapter is concerned that technological determinism is pervasive in public accounts and rhetoric associated with the creation of information societies and the bridging of digital divides. For example, Mark Malloch Brown (2003), former Administrator of the UN Development Programme claims that it is ICTs that are "transforming societies" and calls for ICTs "to deliver revolutionary breakthroughs … giving the world's poor access to the global economy" (Brown, 2000). Bearing this in mind, a second concern of this chapter is to assess the contribution of social shaping approaches to understanding the complex of factors and processes implicated in technology development, particularly as this relates to the adoption and diffusion of ICTs, e-business development and the bridging of the digital divide between developed and developing countries.

The general position regarding social shaping may be enunciated as follows: social processes shape not only the form and features (i.e., the content) of particular technologies, but also the patterns, general characteristics and direction of technologies across whole areas of development and application (Russell & Williams, 2002). Over time, the social shaping approach has been applied to the reshaping or "reinnovation" of technology "on the ground," in the home, office or on the factory floor, and how these activities feed back into upstream activities linked to public policy or corporate strategy decisions about the designs, purposes and uses of potential new technology (MacKenzie & Wajcman, 1985; Russell & Williams, 2002). Central to the social shaping approach is the idea that there are "choices" (though not necessarily conscious choices) inherent in both the design of individual artefacts and systems, and in the direction or trajectory of innovation programs (Williams & Edge, 1996).

Clearly, this type of approach could be of great relevance to analysis of developing countries' efforts to develop information societies and to close the digital gap with developed countries. Yet, a search of major databases, such as ISI Web of Knowledge, yields nothing in this vein. In April 2004, the authors entered all permutations of the key terms "social aspects," "social shaping," "digital divide," "information society," "technology," "e-business" and "electronic business" into ISI Web of Knowledge, searching for research published since 1995. One hundred and two articles were recorded in the database, which admittedly is not exhaustive of work done in the area, but tellingly, not one paper could be said to encapsulate the interaction of technology, policy and society associated with social shaping research in a developing country context (i.e., as distinct from, say the PICT studies of "wired cities" in developed, mainly Western European nations and the STAR project assessing the "digital revolution" in the European Union (EU). There is, therefore, an opportunity, explored in this chapter, to apply a social shaping viewpoint to the analysis of the digital divide, and, in so doing, to identify some factors that may inhibit or promote diffusion of ICTs and e-business practice in a developing country context.

Having outlined the scope and function of the chapter and provided an overview of the relevance of technological determinism and social shaping approaches to its work, the remainder of the chapter is presented as follows. The next section of the chapter carries over discussion of the issues raised here to discuss implications of alternative views of technology in society for policies related to the realization of the information society concept, the diffusion of ICTs within developing countries, and e-business and economic development. Building on this, the third section discusses implications for technology policy and e-business practice stemming from competing views of information society and the digital divide. The final, concluding, section draws together the various strands of the chapter and summarizes its content.

BACKGROUND: INFORMATION SOCIETY CONCEPTS AND DEFINITION OF THE DIGITAL DIVIDE

The following sections connect theories of technology in society to the phenomenon of the digital divide, related in turn to the adoption and diffusion of ICTs, enabling e-business or e-commerce (or electronic government (e-government) or electronic society (e-society)) in developing countries. ICTs are the result of the convergence of the telecommunications and computer technologies and may act as a catalyst to the idea of the "information society," a concept that emerged gradually throughout the 20th century, although widespread usage of the term appeared only in the late 1970s in Japan.

Two camps emerged, one that might be associated with the views of "enthusiasts" and the other with critics of the information society concept (Marien, 1996). Enthusiasts are inclined to the idea that societies benefit from the introduction of ICTs and that the adoption and diffusion of the technology and its impact on society, culminates in the information society. The views of enthusiasts, therefore, are underpinned by technologically determinist thinking, in which ICTs transform society (c.f., Bell, 1973; Masuda, 1980). Critics of the concept include Lyon (1998), who considers the information society to represent a stage beyond industrial capitalism in which the dominant forces in capitalist society find new means of exploitation for profit. Since capitalism has "gone global," it is argued, the freedom of the individual to maneuver, individual, particularly in developing nations has been drastically reduced, most obviously in terms of their national technoeconomic strategies. Further, the process of globalization operates to include or exclude sectors and societies in or from new networks of information— power and wealth—effectively creating "black holes of informational capitalism." These black holes constitute the Fourth World, which comprises "large areas of the globe, such as sub-Saharan Africa ... impoverished rural areas of Latin America and Asia," (Castells, 2000, p. 164) nation states, cities and specific local communities and groups.. The overall concern is that people in less developed countries, regions or districts are marginalized from the new information capitalism and, thus, find themselves excluded from processes of wealth creation and distribution (i.e., their "pauperization" increases and possibly is accelerated). Critics of the information society concept are likely to be concerned with issues concerning the extent of the digital divide, who shapes the adoption and diffusion of ICTs, for what purpose and with what effects (i.e., implications for bridging the digital divide, for e-business, e-commerce and e-government), as well as who wins or loses from ICT implementation and how.

Digital Divide

As mentioned above, a number of countries around the world are planning and developing their own information society policies, though operationalized to differing degrees, at different speeds and in different ways. The result is a disparity of diffusion and adoption of ICTs, where some nations, mostly the developed countries, are diffusing ICT at an accelerated pace compared with others wishing to catch up but have not yet managed to do so (developing countries). An indication of how wide the digital divide is between the developed (high income) and developing and poor (low income) countries may be shown through indicators, such as the diffusion of the telephones (mainline and mobile). For example, data from the World Bank (2000) shows that in developed countries (those with annual gross national product (GNP) per capita greater than $9,360 in 1998 terms), mainline telephone ownership has reached a figure of nearly 600 per 1,000 inhabitants. In developing countries (those with annual GNP per capita of $760 to $9,360 in 1998 terms), mainline telephone ownership is below 100 per 1,000 inhabitants. The disparity is even greater with respect to ownership of mobile telephones, where in developed countries World Bank data shows ownership averaging about 500 per 1,000 inhabitants, whereas in developing countries the figure is less than 100 per 1,000 inhabitants. For "poor" countries (those with annual GNP per capita of less than $760 in 1998 terms), the average diffusion of both mainline telephones and mobiles is minimal.

If one takes the diffusion of ICTs to be indicated by online population, then it could be argued that in developed countries this has matured, indicating that they have become embedded in society. However, in developing countries, ICTs are still in an early adoption phase (c.f., Mansell & Steinmuller, 2000, on the development phases and diffusion rate of technology). Developed countries take from six to 10 years to reach the maturity phase, while developing countries might take more than 20 years to achieve the same feat (see http://www.nua.ie/surveys/how_many_online/world.html).

Asia-Pacific countries clearly illustrates the possibility of a digital divide between developed and developing countries within one geographical region of the world. In developed Asia-Pacific countries, like South Korea, Singapore, New Zealand, Japan and Australia, more than 40% of the population are Internet users. In comparison, developing Asia-Pacific countries, such as Thailand, Maldives, China, Indonesia, India, Vietnam, Laos and Cambodia, are left behind, with less than 8% of their populations being Internet users (International Telecommunications Union (ITU), 2002). Although Malaysia may be categorized as a developing country, Internet diffusion is remarkably high, with more than 30% of the population being Internet users. This could be due to the impact of its comprehensive public policy, Vision 2020.

Much of the above relies upon certain common indicators of the digital divide, typically found in measures developed by the OECD and the U.S. Department of Commerce. These refer to the issue of ownership of or access to information and communications technology (Corrocher & Ordanini, 2002). These focus on the establishment of relevant communication infrastructures and the analysis of differences between individuals, households, businesses and geographic areas pertaining to their opportunity to purchase or to gain access to ITCs. However a different set of indicators now being recognized concerns broader issues than merely infrastructural ones, including the knowledge and capabilities of people to use and to exploit ICT. Here it is recognized that merely offering people a network-connected machine will not ensure that they can use the medium to meet their needs, because they may not be able to take advantage of all that the Web has to offer. Meanwhile, based on their analysis of the digital divide in developed countries, Corrocher and Ordanini (2002) propose some additional elementary indicators, which they consider to constitute "factors of digitalization," dimensions upon which development progress might be evaluated and implications for policy derived. In addition to factors related to diffusion, communication infrastructures, education and skills, attention is drawn to the value of the local IT and telecommunications market, the competitiveness of ICT providers and the state of competition between them.

An apparently important indicator is the "wealth" of the country, normally measured by GDP per capita. For example, Venkat (2002) observes the digital divide to "track" the income divide between countries. Moreover, in a regression analysis of more than 100 countries, Quibria, Ahmed, Tschang and Macasquit (2003) found that GDP per capita is strongly correlated with the diffusion of telephone and personal computers (PCs) and the usage of ICT and the Internet. However, closer examination of a number of African countries, which have roughly the same level of economic wealth (again as reflected in GDP per capita), reveals that these countries have very different levels of telecommunication and Internet diffusion (Wilson, III, & Wong, 2003). This indicates that although the wealth of a country influences the diffusion and adoption of ICT, public policy may be a more important factor related to the creation of a positive ICT-enabling environment. Rwanda, for example, despite its recent political chaos, has been able to construct one of the most modern telecommunications infrastructures in Africa (Wilson, III, & Wong, 2003). Public policies may involve action to enhance ICT infrastructure development through the liberalization of the telecommunications market (Roycroft & Anantho, 2003). Finally, "e-readiness" is a composite measure being used to determine the extent to which a market is conducive to Internet-based opportunities and takes into account a wide range of factors, from the quality of IT infrastructure to the ambition of

government initiatives and the degree to which the Internet is creating commercial efficiencies (Center for International Development (CID), 2004; Computer System Policy Project (CSPP), 2004; Economist Intelligence Unit, 2003). Having presented the plethora of indicators that could be employed to understand the extent of the digital divide and the diffusion (or not) of ICTs and e-business, it is now time to consider views of what has or might be done about it and with what consequences. To begin with, the discussion turns to the technological determinism-social shaping debate, and then it considers implications for ICT diffusion and e-business development.

A SOCIAL SHAPING PERSPECTIVE OF THE DIGITAL DIVIDE AND E-BUSINESS

For technology to make the transition from the potential to the actual requires more than it being technically feasible. There also must be a desire for it, coupled with the ability to pay for it, which economists refer to as "effective demand." Technology is "pushed" by several forces, but it also has to be "pulled" by effective demand (Volti, 1992), which in the developing country context could necessitate demand aggregation policies, pooling at a community level to render provision economic to the supplier (Malecki, 2003). In one version of the linear model of innovation, there is first scientific research or invention; the results of the research are applied, thereby producing a technological application; and finally, the technology is taken up in the marketplace. The concern of this model is how quickly and smoothly a society can adjust to meet the exigencies of new technology.

In arguing against the linear/deterministic model, the social shaping approach contends that there are choices available early in the development and during the implementation of new technologies. Hence, requirements of and negotiations among different social groups and actors are focal points for analysis, and choices among different socio/technical options potentially available at every stage are highlighted. However, for progress towards the information society to proceed in developing countries, it is likely that advanced technologies will be imported (in some instances the technology will be "pushed") from developed countries. This process of transferring in "off the shelf" technology reduces the opportunity of many in developing countries to exercise influence over the design of the innovation early in the development process, potentially leaving few options available during the subsequent implementation of the new technologies.

The argument is reinforced by data supporting the general point that new technologies, including ICTs, are produced for the use of people in developed, rather than developing countries. Figure 1, for example, shows that during the period 1986 to 2000, developed countries accounted for more than 90% of the total number of patents granted in the United States, whereas developing countries patented less than 1%. The U.S. patent data is

chosen due to the United States being the world's largest economy; innovations of a significant nature, such as ICTs, are very likely to be patented there (Archibugi & Pietrobelli, 2003). More pertinent, James (2003) finds that innovations in information technology (IT) tend to be based on incomes in developed, rather than in developing countries where there is a need for lower price basic access, rather than better services, more accessories and higher bandwidth. If the digital divide between developed and developing countries is to be reduced, therefore either the price of access or ownership needs to be drastically lowered, or alternatively, more appropriate lower-cost technology alternatives, based on local needs, need to be found.

The issue of the appropriateness of technology is of significance to the diffusion and adoption of ICTs in developing countries. Studies of ICT projects implemented in developing countries identify problems arising out of the incompatibility of technology and society. For example, Smith (2000) concludes that the biggest hurdle to overcome in developing countries is related

Figure 1. Patents granted in U.S.: Developed, newly industrialized (NICs) and developing countries (Adapted from Archibugi & Pietrobelli, 2003)

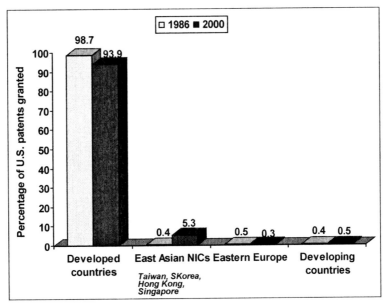

to community expectations and for providers to introduce technology with the understanding of the requirements of the local community. This suggests the need for policymakers and firm-level strategists to attend to "technological culturation" (Loch, Straub, & Kamel, 2003). Though reviewing e-government initiatives in developed countries, Muir and Oppenheim (2002) provide a note of caution for developing countries, too. They observe that policies pursued on the basis of a technical imperative, rather than on the basis of some desirable shared vision of society, risk exacerbating rather reducing the digital divide. In part, this occurs when governments fail to address the problems that citizens may have in using the technology or their "self-efficacy," or self-confidence with using ICTs is underestimated (Bandura, 1997).

On the other side of the coin there are examples of ICT development, which seem more sympathetic to local contexts. For instance, China's "leapfrogging" approach to developing a digital economy has involved combining industrialization and "informatization," and the creation by the State of a Chinese third generation mobile communications standard, to forestall domination of the market by foreign companies, as occurred with mobile telephones (Dai, 2002). James (2002) meanwhile points to the "communal" technologies that could help to provide universal access to rural areas of developing countries, such as village kiosks, wireless technology and removable smart cards to facilitate computer sharing. And in Egypt, attempts to develop technological culturation are reflected in the Ministry of Communications and Information Technology's policy offering free Internet access from late-2001, and the Global Schools Online program, which has brought together governmental, civic and business leaders, "in an effort to integrate Internet technologies within educational systems to strengthen the existing information infrastructure

and to provide the means for community building" (Loch et al., 2003, p. 56). Such moves also relate to a general point made by several researchers concerning the need to address issues of human and social capital and network building to bridge the digital divide and to stimulate development through e-business (Loch et al., 2003; Malecki, 2003; Moodley, 2003).

Other measures at the sectoral level to more specifically promote e-business in developing countries have been identified. These could include establishing a common digital platform to enhance cooperation and knowledge sharing among trading partners across the supply chain, as well as functioning as a route into individual company portals within a sector (Moodley, 2003). They also may require the setting up of support centers or incubators to facilitate suitable firm-level e-business strategies and local ICT sector businesses and capabilities. However the road to e-business may be an uphill one, particularly when firms remain skeptical, owing to their sense of the newness, the risks of e-business and a lack of a critical mass of firms with e-business capabilities. As in and between developed economies, this tendency may be exacerbated according to the "e-unreadiness" of the supply chain, and the extent to which lack of trust across the value chain means that network partners remain unwilling to open electronically access to information. Finally, in some sectors, such as garment retailing and distribution "touch" remains a key aspect of trade likely to impede electronic business or e-commerce. In sectors, serve to inhibit full disintermediation, thus necessitating some capability to combine electronic and personalized communication (Moodley, 2003; c.f., Li, Whalley, & Williams, 2001, on the premature nature of the "death of distance" thesis and the need for firms to be able to conduct business in both physical and electronic spaces).

CONCLUSION

Historians and sociologists of technology have discredited technological determinism, so much so that it has become virtually a term of abuse in academic circles. Nevertheless, the idea that autonomous technology drives social change continues to inform the view that ICTs *per se* have created, or will create, information societies. Connected with this view, ICT infrastructure has been regarded as a tool by which developing countries can change their societies (or specific sectors) in a bid to catch up economically with developed nations. However, a perspective emphasizing the autonomous nature of ICTs is not helpful to understanding the challenges posed by the emergence of ICTs and e-business for developing countries; technological determinism underplays a whole array of factors—social, political and economic—that need to be recognized if the digital divide is to be better understood or ameliorated. The suggestion to invoke a social shaping perspective could help to illuminate the complex factors at play at firm and societal levels. In addition, the appeal of technological determinism remains, partly due to the fact that in their everyday lives most people experience technological development as an external, often remote, process. Thus in developing countries, the ICTs adopted to bridge the digital divide with wealthier nations tend to be the subject of technology push. This is not only by transnational corporations, but also by international organizations, such as United Nations and ITU, on the assumption that the adoption of ICT infrastructure *per se* will drive e-business, e-commerce and economic development. Further, technological determinism endures to the extent that it remains tempting intellectually to imagine that we can discover, and even forecast, the social dimensions of innovations like ICTs (MacKenzie, 1999). Such a view could be inferred from particular configurations of the user implicated in ICT design based on the requirements of users/consumers in developed but not developing countries.

In contrast, application of a social shaping perspective draws attention to other factors of significance to bridging the international digital divide and the promotion of e-business. The chapter has identified a number of factors coevolving with technology development and capable of promoting or hindering diffusion of ICTs, e-business and e-commerce. They have been cited above to include skill and self-efficacy to use ICTs effectively; intellectual, social and human capital; and technological culturation. At the societal level, it is clear that issues of the appropriateness of technology to local needs and the price and ease of access will be important and of concern to technology developers and governments. Developers will need to be mindful of this, if they are to develop markets beyond the saturated West. On the other side of the coin, governments attempt to wrestle with development, while trying to ensure that their countries' economies do not fall further behind developed economies, with firms may be reluctant to award supply contracts to the electronically unready or unwilling. Albeit in a relatively sketchy manner, the chapter has indicated that governments in developing countries do have a role to play in devising policies to stimulate developments in a fashion sympathetic to local expectations or needs. More specifically, at the sectoral level, various aspects of network building, involving the extent and character of relationships across the value chain and levels of trust among the parties concerned, have been identified as significant. Perceptions of the riskiness of doing e-business linked to the newness of the phenomenon and the paucity of firms with e-business capabilities also appear to be crucial factors. Sectoral and national level actions have been identified here, including the establishment of common electronic portals to facilitate interfirm collaboration and support centers to generate and to share best practice with regard to e-business strategies.

Finally, it should be said that there remains much work to be done on analyzing the digital divide and the implications for e-business development. This may extend and complement prevailing concerns of social shaping research with technology development in the "North" and with IT in the workplace. Some opportunities lie in analyzing the extent to which a technology push actually reduces the number of agencies within developing countries adopting ICTs and examining the different visions or scenarios informing technology development. Future research could look into the nature of public policies and corporate e-business strategies in and among different developing countries, identifying actions and interactions, which mediate the selection environment, or lead to the development of more appropriate technology compatible with local contexts. Also, the future points to the application of social shaping approaches to the analysis of innovations downstream, concerning the manner in which firms and consumers use ICTs, more or less as intended by the developer, more or less for the purposes intended, and with greater or lesser difficulty than expected.

REFERENCES

Archibugi, D., & Pietrobelli, C. (2003). The globalisation of technology and its implications for developing countries; Windows of opportunity or further burden? *Technological Forecasting and Social Change, 70*(9), 861-883.

Bandura, A. (1997). *Self-efficacy: The exercise of control.* New York: Freeman.

Bell, D. (1973). *The coming of the post-industrial society.* New York: Basic Books.

Brown, M. M. (2000, July 3). *The challenge of information and communications technology for development* [speech]. Retrieved January 22, 2004, from http://www.undp/dpa/statements/administ/2000/july/3july00.html

Brown, M. M. (2003, December 11). *World Summit on the Information Society, Geneva.* Retrieved January 22, 2004, from http://www.undp.org/dpa/statements/administ/2003/december/11dec03.html

Castells, M. (2000). The informationage: Economy, society and culture. *Volume III: The end of the millennium* (2nd ed.). Oxford: Blackwell.

Center for International Development (CID). (2004). Harvard, Retrieved January 13, 2004, from http://www.readinessguide.org

Computer System Policy Project (CSPP). (2004). Retrieved January 13, 2004, from http://www.cspp.org/projects/readiness

Corrocher, N., & Ordanini, A. (2002). Measuring the divide: A framework for the analysis of cross-country differences. *Journal of Information Technology, 17*(1), 9-19.

Dai, X. (2002). Towards a digital economy with Chinese characteristics. *New Media and Society, 4*(2), 141-162.

Ducatel, K., Webster, J., & Herrmann, W. (2000). Information infrastructures or societies? In K. Ducatel, J. Webster, & W. Herrmann (Eds.), *The information society in Europe.* Lanham, MD: Rowman and Littlefield.

Economist Intelligence Unit. Retrieved January 12, 2004, from http://www.eiu.com/ereadiness

International Telecommunications Union (ITU). (2002). Retrieved January 12, 2004, from http://www.itu.int/ITU-D/ict/statistics/at_glance/basic02.pdf

James, J. (2002). Universal access to information technology in developing countries. *Regional Studies, 36*(9), 1093-1097.

James, J. (2003). *Bridging the global digital divide.* Cheltenham, UK: Edward Elgar.

Li, F., Whalley, J., & Williams, H. (2001) Between physical and electronic spaces: The implications for organisations in the networked economy. *Environment and Planning A, 33,* 699-716.

Loch, K. D., Straub, D. W., & Kamel, S. (2003). Diffusing the Internet in the Arab world: The role of social norms and technological culturation. *IEEE Transactions on Engineering Management, 50*(1), 45-64.

Lyon, D. (1988). *The information society: Issues and illusions.* London: Polity Press.

MacKenzie, D. (1999). Technological determinism. In W. Dutton (Ed.), *Society on the line: Information politics in the digital age* (pp. 39-41). Oxford: Oxford University Press.

MacKenzie, D., & Wajcman, J., (Eds.) (1985). *The social shaping of technology.* Milton Keynes, UK: Open University Press.

Malecki, E. (2003). Digital development in rural areas: Potentials and pitfalls. *Journal of Rural Studies, 19*(2), 201-214.

Mansell, R., & Steinmuller, E. W. (2000). *Mobilizing the information society: Strategies for growth and opportunity.* Oxford: Oxford University Press.

Marien, M. (1996). New communications technology. *Telecommunications Policy, 20*(5), 375-387.

Masuda, Y. (1980). *Managing in the information society.* Oxford: Basil Blackwell.

Moodley, S. (2003). The challenge of e-business for the South African apparel sector. *Technovation, 23*(7), 557-570.

Muir, A., & Oppenheim, C. (2002). National information policy developments worldwide I: Electronic government. *Journal of Information Science, 28*(3), 173-186.

Quibria, M. G., Ahmed, S. N., Tschang, T., & Macasquit, M. L. R. (2003). Digital divide: Determinants and policies with special reference to Asia. *Journal of Asian Economics, 13,* 811-825.

Roycroft, T. R., & Anantho, S. (2003). Internet subscription in Africa: policy for a dual digital divide. *Telecommunications Policy, 27*(1/2), 61-74.

Russell, S., & Williams, R. (2002). Concepts, spaces and tools for action? Exploring the policy potential of the social shaping perspective. In K. H. Sorensen & R. Williams (Eds.), *Shaping technology, guiding policy: Concepts, spaces and tools* (pp. 37-132). Cheltenham, UK: Edward Elgar.

Smith, R. (2000). Overcoming regulatory and technological challenges to bring Internet access to a sparsely populated, remote area. *First Monday 5*(10). Retrieved December 1, 2003, from http://firstmonday.org/issues/issue5_10/smith/index.html

Venkat, K. (2002). Delving into the digital divide. *IEEE Spectrum,* February, 14-16.

Volti, R. (1992). *Society and technological change* (2nd ed.). New York: St. Martin's Press.

Williams, R., & Edge, D. (1996). The social shaping of technology. *Research Policy, 25*(6), 865-899.

Wilson, E. J., III, & Wong, K. (2003). African information revolution: A balance sheet. *Telecommunications Policy, 27*(1/2), 155-177.

World Bank. (2000). Retrieved December 6, 2003, from http://devdata.worldbank.org/external/dgsector.asp?W=0&RMDK=110&SMDK=473895

About the Authors

Feng Li (Feng.li@ncl.ac.uk), PhD, is chair of e-business development and the convener of the Management Subject Group at the University of Newcastle upon Tyne Business School (UK). His research has focused on using information and communication technologies to facilitate the development of new strategies, business models and organisational designs in both private and public sector organisations. He is a council member of the British Academy of Management (BAM) and chair of the BAM E-Business and E-Government Special Interest Group (SIG). His recent work on Internet banking strategies and business models and on the evolving telecommunications value networks and pricing models has been extensively reported by the media. His latest book, *What is e-Business? How the Internet Transforms Organizations*, was published by Blackwell Publishing Ltd. (2006).

* * *

Eddie Blass (Eddie.Blass@ashridge.org.uk), is a senior researcher at Ashridge Business School (UK) whose doctorate in education focused on the corporate, virtual and global university of the future. Formerly a senior lecturer in human resource management, Dr. Blass' research focus spans the fields of education and leadership with a particular focus on where we are going, rather than where we have been.

Norman Bonney (n.bonney@rgu.ac.uk), is a senior research fellow at the Aberdeen Business School, The Robert Gordon University (RGU), Garthdee, Aberdeen (UK).

Roongrasamee Boondao (roong@bus.ubu.ac.th), is a lecturer in management information system at the Faculty of Management Science, Ubon Rajathanee University (Thailand). She received her doctorate in information management from Asian Institute of Technology (Thailand), and her master's degree in business systems from Monash University (Australia). Her research interests include electronic government, electronic policing, Bayesian networks for crime analysis, and geographic information systems for crime control. Her papers were presented at the 8th Pacific Rim International Conference on Artificial Intelligence, the 4th WSEAS Conference on Information Systems and Map Asia 2003 and 2004. Her research papers have appeared in the journals *WSEAS Transactions on Information Science and Applications* and *WSEAS Transaction on Circuits and Systems*.

Raluca Bunduchi (r.bunduchi@abdn.ac.uk), is a lecturer in management at the University of Aberdeen Business School, Aberdeen (UK). Her current research focuses on technology management and the development and adoption of e-business in organizations. She was a research fellow at the University of Edinburgh, where she looked at the development and adoption of e-business standards. She studied for her doctorate in the Department of Management Science at Strathclyde Business School, examining the use of Internet technologies and their implications for the nature of business relationships within and across organizational boundaries.

Chi-Chang Chang (threec@saturn.yzu.edu.tw), is a lecturer in the Department of Computer Science & Information Management at Hung Kuang University, Tai Chung (Taiwan). He is also finalizing his doctoral thesis at Yuan-Ze University in the subject of chronic-disease risk modelling. His primary research interests are in the areas of medical decision analysis, reliability engineering, stochastic processes, fuzzy theory, and e-government. He has published in the *European Journal of Operational Research*, the *International Journal of Technology & Management*, the *Journal of Universal Computer Science*, the *Journal of Management & Systems*, the *Journal of Shin Sheng*, and the *Journal of Quality*, among others.

Yi-Fen Chen (fen1307@ms21.hinet.net) is an assistant professor in the Department of International Trade at the Chung Yuan Christian University, Chung Li (Taiwan). Her research interests include Internet marketing, service management, electronic commerce and information management. She has published in *Psychology & Marketing* and *Journal of Shin Sheng*.

Thomas Connolly (CONN-CI0@wpmail.paisley.ac.uk), is a professor in the School of Computing at the University of Paisley (UK). His specialties are online learning, games-based e-learning and database systems. He has published papers in a number of international journals, including the *Journal of IT Education* and *Computers & Education*, as well as authoring the highly acclaimed books *Database Systems: A Practical Approach to Design, Implementation, and Management* (Addison Wesley Longman) and *Database Solutions* (Addison Wesley Longman). Professor Connolly also serves on the editorial boards of several international journals as well as managing large-scale externally funded research projects.

Nikhilesh Dholakia (nik@uri.edu), is professor of marketing, e-commerce and international business at the University of Rhode Island (USA). Dr. Dholakia's research deals with technology, innovation, market processes and consumer culture. He has published extensively in the fields of marketing, e-commerce and consumer culture. Among his books are *Consuming People: From Political Economy to Theaters of Consumption* (Routledge, 1998), *Worldwide E-Commerce and Online Marketing: Watching the Evolution* (Quorum, 2002), and *M-Commerce: Global Experiences and Perspectives* (Idea Group Publishing, 2006).

Andrew Ettinger (Andrew.ettinger@ashridge.org.uk), is director of learning resources at Ashridge Business School (UK). He heads up a team that produces the virtual learning resource centre (VLRC), an e-learning product that is subscribed to globally by over 150 organizations. He frequently speaks at conferences and has completed several consultancy assignments. He was a fellow of the Institute of Information Science and European Business Librarian of the Year (1998).

Audley Genus (audley.genus@ncl.ac.uk), is senior lecturer in technology policy and strategy at the University of Newcastle upon Tyne Business School (UK). He has written extensively on the link between radical or large-scale technological innovation, change in organizations and developments in society more generally. His research has been published in a number of highly regarded peer-reviewed journals, such as *Research Policy, Technology Analysis & Strategic Management,* and *Technological Forecasting & Social Change.* The most recent of his three books is *Decisions, Technology and Organization* (Gower).

Veronica M. (Ronnie) Godshalk (vmg3@psu.edu), is an associate professor in the Department of Management and Organization at the Pennsylvania State University (USA). She teaches courses in organizational behavior, organizational change, strategy, communication skills and career management. She has been on the faculty at Penn State for 15 years. Dr. Godshalk's research interests include issues surrounding career management, mentoring, stress and the intersection of work and nonwork domains. She has published articles in the *Journal of Vocational Behavior, Journal of Organizational Behavior, Group & Organization Management* and the *Journal of Management Systems.* She published a book, *Career Management* (2000) with co-authors Jeff Greenhaus and Gerry Callanan. She is an active member and presenter in professional associations, such as the Academy of Management and the Society for Industrial and Organizational Psychology. Dr. Godshalk had worked in the computer industry in sales and sales management prior to entering academia and has been a consultant for several *Fortune 500* companies.

Shahizan Hassan (shahizan@uum.edu.my), is an associate professor at the Faculty of Information Technology, Universiti Utara Malaysia (Malaysia). He completed his doctorate in information systems from the University of Newcastle upon Tyne (UK), his master's in information technology from the University of Nottingham (UK), and his bachelor's from the Manchester Metropolitan University (UK). His research interests include electronic government, knowledge management, Web design and evaluation, and the impact of information technology on society.

Bogdan Hoanca (hoanca@nero.scob.uaa.alaska.edu), is an assistant professor of management information systems at the University of Alaska Anchorage (UAA) (USA). Before joining UAA, he cofounded, started up and sold a company that builds components for fiber-optic communications. He also helped start and consulted with a number of other start-up companies in optical-fiber communications. Dr. Hoanca received a doctorate in electrical engineering (1999) from the University of Southern California (USA). His current research interests revolve around technology, and in particular, e-learning and societal implications of technology as well as privacy and security.

Viki Holton (viki.holton@ashridge.org.uk), is a senior researcher with Ashridge Business School (UK). Her interest areas include surveying current trends in learning and development, human resources, equal opportunities and diversity issues. She is a member of the editorial board of two journals, *Women in Management Review* and *Career Development International.*

Petar Jovanovic (petarj@fon.bg.ac.yu), is a professor of management and project management at the Faculty of Organizational Sciences, University of Belgrade (Serbia). He has worked in several companies and is employed as a professor by the University of Belgrade (since 1978). Jovanovic also served as a dean of faculty (1991-1996). He has published 20 books related to management and many papers. He was consultant for several companies and has managed several investment projects. He is a founder and president of the Yugoslav Project Management Association and editor-in-chief of *International Journal Management*, published by the Faculty of Organizational Sciences. His research interests include project management, project appraisal, strategic management, change management and general management.

Olufemi Komolafe (o.komolafe@rgu.ac.uk), earned a bachelor's degree from Obafemi Awolowo University (Nigeria), and a master's in computing (2004) from The Robert Gordon University (RGU) (UK). He is a research associate on a DTI/ESRC-funded Knowledge Transfer Partnership project between RGU and Pathways Services Plc at RGU and is working on database development.

Spyridoula Lakka (lakka@di.uoa.gr), received a degree in mathematics at the National and Kapodistrian University of Athens (Greece), and a master's degree with distinction in software engineering from The University of Liverpool (UK). She is a high school teacher of informatics and computer science, and during the last year, she has been a researcher at the Department of Informatics and Telecommunications of the National and Kapodistrian University of Athens. Her research interests are in the area of open contribution and open-content projects, social networks, techno-economics and diffusion of high technology and informatics.

Nikolas E. Lionis (nlionis@di.uoa.gr), is an adjunct lecturer in the Department of Informatics and Telecommunications and the Department of Economics at the National and Kapodistrian University of Athens (Greece). He received his bachelor's in economic science at the National and Kapodistrian University of Athens and his master's with commendation in economics and finance at the University of Bristol (UK), where he also received his doctorate (2003). His recent research interests are in the area of game theory, industrial organization and network economics.

Marko Mihic (mihicm@fon.bg.ac.yu), is a teaching assistant at the Faculty of Organizational Sciences, University of Belgrade (Serbia). He is member of the Yugoslav Project Management Association, International Project Management Association and European Central-East Network of National Project Management Association. He was consultant for several companies and the Serbian government on project management system implementation, strategic management, public-sector management and so forth. He has published papers in several international symposia and journals. His research interests are in the area of project management, project appraisal, strategic management, change management and e-business.

Kenrick Mock (kenrick@uaa.alaska.edu), received his doctorate in computer science (1996) from the University of California, Davis (USA). He is an associate professor of computer science at the University of Alaska Anchorage (USA). His research centers on complex systems, information management, artificial intelligence, computer security and technological innovations in education. Dr. Mock has previously held positions as a research scientist at Intel Corporation and as CTO of the Internet start-up company, Unconventional Wisdom.

Mohd Ali Mohamad Nor (Malimnor@aol.com), is a doctoral student in the at University of Newcastle upon Tyne Business School (UK). His research focuses on efforts to close the digital divide between urban and rural areas of Malaysia.

Anil M. Pandya (anil-pandya@sbcglobal.net, a-pandya@kellogg.northwestern.edu), is a professor of marketing at Northeastern Illinois University, Chicago (USA), and an adjunct professor of marketing in the College of Industrial Engineering and Management Science at Northwestern University in Evanston, Illinois (USA). His scholarly research has appeared in the *European Journal of Marketing, Journal of Macromarketing, Research in Marketing, Journal of Finance and Strategy*, and *Journal of Electronic Commerce in Organizations*. He teaches in the area of marketing management and international marketing. His research interests are in investigating the strategic issues related to the recent failure of the B2C electronic-commerce firms.

Dejan Petrovic (dejanp@fon.bg.ac.yu), is a professor of project management and investment management at the Faculty of Organizational Sciences, University of Belgrade (Serbia). He is member of the management board of the Yugoslav Association of Project Management (YUPMA) and the assembly of the International Public Management Association (IPMA). He was consultant for several companies and has managed several investment projects. He has published many papers about project and investment management.

Mark Stansfield (stan-ci0@wpmail.paisley.ac.uk), is a senior lecturer in the School of Computing at the University of Paisley (UK). He has a doctorate in information systems and has published papers on online learning, games-based e-learning, information systems and e-business in a number of international journals that include the *Journal of Further and Higher Education*, the *Journal of Electronic Commerce Research*, the *Journal of IT Education*, and *Computers & Education*. He also serves on the editorial boards of several international journals.

Elizabeth Tait (e.j.tait@rgu.ac.uk), received her master's in politics (2002) from Glasgow (UK), and her master's in electronic information management (2004) from The Robert Gordon University (RGU), Aberdeen (UK). Dr. Tait is a research assistant in the Aberdeen Business School, RGU and is working on a doctorate on e-democracy in Scotland.

Horst Treiblmaier (horst.treiblmaier@wu-wien.ac.at), is an associate professor of information systems at the Vienna University of Economics and Business Administration (Austria). He earned his doctorate in management information systems at the Vienna University of Economics and Business Administration. His research interests include communication strategies for electronic commerce, Web site analysis and electronic customer relationship management (eCRM). His work has appeared in journals such as *International Journal of Electronic Business Management, Schmalenbach Business Review, Electronic Markets, Transactions on Advanced Research, International Journal of Technology, Policy and Management*, and *International Journal of Mobile Communications*.

Nitin Kumar Tripathi (nitinkt@ait.ac.th), is an associate professor of remote sensing and geographic information system at the Asian Institute of Technology (AIT) (Thailand). He received his master's and doctorate in remote sensing from the Indian Institute of Technology (India). He has received the DAE Young Scientist Award (2004) from India's Department of Atomic Energy. He received Career Award for Young Teachers (1995) from the All India Council for Technical Education. He is also editor-in-chief of the *International Journal of Geoinformatics*, which is a peer-reviewed research journal. His research interests are application of geoinformatics for disasters, such as floods and landslides, sustainable development and technology development in the areas of wireless and Internet geographic information systems (GIS). He is involved in teaching and training related to GIS at AIT.

Dimitris Vartoutas (arkas@di.uoa.gr), holds a physics degree and a master's and doctorate in communications and techno-economics from the University of Athens (Greece). He is a lecturer on telecommunications techno-economics in the Department of Informatics and Telecommunications at the University of Athens. He has participated in numerous European research and development projects. His research interests include optical, microwave communications and techno-economic evaluation of network architectures and services. He has published more than 40 articles in refereed journals and for conferences in the area of telecommunications, opto-electronics and techno-economics, including leading Institute of Electrical and Electronics Engineers Inc. (IEEE) journals and conferences.

Index